T0198578

SOUL LESSONS
FROM THE

Light

HOW
SPIRITUALLY TRANSFORMATIVE EXPERIENCES
CHANGED MY LIFE

Yvonne Kason, M.D.

iUniverse®

SOUL LESSONS FROM THE LIGHT
HOW SPIRITUALLY TRANSFORMATIVE
EXPERIENCES CHANGED MY LIFE

Copyright © 2022 Yvonne Kason.

All rights reserved. No part of this book may be used or reproduced by any means, graphic, electronic, or mechanical, including photocopying, recording, taping or by any information storage retrieval system without the written permission of the author except in the case of brief quotations embodied in critical articles and reviews.

iUniverse books may be ordered through booksellers or by contacting:

iUniverse
1663 Liberty Drive
Bloomington, IN 47403
www.iuniverse.com
844-349-9409

Because of the dynamic nature of the Internet, any web addresses or links contained in this book may have changed since publication and may no longer be valid. The views expressed in this work are solely those of the author and do not necessarily reflect the views of the publisher, and the publisher hereby disclaims any responsibility for them.

Any people depicted in stock imagery provided by Getty Images are models, and such images are being used for illustrative purposes only. Certain stock imagery © Getty Images.

Cover design by GetCovers
Author Photo: Ronald Miller Photography

Scripture quotations marked KJV are from the Holy Bible, King James Version (Authorized Version). First published in 1611. Quoted from the KJV Classic Reference Bible, Copyright © 1983 by The Zondervan Corporation

ISBN: 978-1-6632-4609-7 (sc)
ISBN: 978-1-6632-4610-3 (e)

Library of Congress Control Number: 2022917975

Print information available on the last page.

iUniverse rev. date: 05/08/2023

Praise for Soul Lessons from The Light

"'Soul Lessons from the Light" by Dr. Yvonne Kason is truly remarkable. Having undergone five Near-Death Experiences and several additional "Spiritually Transformative Experiences" the author is one of the world's foremost experts in the realm of survival of consciousness and the afterlife. Dr. Kason takes the reader on a mystical journey into the mind of her genius and beyond our world into the divine. Her engaging writing style makes even the most esoteric of metaphysical experiences relatable to the reader. This must-read book not only describes Spiritually Transformative Experiences, reading it is a Spiritually Transformative Experience."

Mark Anthony, JD Psychic Explorer®
Author of *The Afterlife Frequency*,
Evidence of Eternity and *Never Letting Go*.

"Dr. Yvonne Kason contributes tremendously to the understanding of Spiritually Transformative Experiences in this beautiful and highly personal book. Her own experiences are remarkable and provide a great roadmap for others to understand their own spiritual experiences. Dr. Kason is a consummate researcher with an excellent academic background—and a deeply spiritual leader in this growing field. This book is extraordinary!"

Anne Archer Butcher, M.A.
Author of *Five Blue Rings*,
Board member, Spiritual Awakenings International.

"*Yvonne Kason, a noted Canadian physician, and a multiple near-death experiencer, has written one of the great spiritual autobiographies of our time in chronicling her journey from a childhood NDE to becoming a modern mystic and an illumined soul. Her story, which includes overcoming a twelve-year battle from a traumatic brain injury, is not only deeply inspirational and rivetingly dramatic, but contains profound soul-truths that also make her book a treasury of spiritual wisdom.*"

Kenneth Ring, Ph.D.
Professor Emeritus of Psychology, University of Connecticut,
Co-Founder, International Association for Near-Death Studies,
Author of *Lessons from the Light*.

"*In this remarkable and uplifting book, Yvonne Kason brings to bear her insights as a physician who has had five near-death experiences, each one different, but all pointing toward a consistent message of hope and love. Her account of her spiritual odyssey, and the miraculous healing of her brain after traumatic injury, are inspirational testimonies to the human spirit and to the Higher Power behind the universe.*"

Bruce Greyson, M.D.
Carlson Professor Emeritus of Psychiatry &
Neurobehavioral Sciences, University of Virginia,
Co-Founder, International Association for Near-Death Studies.

"*Dr. Yvonne Kason takes us on the path of a modern day mystic. We witness the moments when the Divine absorbs her, releasing knowledge held in her of a vast and all loving Presence. We witness moments when her awareness expands allowing her to view a larger tapestry of life and her place in it. We observe the struggles such awareness provoke that temper the personality, heal old wounds and reconnect her to her Soul's journey. She shares this walk of a mystic through the relationship revealed with her "Higher Power" from the times reported during these mystical encounters as a child, a young adult and as a professional and devotee. Dr. Kason's ability to courageously share these experiences woven with the medical and psychological understandings of such states will not only give validity to others walking this path, but will help them to integrate these states into everyday life. …We thank you, Dr. Kason, for the bridge of understanding you have constructed. The march to wholeness is at hand!*"

Jyoti Ma (Jeneane Prevatt, Ph.D.)
Spiritual Director, Center for Sacred Studies,
Founder, The Fountain for the Natural Order of Our Existence,
Author of *An Angel Called My Name*.

"Dr. Yvonne Kason presents an extraordinary account of her multiple near-death experiences, and other Spiritually Transformative Experiences, which occurred throughout her life. It is rare to find such a rich and deep disclosure by a medical professional, allowing readers a glimpse into the private struggles and celebrated victories as Dr. Kason engaged her experiences head on.

This book is for those who have had a spiritual experience, and may have struggled to accept it into his or her life, but nevertheless found meaning and purpose from the experiences themselves. It is also for those who may have a friend or relative who has struggled with a near-death or similar experience, and in witnessing this struggle became curious about what it might be like to go through the experience ... It may even be for those facing end-of-life challenges, who wish to gain comfort as she or he nears the earthly veil from which only a handful have returned.

... Spiritually Transformative Experiences (STEs, as coined by Dr. Kason) impact a person's overall developmental process...Dr. Kason has provided us a view into a life influenced by many large and small STEs, each with its own impact. ...I invite you to join Dr. Kason as she opens the door to her inner world and invites you to travel with her along her path..... She has helped many, and will continue to do so through her books, including "Soul Lessons from the Light"."

Ryan Rominger, Ph.D.
Past-President, American Center for the Integration
of Spiritually Transformative Experiences,
Adjunct Research Faculty, Sofia University &
California Institute of Integral Studies,
Associate University Research Chair,
University of Phoenix,
School of Advanced Studies,
Center for Leadership Studies and Educational Research.

Dedicated to

Paramahansa Yogananda

and

Mahavatar Babaji

Thank You.

CONTENTS

INTRODUCTION

My life has been molded and profoundly blessed by powerful Spiritually Transformative Experiences over the course of my lifetime: five extraordinary Near-Death Experiences, mystical experiences, out-of-body experiences, a kundalini awakening, clairvoyance, clairaudience, past-life recall, and more. These inspiring and moving Spiritually Transformative Experiences, a term I coined in 1994, have dramatically changed me and propelled my life in an increasingly more spiritual direction.

At the hand of the Divine sculptor, I have become one of a rare breed, someone who has had multiple Spiritually Transformative Experiences and multiple Near-Death Experiences, a modern-day mystic. But I know I am not alone. I know for a fact that people all around the world are also having spiritual awakenings of many types, and are having Spiritually Transformative Experiences too. I know this to be true as the president and co-founder of *Spiritual Awakenings International*® and based on over 40 years of research as a medical doctor.

In this book, I will share my personal story of how I learned about Spiritually Transformative Experiences first-hand through my own experiences. I'll share the intimate details of some of my most powerful Spiritually Transformative Experiences, including the stories of all five of my Near-Death Experiences, and reflect on the many life-changing after-effects each had on me and the course of my life. As I look back and reflect upon these spiritual experiences, I will share the many deep soul lessons that I learned through my repeated journeys to the other side and into heaven, the realm of the light and unconditional love of the Higher Power.

Although I started having Spiritually Transformative Experiences in my childhood, at that young age I did not recognize them as being anything out of the ordinary. My kundalini awakening with a full-blown mystical experience occurred while I was in medical school. This first awakened me to the reality of spiritual and paranormal experiences being possible to the average person, rather than limited to saints and yogis. As a young doctor, my first adult Near-Death Experiences in 1979 confirmed that fact.

These experiences also transformed me, causing a marked increase in my spiritual yearning. Together, the Spiritually Transformative Experiences that I was having propelled me on a personal and professional quest to understand diverse spiritual and paranormal experiences. They prompted me as a young medical doctor to become a Spiritually Transformative Experience researcher in my private time. Over the years, many people who had undergone similar Spiritually Transformative Experiences began to confide in me as patients in my medical practice, and thus with time my medical career became increasingly focused on counseling patients who had undergone powerful paranormal and spiritual experiences. However, my research into Spiritually Transformative Experiences remained private for many years. I was in the closet because, as I will describe in this book, my Spiritually Transformative Experiences were not understood or accepted by those around me.

To my great astonishment, the Divine hand touched me again in 1990 with a powerful *calling mystical experience.* This was a strong prompting from Spirit to come out of the closet and publicly specialize my medical practice in Spiritually Transformative Experiences. I followed this inner guidance. Then as a spiritual confirmation of the validity of my decision, I felt blessed with another powerful mystical experience. I had another Near-Death Experience in 1995 that opened me to yet deeper mystical states of consciousness afterward.

I first described my dramatic plane crash Near-Death Experience as a young doctor and my resulting research quest in my 1994 book, *A Farther Shore.* In it, I first coined the phrase *Spiritually Transformative Experiences* to describe the broad range of powerful spiritual and paranormal experiences happening to many people. I found that Spiritually Transformative Experiences all tend to change the experiencer's values and attitudes into a more spiritual direction. They may also begin a long-term process of psychological and spiritual transformation.

In 2000, I wrote *Farther Shores,* a revised and updated version of *A Farther Shore,* to share my deeper insights and increasing medical understanding of all types of Spiritually Transformative Experiences. I was delighted at how well both books were received by readers all over the world.

To my great wonder and amazement, the Divine hand touched me with yet another extremely powerful mystical experience, a white light Near-Death Experience on November 8, 2003, when I sustained a traumatic brain injury in a slip and fall accident and instantly died. After a profoundly beautiful welcome to the other side by saintly beings of light, and receiving many revelations in the loving white light realm of the afterlife, I later returned to my body to find myself seriously injured with a traumatic brain injury.

For twelve years following that 2003 traumatic brain injury, I thought my previous life as a practicing medical doctor and as an author and speaker, my life before the brain injury, were permanently gone. Certainly, my continuing medical challenges made it physically impossible for me to practice medicine any longer. For twelve years, I thought my ability to write books, engage in public speaking, or do volunteer work of any kind had also been permanently lost. However, to my great amazement and delight, on February 24, 2016, I experienced a miracle.

Through the grace of God, I had a miraculous and sudden brain healing – a miracle of neuroplasticity of the brain. As I describe later in detail, this Spiritually Transformative Experience suddenly and unexpectedly, with an eruption of white light in the center of my brain, healed me. The traumatic brain injury was healed abruptly and my writing-inspired creativity spontaneously was re-awakened. After years of complete loss, it was as if my brain and creativity had awakened from a twelve-year slumber!

After that miraculous day of healing, I felt like a caged bird finally set free. I rejoiced that at last, through my new books, I was able to express in writing the knowledge, life experience, and wisdom that had been locked inside my head for the previous twelve years due to the traumatic brain injury. The inspiration for several books flowed through my consciousness, together with the inner guidance to "pass on what you have learned."

I wrote the first drafts of two new books in less than a year following my spontaneous brain healing: *Touched by the Light: Exploring Spiritually Transformative Experiences* and this book, *Soul Lessons from the Light,* my personal story. These two new books form a permanent written testimonial documenting the extraordinary miracle that I experienced. Through the miracle of my healing, I have been able to continue writing books, and resume public speaking and serving others through volunteer work.

Later, inspired by a powerful download of inner guidance, I co-founded *Spiritual Awakenings International* www.spiritualawakeningsinternational. org, a non-profit charitable organization, and became the founding president. Spiritual Awakenings International's mission is to raise awareness globally about the whole spectrum of Spiritually Transformative Experiences. Thus, I am now *passing on what I have learned* through my new books, talks, and through my volunteer work with Spiritual Awakenings International.

I am very aware that I am not the only person having powerful spiritual awakenings with Spiritually Transformative Experiences. There are clearly documented testimonials of hundreds of mystics and seers for thousands of years written in the mystical literature of all sacred traditions. In addition, hundreds of people from all walks of life, from all over the world, have shared their stories with me, each one a powerful story of their own Spiritually Transformative Experiences. In fact, this leads me to conclude that there is a *global* spiritual awakening happening on our planet right now.

At the conclusion of this book, I will also introduce the model of *Purifying the Heart* to describe the successive stages spiritual seekers move through over the years in their evolution and spiritual growth. I think this beautiful model will greatly help others understand the stages and shifting focuses in the long-term spiritual transformation process of spiritual awakening.

I hope others will find inspiration and insight from this book. I believe my personal spiritual stories can help to validate others having similar experiences. I also hope to inspire and uplift readers, through deepening their love and trust for the incredibly loving Higher Power, God. I also hope the miracle of my sudden brain healing will give encouragement to readers as they face their own life challenges. Finally, I hope my readers will be reassured that in God all things are possible, miracles do happen, and they are happening for all of us all the time. There is always hope for a brighter tomorrow!

Yvonne Kason MD, December 2022

Chapter 1

MY CHILDHOOD NEAR-DEATH EXPERIENCES

I now realize that I had two Near-Death Experiences when I was a child. I did not realize this for most of my life because as a child aged five years and then eleven years when my Near-Death Experiences (NDEs) happened, I did not label these experiences as anything unusual. I just accepted my out-of-body experiences during these close calls as normal childhood events. As a child, I knew no better. I had no idea these experiences were considered paranormal.

As an adult, I also didn't recognize my childhood Near-Death Experiences for many years, because they were both out-of-body type NDEs. These were very different from my adult Near-Death Experiences, which were all mystical/white light experiences - events that were much more powerfully transformative than my childhood NDEs. Thus for many years, I did not link the experiences together. It was only recently, with my deepened understanding gained over many years of studying the great diversity of NDEs, that I slowly came to realize that my two childhood out-of-body experiences were in fact childhood Near-Death Experiences.

Yvonne Kason, M.D.

My First Childhood Near-Death Experience – Age 5 years

My first childhood Near-Death Experience happened when I was five years old. It happened during the summer before kindergarten. My maternal grandparents lived in Switzerland, and I had traveled there with my parents and siblings to visit my grandparents that summer. All my life I have clearly recalled this unusual near-miss incident that happened while we were standing on a train station platform in a small town in Switzerland, waiting for a train to arrive at the station.

I was born and raised in Toronto, Canada. Both my parents were born in Europe, and after World War II ended, they immigrated together to Canada. My father was born in Poland, and most of his siblings had also immigrated to Canada. My mother was born in Switzerland, and her parents, my grandparents, continued to live in Switzerland, in a scenic small town in the foothills of the Swiss Alps. My parents regularly took our family, my two brothers, my sister, and me, on summer vacations to visit our relatives in Switzerland. My grandparents were kind and loving people who opened their home to our good-sized family of six. Therefore, while in Switzerland we would stay in my grandparents' home, which overlooked a pasture of cows grazing, and rolling hills.

I have fond childhood memories of the sounds of visiting in my grandparents' home in this tiny Swiss village: the regular low-pitched gonging of the local church bells that loudly marked the hour, half-hour, and quarter-hour, plus the gentle ringing of the cowbells many of the cows grazing in the neighboring pasture had fastened under their necks. This chorus of country village sounds seemed like beautiful Swiss music to my young ears as a child.

We often traveled around Europe during our vacations there. As I recollect happily visiting my many relatives, aunts, uncles, and godparents, who lived in various locations around Switzerland, I recall joyously playing with my cousins who were close to my age. On weekends, when he was not working, my grandfather regularly drove us on outings to scenic locations all over Switzerland and into nearby Germany and Lichtenstein. We visited historic castles, took lifts up to mountain peaks with panoramic vistas, and traveled to have lunch at my grandfather's favorite restaurants, some of which were nestled at beautiful lakeside locations. My summer holidays in Switzerland were the highlights of my childhood.

During our Switzerland visit when I was five years old, my parents took us on a short trip by train, perhaps to visit a relative. The Swiss train system is very well developed, punctual, and clean, leading most Swiss to travel regularly by train. As a curious young child, I eagerly looked around with great interest as we waited at the local train station. This was something new for me, traveling by train in Europe.

As I waited on the platform, I did not hold a parent's hand. My younger brother and sister were being held by them instead. An energetic blonde-haired blue-eyed youngster, I freely gazed around me. I watched intently as a station attendant jumped down off the platform onto the railway tracks, then quickly climbed up onto the next platform on the far side of the tracks. *Oh, that looks like fun,* I thought to myself, thinking about how I enjoyed climbing in playgrounds. I decided to do the same thing. I immediately leaned forward and began to jump down onto the railway tracks.

Suddenly, it felt like time stood still. While I was midair, time froze. It was as if my life were a movie, and the movie had frozen at one specific frame. My thoughts continued to flow, but the world around me seemed to have stopped, frozen in time. I suddenly found myself, or more accurately my point of perception, floating ten or twenty feet above my body, viewing the motionless scene below me.

From this viewpoint above my body, I could clearly see what I had not realized when I began to jump. I saw my tiny body poised in mid-air, at the beginning of my jump off the platform onto the tracks. However, from the vantage point above my body, I could also see that I was jumping directly in front of a rapidly oncoming train arriving at the station. Strangely, although it appeared that the train was about to hit my child-size body, while floating out-of-body watching the scene of the accident about to happen I did not feel any fear. Somehow I felt a powerful sense of peace and stillness. I felt calm and unafraid. *Oh, I see. I'm about to be hit by a train,* I calmly thought.

In the next instant, the movie of my life started moving forward again. Out of nowhere, a large adult's hand suddenly grabbed my tiny body from behind and pulled me back onto the platform. Suddenly I found myself back in my body again, standing on the station platform. The next instant I felt a strong gust of wind on my face, as the oncoming train rapidly pulled into the station on the tracks in front of me. My parents took me firmly by the hand and immediately started to scold me vigorously, after thanking the man who had pulled me back onto the platform.

I felt stunned by the whole incident. I felt shocked. *What just happened?* I wondered. I felt confused. I did not understand what had just happened to me. I did not feel frightened by the incident. Strangely, I felt very calm about it, perhaps because of the peace and calm I felt while out-of-body. However, as a young child at the time, I was frightened by the scolding I received. Therefore, I did not speak to my parents or grandparents about this train near-miss accident and out-of-body experience afterwards, for fear of bringing on another scolding.

As a child, it never crossed my mind that anything paranormal or unusual had happened when I went out-of-body. It is fascinating to me now, as an adult, that this childhood close-call and out-of-body experience has been etched in my memory all my life. The memory remains unusually clear in my mind to this day. I now know that this was my first Near-Death Experience, which I will explain later.

My Second Childhood NDE – Age 11 years

My second Near-Death Experience happened to me in 1964 when I was an eleven-year-old child. For most of my life, I did not realize that this unusual childhood experience was also a Near-Death Experience. But now, I realize that this was indeed an NDE as well.

This NDE happened when I suffered a serious head injury in a major car accident. This occurred while my family and I were moving from Toronto, Canada, to Los Angeles, California in 1964. At the time, I was still a child in all aspects because puberty had not begun yet, and I still had an optimistic wide-eyed innocence about the world and life. At that age, life seemed to me to be a great adventure, one that still lay undefined in front of me.

My father had decided that our family would immigrate to the USA and move to Los Angeles, California. All legal immigration paperwork had been completed, and the entire family had received green cards, permitting us to move to the USA as immigrants. As an eleven-year-old child, I didn't really understand why we were moving, but I trusted my father's decision. I guessed that my father thought California would offer him better opportunities for his business success.

Dad planned the move with our entire six-member family, including mom, dad, my two brothers, my sister, and me, driving together across the continent in our large family station-wagon car. The drive from Toronto to Los Angeles would take about one week. Our former Toronto home had been sold, and our personal belongings and household furniture had all been packed into a moving van. It was scheduled to meet us upon our arrival at our new home in Los Angeles, about one week later.

As we set off for our cross-continental drive, our car was full to the brim. Mom and Dad were seated in the front on the bench-style seat. Dad would be doing all the driving. The four children were all seated in the second-row bench-style seat, my sixteen-year-old brother, my eight-year-old sister, my six-year-old brother, and eleven-year-old me. The rear luggage area of the station-wagon was filled, packed tightly with the suitcases of six people. This was before the age of seatbelts in cars, and thus we four children were all squeezed together, seated irregularly to fit on the second-row bench-seat without any seatbelts on.

The Car Accident

As we left Toronto and drove west out of the city along the highway, I thought we were beginning a big adventure. Relaxed and quite excited, I looked out the car window at the passing scenery. Less than an hour after we left Toronto, as we were speeding along the highway, I recall suddenly feeling the car lurch sharply. I remember asking Dad "What's that?"

"Probably a flat tire," my father replied as he struggled to control the veering car. From that point onwards, I have no worldly memories until several days later, when my body regained consciousness in the hospital. I was later told that I had lost consciousness during the accident, presumably around the time my worldly memories ended.

My parents later described to me the details of the events that transpired after I lost consciousness during the car accident. It all happened very quickly, they said. Our fully loaded car had been traveling at high speed along the highway when the flat tire struck. The heavy car swerved abruptly with the "pop" of the flat tire exploding, and then veered sharply off the road onto the highway's graveled soft shoulder. It then plunged down into the wide, deep ditch beside the highway. The station-wagon flipped over as it plummeted into the deep ditch, rolling over at least once, perhaps twice. The vehicle finally came to a stop at the bottom of the ditch, with its roof collapsed and compressed, and with the car body dented and smashed from the impact of the rolls.

Several of my family members were seriously injured during the accident. Dad had been gravely injured in the driver's seat. He had fractured several ribs and dislocated a shoulder from impacts with the steering wheel and car frame during the accident. The top of Dad's head had also suffered huge lacerations, and he was bleeding profusely from these large scalp cuts. His face and body were covered with blood when the ambulance finally arrived. Mom in the front seat passenger area had also suffered many deep and large lacerations from broken glass, especially on her neck and on her arms.

My eight-year-old sister had been thrown through a window of the car and landed on the pavement a short distance from the car's wreckage. She broke her arm when she landed and suffered many large cuts to her face from glass and pavement. Miraculously my two brothers, aged six and sixteen, were essentially unharmed in the accident. Somehow they were both protected during the accident, wedged between the cushions of the front bench-seat and the second-row bench-seat. They were able to walk away from the accident, quite shaken emotionally, but physically suffering only minor scratches.

Several passing vehicles stopped to offer help, and one passerby called for an ambulance. Another person who stopped happened to be a Catholic priest. My father was obviously severely injured, bleeding profusely from his huge head lacerations. The priest thought that my father would likely die quickly from his serious injuries, and would not survive the ambulance drive to the hospital. Therefore with my father's consent, the priest performed the last rites on my father while we all waited for an ambulance to arrive.

After the ambulance arrived, its crew managed to pull my father and mother out of the front seat of the crushed and tangled car wreckage. My two brothers were pulled out of the compacted second-row seat area. They were placed on the highway shoulder next to my injured parents. My sister, crying in pain with her broken arm, was also located and placed beside my parents on the roadside.

My father recounted to me many times in the past, how he could barely see during the car accident's aftermath and rescue, due to the quantity of blood pouring down his face and into his eyes. However, dad remembered vividly that he kept counting his children beside him….one, two, three. One child was missing he realized. One daughter is missing, he thought. "My daughter!" dad exclaimed.

It was true. I was indeed missing. My body was not visible in the car wreckage or around the car at the scene of the accident, so the rescuers thought they had found all the car's passengers. However, my body had not yet been found. "My daughter," my father repeated again and again.

Unfortunately, the rescuers thought that dad was confused or in a delirious state, carrying on about his daughter. They thought dad was referring to my injured sister, who had already been retrieved. Thinking all the passengers had now been accounted for, they did not search further for a second daughter.

I am told that a casual passerby finally found my unconscious body. This passerby for some reason decided to look in the compacted luggage area of the crushed station wagon wreckage, perhaps to see if any of the luggage could be salvaged. To their surprise, when they pried one of the suitcases out of the crushed rear of the station wagon, they could see a child's body part protruding from among the luggage. It was my unconscious body. "There's another one in here," they exclaimed. It was only then that the rescuers finally found me, and with difficulty pulled my body out of the car's wreckage.

Dad told me that he could only finally relax then, after I was finally discovered and brought to his side on the shoulder of the road. Dad then breathed a sigh of relief while the paramedics continued in their efforts to control his heavy bleeding and stabilize his condition. Dad then knew, to his great relief, that all four of his children had been found, and they had all survived the accident.

We guess that somehow during the jolts, swerves, and rolling of the car into the deep ditch during the accident, my unrestrained child-sized body had been thrown up and back out of the second-row seat area, into the luggage area in the rear of the car. During either the impact or the rolls, I sustained a serious head injury. When the car finally came to a stop in the ditch, I lay unconscious, out of sight, covered by the suitcases in the crushed rear luggage area.

After we were all pulled from the car wreckage, we were taken by ambulance to a nearby hospital, where my father, mother, sister, and I were immediately admitted for treatment of our respective injuries. We all gradually recovered from our various physical injuries. I was hospitalized for two weeks, due to my head injury and a less serious neck injury. My parents informed me that I remained unconscious for the first several days that I was in the hospital. Their memory for the details of my medical condition and recovery was not clear, however, because they, too, were seriously injured and hospitalized.

My Out-of-Body Near-Death Experience

My last worldly memory of this car accident was the sensation of a sudden sharp jolt of the car as we were speeding along the highway. I also recall asking Dad, "What's that?" and hearing my father's reply. I have no worldly memory for the next few days. However, I do have other memories.

My next memory is of my spirit and point of perception floating above the car wreckage, immediately after the accident. My unconscious physical body was buried under the luggage of the mangled station-wagon. I clearly recall viewing my injured father from several feet above him, while he lay injured at the roadside. I inwardly felt and heard my father calling out for me, as from above I heard him cry out, "My daughter." It felt to me as if my soul somehow knew that Dad was calling out for me, and this call from his soul had drawn my out-of-body spirit to move to him briefly. My memory then abruptly shifts to a short time later, in a different location.

My next clear memory is of my spirit and point of perception floating up by the ceiling above my unconscious body in the emergency room of a nearby hospital. By that time, my injured body had been taken there by ambulance. I watched from above as my body lay motionless on a surgical table in a room in the emergency department. It seemed as if the physical ceiling of the room had been removed or had become transparent, allowing me to view the scene unfolding below, as my spirit floated fifteen feet or so above my body. I could see the colors and detail of my clothes as my physical self lay with limp unmoving limbs.

Below me, I could clearly see the shiny metallic curved top surface of the large disc-shaped operating room light which hung over the table, suspended from the ceiling. I watched from above as two male medical personnel bent over my unconscious body, examining me and trying to revive me. I guessed that they were doctors. As I watched the events occurring around my body below, I felt no pain or distress. I felt still, completely peaceful, and totally unafraid.

Returning to My Body

My next memory is a few days later when I abruptly awoke in my previously unconscious body. I distinctly recall the moment that I awakened. It felt as if I were waking from a very deep sleep. I was slightly disoriented at first. I looked around me, to try to figure out where I was. I discovered myself to be in a bed in a children's ward in a hospital. It was nighttime, and my room had very dimmed lights. I found myself wearing a hospital gown, laying in a children's hospital bed with the railings pulled up high on both sides. There were other children in my room who were asleep in their respective beds.

I recall that upon waking I had a very strong urge to go to the washroom to pass urine. I didn't realize the nurses had put me in diapers while I was comatose, something I had outgrown many years earlier. Therefore, I sat up in my bed and looked around for a washroom. I could not see a washroom nearby. I would have to walk down the hall to find a washroom, I thought. Disconnecting myself from whatever medical lines had been attached to me, I then carefully climbed over the bed railing and out of the bed.

Peering out of the doorway of my hospital room, I saw a long semi-lit hallway to my left. I started slowly walking barefoot down the hospital corridor in search of a washroom. A disgruntled nurse suddenly appeared from nowhere at the end of the hall and rushed down the hall towards me. "You should not be out of bed," she scolded me.

"But I have to pee!" I responded.

The nurse hustled me back into my bed and insisted that I wait for her to bring me a bed pan before I could finally relieve myself. I did not want to urinate into a diaper. It took me a few days after I awoke to learn and adjust to the hospital's rules and routines. I was eventually discharged from the hospital after about two weeks of care.

I have always had a clear memory of my out-of-body experience while I was unconscious after the childhood car accident, as well as for my moment of re-awakening in my body. In addition, these memories have remained very clear in my mind, even though the events occurred over fifty years ago. It is interesting to me that my out-of-body memories are much shorter in duration than the actual period that I was unconscious. It felt to me as if I had been "asleep," in a deep sleep with no awareness, during the remainder of the time I was unconscious and for which I have no memory.

Now, many years later, I have realized that this childhood out-of-body experience that I had while unconscious after the 1964 car accident, was in truth my second Near-Death Experience. Unknown to me as a child, these childhood NDEs were a herald of many more extraordinary consciousness experiences that lay in store for me in my adult life ahead.

Chapter 2

REFLECTIONS ON MY CHILDHOOD NDES AND THEIR AFTER-EFFECTS

After my train station Near-Death Experience at the age of five, I did not talk to anyone about what I had experienced during the mishap. As a child, I felt embarrassed and a bit ashamed to have angered my parents by trying to jump onto the railway tracks. I had not realized the danger when I started to jump. I certainly did not want to bring up the incident with my parents and risk another severe scolding.

Further, I had no idea at that young age that anything out of the ordinary had happened to me when I had the out-of-body experience. Even for most of my adult life, and although I was a researcher of NDEs and other Spiritually Transformative Experiences (STEs), I did not recognize that this childhood experience was a Near-Death Experience. I finally arrived at this conclusion only a few years ago, when I reflected objectively upon the number of NDE features I had during this childhood experience. Then I finally came to the realization, that I had my first Near-Death Experience at the age of five years, in the train near-miss incident.

Yvonne Kason, M.D.

Characteristics of Near-Death Experiences

I and others who had Near-Death Experiences have faced many challenges in striving to understand these unusual incidents of consciousness because NDEs were unknown or misunderstood for many years. In recent years, confusion about Near-Death Experiences is also occurring. It's because some people in the general public have begun to loosely refer to any or all close-call events, severe frights, or brushes with death, as a near death experience, even when no true NDE occurred according to the defining features used by Near-Death Experience researchers today.

Therefore, before I go on to reflect on my childhood NDEs, I think it important that I outline the characteristics of Near-Death Experiences. They are one sub-type of Spiritually Transformative Experiences.

The term *Near-Death Experience* was first coined by Dr. Raymond Moody MD, in his ground-breaking 1975 book *Life After Life*. Dr. Moody identified fifteen general NDE features. Dr. Moody's NDE features have become standard identifying factors used by professionals in the field.

Although most NDEs do not contain all of the features Dr. Moody lists, most have at least eight of the fifteen features. They usually occur in the general order listed. As I discuss in detail in *Touched by the Light,* my research and professional work with NDE experiencers confirmed Dr. Moody's definitions and revealed that the number of NDE features people experience tends to increase with the length of time they were close to death or deceased.

A Near-Death Experience is defined as a paranormal experience, an out-of-body and/or mystical experience, that occurs to some people when they are clinically dead and later resuscitated, physically close to death, unconscious, or psychologically facing imminent death or severe trauma. They include at least five of the following of Moody's NDE features:

1. *Ineffability.* NDEs have dimensions and aspects that are beyond words and cannot be adequately described to others.
2. *Auditory awareness.* Clairaudience. Experiencers may have clear and accurate recall of hearing what others said around their body while they were unconscious or clinically dead.

3. *Strong feelings of peace.* A feeling of peace, comfort, and tranquility comes to the experiencer. Fear either dissolves or is completely absent. Pain is also absent.

4. *Unusual inner sounds.* Experiencers may hear inner sounds such as buzzing, ringing, roaring, wind blowing, distant wind chimes, celestial music, or music of the spheres.

5. *Floating out of the body.* An out-of-body experience.

6. *Dark tunnel.* Experiencers may have a sensation of moving away from the physical body through a long, dark passage or tunnel, or a dark expanse of space, with a bright light at the far end.

7. *Meeting spirits.* Mystical Visions – seeing beings of light. Experiencers may see and mentally communicate with loving spirits, often luminous spirits of departed loved ones, relatives, or friends, or they may see luminous spirits of saints, an angel, a Spiritual Master such as Jesus, or orbs of light.

8. *White Light Experience.* A Mystical Experience. Encountering or being immersed in indescribable white light that emanates a powerful aura of intense love and unconditional acceptance. Mystical revelations and/or illumination may occur in the white light, with new knowledge, life messages, or spiritual teachings being revealed, or even prophecy of future events being shown.

9. *Life review.* Experiencers may have a review or rapid re-experiencing of all or some significant life events, including ones that may have been forgotten or repressed. Some can sense the thoughts and feelings of others during the life review.

10. *Life barrier.* Experiencers may perceive a barrier or border that they cannot cross if they are going to return to the physical body. Some experiencers are given a choice of whether or not to return to their physical body. Others are simply told that they must now return.

11. *Abrupt return to the body.* Experiencers may have the sensation of rapidly traveling back down through the tunnel into their body and/or suddenly being pulled down, sucked down, or being sucked back into the physical body. The sensation of abruptly re-entering the physical body is sometimes instantaneous, or with a sudden jolt or gasp of breath.

12. *Conviction of the reality of the experience.* Experiencers may have an absolute certainty that the experience was real and not a fantasy or a dream—even in the face of disbelief or ridicule. Experiencers usually have an unusually clear memory of the experience, which may remain exceptionally clear in their memory for many years, or even for the rest of their lives.

13. *Transformational impact.* Experiencers have after-effects resulting in their lives becoming changed in one or more ways: (a) *psychologically* (b) *spiritually*; and/or (c) *psychically.*

14. *New views of death.* Experiencers lose their fear of death and have an increase in the certainty that the spirit lives on after the death of the physical body.

15. *Independent corroboration.* Veridical perceptions. Events the experiencer observed on the physical plane during their out-of-body experience are corroborated by other people or evidence.

It is important to note that not everyone who is close to death or is clinically dead, flatlined, and then resuscitated, has a Near-Death Experience, as defined by the above NDE features. Certainly, a close call, a fright, or even a cardiac arrest that does not have any of the above features is not, by definition, a NDE. I, like other NDE researchers today, only use the term "Near-Death Experience" to refer to a brush with death which includes a paranormal out-of-body experience and/or mystical experience with five or more of the features from Dr. Raymond Moody's NDE criteria as listed above. As I will outline in this book, all five of my Near-Death Experiences had multiple features listed in Dr. Moody's criteria.

It is interesting to note that Near-Death Experience researchers have found that individuals who have been close to death on more than one occasion, may report no NDE at all with one brush with death, and then a clear NDE with another close-call. We do not yet know why some people have NDEs and others do not, or why the same person may have an NDE with one brush with death, and not with another.

Sadly, some people criticize the multiple NDE Experiencer, saying, "What's wrong with you that you had so many Near-Death Experiences? Are you accident-prone? Are you clumsy?" The multiple Near-Death Experiencer needs support for the many traumas they've been through, not criticism. But it is important to note that an NDE is also a Spiritually Transformative Experience, and for some people, these incidences may be an opportunity to grow and transform in a radical way.

NDE Features of my First Childhood Near-Death Experience

Comparing the features of my train station out-of-body experience at age five with the above NDE features first defined by Dr. Moody, it is clear that my experience included seven of the fifteen classic NDE features. This definitely makes my train station experience fall within the parameters of a Near-Death Experience. These features were:

1. *Ineffability*: The experience had aspects that were beyond words, and are difficult for me to describe to others. The fact that worldly time seemed to stand still while my thoughts continued to flow, is particularly difficult to describe.
2. *Strong feelings of peace*: During my experience, I felt remarkably peaceful, very calm, and totally unafraid, although I was facing what looked to me like imminent death.
3. *Floating out of body:* I recall my spirit and point of perception suddenly moved up out of my physical body, to about twenty feet or so above my body, allowing me to view my surroundings, including the rapidly approaching train arriving at the station.
4. *Abrupt return to the body:* I clearly remember abruptly finding myself and my point of perception back in my body, after a stranger's hand suddenly pulled my body back onto the train platform. Time began to move forward again at this same moment.
5. *Conviction of the reality of the experience:* I have always had a clear memory of my out-of-body experience in the train station incident, and this memory has remained extraordinarily clear in my mind, despite the passage of sixty years now.
6. *Transformational impact:* This event transformed my thinking afterwards, in that having this out-of-body experience caused me, as a child, to think that I was able to fly.
7. *Independent corroboration:* Veridical Perceptions. My perception while out-of-body that a train was rapidly pulling into the station

was confirmed after the NDE when my family and I later witnessed the train pull in.

After-Effects of my first NDE

Looking back, it is difficult to say for certain whether or not this childhood Near-Death Experience transformed me psychologically or spiritually, because I was such a young child when it occurred. I was still early in my growth and development process. I hadn't even started kindergarten yet.

However, what I do recall is that in the months immediately following this childhood incident, when I started kindergarten in September, I was convinced that I could fly. In my mind as a child, my understanding of the out-of-body incident was that I had been flying that day at the train station.

I clearly recall that I was so strongly convinced that I could fly, that when I made a new friend in kindergarten I promptly confided in him that I could fly. He laughed at me and said it was impossible that I could fly. I was so convinced that I was able to fly that I told him I would prove it.

That day after kindergarten class finished, I walked with my young friend to the garden fence in front of my home. Confidently, I climbed up to the top of the fence and jumped off with my arms outstretched, to prove to my new friend that I could indeed fly.

I immediately tumbled down to the ground. My friend laughed, saying, "I told you that you couldn't fly," and walked away. I sat on the ground in shock and disbelief. I felt surprised – puzzled and confused. I did not understand why I had not been able to fly, when I had a clear memory of flying a few weeks earlier while I was in Switzerland.

As an adult, I now realize that this childhood belief that I could fly was simply the way my innocent childhood mind interpreted the experience of being out-of-body during my first Near-Death Experience.

Reflections on my Car Crash NDE at age 11 Years

After the car accident when I was eleven, my family and I slowly recovered from our respective physical injuries. Although I was discharged from the hospital about two weeks after the accident, my father, who was most seriously injured of all of us, was hospitalized longer for treatment of his injuries. My family lived temporarily in a relative's home in Toronto until he was finally discharged from the hospital. When all six of us were strong enough for the trip, we flew to Los Angeles by airplane, to complete our move.

Immediately after the car accident, I did not speak to my parents or anyone else about the out-of-body experience that I had while I was unconscious. As a child, I simply did not realize that this experience was unusual. Because I did not know otherwise, I thought my experience was normal for somebody who had received a head injury and went into a coma as I had. But now, fifty years later, and after my many years of research into NDEs and other Spiritually Transformative Experiences, I realize that my experience in this childhood car accident was indeed a Near-Death Experience.

NDE Features of my Near-Death Experience at age 11

Comparing the features of my out-of-body experience while unconscious at age eleven with the NDE features first defined by Dr. Moody, we see that my experience included eight of the fifteen classic features. These were:

1. *Ineffability*: The experience had aspects that were beyond words, and are difficult for me to describe to others.
2. *Auditory awareness*: Clairaudience. While I was unconscious, buried under luggage in the car wreckage, my out-of-body spirit clearly heard and felt my injured father calling out for me. "My daughter," he cried.
3. *Strong feelings of peace*: During my experience, I felt extremely peaceful, very calm, and totally unafraid. I felt no pain.

4. *Floating out of body:* I clearly recall my spirit and point of perception floating out of my physical body, allowing me to view my injured father at the site of the crash briefly, then later observe my unconscious body being treated by doctors in the emergency room of the hospital.

5. *Abrupt return to the body:* I clearly remember suddenly waking up in my physical body, now laying in a bed in a hospital children's ward.

6. *Conviction of the reality of the experience:* I have always had a clear memory of my out-of-body experience in the car accident, and this memory has remained extraordinarily clear despite the passage of over fifty years.

7. *Transformational impact:* The NDE definitely transformed me psychically. I found myself having new psychic experiences after the NDE. I started being able to see ghosts or spirits. Because I was just a child at the time, I am not certain whether or not the NDE also transformed me psychologically or spiritually. However, I think the NDE may have increased my spiritual convictions and broadened my spiritual views.

8. *Independent corroboration:* Veridical Perceptions. My father corroborated for me what I saw and heard while out-of-body, that he had called out for me, as he lay injured on the roadside. In addition, many years after the accident I entered medical school and became a doctor. In my training and career as a medical doctor, I often saw the large disc-shaped operating room lights, which were exactly as I had viewed from a top-down perspective during my NDE. As a child, however, I had never previously seen such operating room lights before my NDE.

At the time of my out-of-body experience and for many years afterwards, I thought this experience to merely be a normal one, an inner experience had by everyone who received a head injury and became unconscious for a period of time. After reviewing Dr. Moody's NDE features that occurred during my out-of-body experience at the age of eleven years, it becomes clear that this was indeed a Near-Death Experience, my second NDE.

Immediate After-Effects

As I reflect on the immediate after-effects of my Near-Death Experience as an eleven-year-old, I wonder how it might have impacted and transformed me. Physically, my body slowly recovered from the injuries I sustained in the car accident. I was not permitted to run or jump for several months after the accident due to my head injury and neck injury. When I did begin to participate in school sports again, I remember feeling that my body was much more awkward and poorly coordinated than before the accident. I felt oddly clumsy, especially when using my arms. This awkward clumsiness gradually disappeared with time.

When I grew into a teenager, I developed problems with severe recurrent headaches. My doctors presumed my recurrent headaches were a physical after-effect from the head and neck trauma suffered in the childhood car accident. These physical after-effects seemed to be caused by the physical injuries I sustained in the accident, and did not seem related to my having had an NDE.

Psychological After-Effects are Unclear

It is difficult for me to judge whether or not I changed psychologically after this Near-Death Experience, because I was only a young child. It is really impossible to tell so many years later. I have only very spotty memories of my life and worldview before the age of eleven years. My early childhood memories are mainly of normal family events, and some grade-school teachers and classmates.

I recall no adults ever commenting to me that my personality had changed in any way after the car accident. My school performance certainly did not change after the NDE. I was considered academically gifted as a young child and had been placed in a special accelerated school program several years before the car accident. My academic abilities did not seem to be affected in any way by the head injury, or by the NDE. I continued to excel in school afterwards, and was again placed in advanced classes. My academic excellence continued throughout high school and university, enabling me to eventually enter medical school.

Yvonne Kason, M.D.

Psychic After-Effect – I Could See Ghosts

One change that occurred in me after my second NDE stands out clearly in my memory. After this childhood NDE, I became temporarily prone to some new psychic experiences. In the months after the NDE, I clearly remember being frightened by what I was seeing at night, namely ghosts.

After my family moved into our new home in Los Angeles, when I lay in my bed at night I could clearly see ghosts, wispy wraith-like spirits, moving in space around and above me. This new psychic phenomenon scared me. As a child, I interpreted these sightings as proof that the house we had moved into was haunted. However, nobody else in my family was having any experiences suggesting that the house was indeed haunted. My parents dismissed my concerns. They probably thought I was imagining things because I was emotionally upset by the move, or due to the trauma of the car accident.

I recall that in my efforts to deal with these frightening apparitions, with childhood innocence I prayed intently to God, asking Him to protect me from the ghosts that I was seeing. I also refused to sleep alone in my assigned bedroom. My parents consoled my fears by allowing me to sleep in the same bedroom as my younger brother and younger sister, as I insisted. I felt much safer at night with my two siblings in the room beside me, despite the fact I continued to see ghosts around me.

I had never seen ghosts or spirits before this Near-Death Experience, and within a year after the NDE I stopped seeing them altogether. Now, as a medical doctor who has researched NDEs, I realize that this period of seeing ghosts or spirits was likely due to the NDE's psychic transformational impact on my consciousness.

Many Near-Death Experience researchers, including myself, have noted that people who have had an out-of-body type of NDE, often find themselves having new or increased psychic experiences after the NDE. It is as if the out-of-body experience, which is held to be a type of psychic phenomenon, leaves the NDE experiencer's brain and/or consciousness more capable of perceiving other psychic phenomena after the NDE. Thus, my young eleven-year-old self was able to psychically perceive ghosts or spirits for some time after my out-of-body NDE. Then, with time, this new psychic ability went away.

Spiritual After-Effects

I am not certain whether or not my Near-Death Experience at age eleven had any transformational effect on me spiritually, but I do think it may have increased my spiritual drive and spiritual focus. I do not recall how strong my spiritual drive was as a young child. However, I recall that I had a very strong spiritual impulse during my pre-teen and teen years following that second NDE.

I recall that about one year after it, at the age of twelve, when a school friend of mine who was a devout Roman Catholic told me about a possible life vocation as a nun, a life dedicated to loving God and serving God, I was very attracted to this concept. Although I was raised as a Protestant Christian in the United Church of Canada, when I learned of the possibility of becoming a nun, I seriously considered becoming a nun within the Catholic Church.

Later that same year, when I was still twelve, I caught some illness with a high fever a couple of days before Christmas. My fever was still high the evening before Christmas. My mother told me that if my fever did not come down by the next morning, I would have to stay in bed and miss the family Christmas celebration the next day. I remember being absolutely heartbroken at the prospect of possibly missing what, as a child, I considered to be the high point of the year, our family Christmas celebration.

I recall sobbing into my pillow and with childhood innocence intently and earnestly praying to God, "Dear God, please, please, please heal me for Christmas.....If you heal me for Christmas, I will do anything you want me to do in this life... but, please, please, please heal me for Christmas."

The next morning when I awoke, my fever had come down. The illness had gone away overnight. I was ecstatic that I was able to get up and attend our family's Christmas celebration. In my heart, as a twelve-year-old child, I believed that God had answered my prayers, that I had been healed by a miracle that night.

I do not recall any single episode that I prayed with such intense fervor as a young child before my NDE at age eleven. But I clearly recall these two incidents which occurred shortly after this Near-Death Experience, when I prayed with deep conviction and fervent heartfelt intensity, first for protection from ghosts, and later for a healing in time for Christmas. Perhaps my deep conviction and faith in the power of God and my attraction to becoming a nun at age eleven and twelve were to some degree after-effects of my car-accident NDE.

My Soul Lesson – I am a Soul, not just a Body

As I look back and reflect upon what soul lesson I learned from my first two Near-Death Experiences, as a child of five years and then as a child of eleven years, I realize that I learned that I am a soul or spirit, and not just a physical body. Although I did not have the words to express this realization when I was a child, I had experienced twice by the age of eleven years that my soul or spirit could leave the body in certain circumstances.

During my childhood out-of-body Near-Death Experiences, I found that I was still very much awake and alive when my soul separated from my physical body. Thus, I discovered that I was more than just the physical body. I also learned that although out-of-body, my soul could once again re-enter, and reside in my physical body. Although as a child I did not stop to analyze them, my childhood Near-Death Experiences clearly taught me that I am a soul, not just a physical body, but a soul having a physical experience.

Later After Effects – Spiritual Thinking Outside the Box

As I grew into a teenager, my strong spiritual impulse continued. During my early teens, I became very active in my local United Church of Canada, teaching Sunday school and singing in the church choir. Quickly, I began to think outside the box. I became interested in broader spiritual topics which went beyond the parameters of the religion in which I was raised. I became curious about yoga, meditation, Native American spiritual traditions, and Eastern religious philosophies.

Perhaps I was influenced as a teenager by the music and the spiritual exploration in India of my music idols at that time, the Beatles. It is also possible that I was influenced by the mentality of the hippie generation of which I was a part, and the flower-power philosophy of peace, love, and rock and roll.

My thinking outside the box was evident in an oral presentation I prepared and gave to my high-school French class when I was sixteen, with a spiritual theme that startled my teacher. I stated in French, "I think the world is on the brink of a spiritual revolution in consciousness. Raising the spiritual consciousness of the planet is the only way I think the world will be able to survive our many wars, crises, and misunderstandings between people and between nations..." I recall most of my classmates selected a far more mundane topic for their French oral presentations.

In the late 1960s and early 1970s, during high school and early university, I read, among other things, the writings of Alan Watts, Timothy Leary, and Carlos Castaneda, and became fascinated with their discussions of mystical states of consciousness. They said mystical states could be glimpsed through the use of hallucinogenic drugs such as LSD. But it quickly became clear to me that people should be able to reach these mystical states of consciousness, which I considered glimpses of the Divine, without the use of drugs.

My spiritual inquiry and thinking outside the box continued throughout my university and medical school years. Because I had moved away from home in Toronto to attend McMaster University in Hamilton, Ontario, I was no longer active in my local church. Although my university life was fairly normal in most ways, filled with lots of studying and weekends socializing with other students, I also joined a university hatha yoga class. I was introduced to meditation there and began to practice hatha yoga regularly. This new daily practice of meditation ultimately changed the course of my life, beginning with an explosive spiritual experience a few years later.

Chapter 3

MY SPIRITUAL AWAKENING: DISCOVERING SPIRITUALLY TRANSFORMATIVE EXPERIENCES

"In my Father's house are many mansions." (John 14:2)

Much to my wonder and amazement, my childhood Near-Death Experiences were just the beginning of an inspiring lifelong spiritual awakening journey, punctuated with multiple Spiritually Transformative Experiences (STEs) including five NDEs. I am now one of a rare breed, someone who has had multiple Spiritually Transformative Experiences and multiple Near-Death Experiences, a modern-day mystic. Each STE and NDE I had was unique. However, although they were similar to the others in some ways, each differed from the others in many ways.

All the Spiritually Transformative Experiences throughout my lifetime, including all five of my Near-Death Experiences, had one thing in common, confirming that I am truly a soul, not just a physical body, and that my soul exists beyond my physical body. Starting in my childhood, I repeatedly experienced my soul leaving my body and returning again, and that my soul would indeed live on after the death of the physical body, just as the founders of the world's great faiths have attested.

Further, each STE gave me a brief glimpse of an aspect of a reality greater than the physical, a multi-dimensional universe, with many glimpses of the Divine Higher Power underlying and interpenetrating the universe. They revealed to me that our Higher Power, what I call God and others may call Spirit, Brahma, Creator, the force, or other names, is immensely vast, infinitely intelligent, and profoundly loving in nature. These STEs and NDEs deeply affected me, and ultimately changed my life path.

The similarities plus the differences between my multiple Spiritually Transformative Experiences including my five NDEs have drawn me to conclude, as Jesus Christ once said, "In my father's house are many mansions." (John 14:2) To me, this means that in God's infinite universe of matter and consciousness, there are infinite dimensions, aspects, and facets. Therefore there are many ways that our loving Higher Power God may reveal glimpses of Its complex, infinite reality to us – as glimpses of many diverse rooms in the Creator God's immense mansion of loving universal creation.

As I share in detail the stories of several of my most powerful and life-changing STEs including all five of my NDEs, I will reflect upon them, both personally as an experiencer, and professionally as a medical doctor and STE researcher. I will reflect on each STE's after-effects, the ways in which each seemed to uplift me and change me in many positive ways, and the soul lessons that I learned from them. I will describe how many STEs seemed to launch me forward onto my next spiritual life-stage.

I will also describe the struggles and the challenges I encountered in striving to understand my extraordinary experiences, and how all my STEs were misunderstood for years, particularly my NDEs and kundalini awakening. You will see how my STEs were often mislabeled, critically judged, and/or minimized by others, sometimes ridiculed, called such things as a hallucination or a flight of my imagination, or dismissed as nothing of significance. You will learn how I felt compelled to live in the closet for many years, not disclosing my experiences to those around me. Unfortunately, I know I am not alone. I know many other STE experiencers have had similar struggles.

Yvonne Kason, M.D.

Researching Spiritually Transformative Experiences

Propelled by a quest to understand my own experiences and the subsequent transforming after-effects, and by my desire to help others who had similar experiences, I spent the last 40 years researching Spiritually Transformative Experiences. I started by reading many books about mystical experiences. This included medical, psychological, and spiritual books from the mystical traditions of many religions and sacred paths. I researched further by learning directly from STE experiencers, by counseling people who had many types of STEs. In 1990, I co-founded the Kundalini Research Network and did further research as Chair of the Kundalini Research Network's Questionnaire Research Project. In my books, *A Farther Shore, Farther Shores*, and *Touched by the Light*, I describe what I learned through my research and clinical experience, and give many case stories of STEs happening to people today.

What are Spiritually Transformative Experiences?

I first coined the term *Spiritually Transformative Experiences* (STEs) in 1994 in my book *A Farther Shore*, to describe the wide range of powerful spiritual and paranormal experiences that I and many others were having. I found all types of STEs tend to transform the experiencer's values and beliefs in a more spiritual direction, and often begin or speed up a long-term process of psychological growth and spiritual deepening. I described STEs in greater detail in *Farther Shores*, and in most up-to-date detail in *Touched by the Light*.

I define Spiritually Transformative Experiences in the following six categories:

1. Mystical experiences of many types;
2. Near-Death Experiences;
3. Kundalini or spiritual energy awakenings;
4. Psychic awakenings, including out-of-body experiences, past-life recall, clairaudience, clairvoyance, clairsentience, mediumship, channeling, trans-dimensional experiences, and more;

5. Other death-related STEs, including death-watch experiences, death-bed experiences, After-Death Communications; and

6. Inspired creativity and genius.

In my professional research and personal experience, I found that each person's STEs give them glimpses of a greater reality, of an expanded range of consciousness, and often glimpses of the Divine power behind the universe. These glimpses differ slightly one from the other but share many common features. In addition, Divine glimpses perceived by one individual in several of their NDEs or several STEs may also be quite different one from the other – like glimpses of different rooms of a vast mansion.

But despite the differences, there is virtually universal agreement on the overall nature of the owner of the mansion. The Divine glimpses, the expanded range of consciousness occurring in STEs, reveal a multidimensional universe permeated with an expansive cosmic consciousness, a Higher Power, an infinitely intelligent loving force that underlies all creation and which exudes profound unconditional love for all of humanity. This was true for me and my glimpses of the Divine in my multiple STEs.

My Spiritual Awakening – A Kundalini Awakening

My first adult STE was a Kundalini Awakening in 1976. As I will describe in detail later, while deep in meditation, I suddenly heard a loud inner roaring sound at the same time as I felt a powerful energy move up my body and spine. My consciousness rose up out of my body and expanded to fill a vast space. I then slipped into what I now know to be a mystical experience. I felt tremendous love and joy throughout the expansion.

Following this powerful meditation experience, I began to notice unusual physical sensations, rushes of energy up my spine, energy sensations at my chakra points, unusual inner sounds, and more. It took me many years to come to an understanding that what I had experienced in 1976 was a kundalini awakening and that the unusual physical sensations I was feeling are known signs of an activated kundalini.

Yvonne Kason, M.D.

1979 Mystical Experience – a Medevac Plane Crash NDE

A dramatic experience in 1979 began my lifelong quest to understand Near-Death Experiences and mystical experiences. On March 27, 1979, when I was a young doctor on a medevac flight, I came close to death when the plane crashed. I suddenly found my spirit lifting out of my body and moving upwards into a place filled with a profoundly loving white light, a loving light that I sensed to be coming from the Higher Power, what I call God.

For years afterward I did not know what to call my extraordinary experience. I had no vocabulary to accurately describe the experience. It was beyond words in many ways. The best term I found was a *mystical experience*. This propelled me, as a young doctor, onto a quest to understand mystical and paranormal experiences from a modern Western medical and psychological perspective. It also drove me on a personal spiritual quest. I became a spiritual seeker, wanting to come to a deeper spiritual understanding of what I had glimpsed. Additionally, the mystical experience seemed to launch me onto an accelerated path of spiritual transformation of my consciousness with impacts on my body, mind, and spirit that I did not understand, and that seemed beyond my control.

At the time of my 1979 mystical experience/NDE in the airplane crash, there was very little awareness about mystical experiences or Near-Death Experiences, both within the medical profession and in the public eye. Trying to understand my own experience, I began to research the literature. I first explored many books about mystical experiences. Later I discovered the writings of Dr. Raymond Moody.

I learned that in 1975, he had documented many cases of people having out-of-body and/or white-light mystical experiences while clinically dead and then later resuscitated, or while very near death. As I mentioned in Chapter 2, Dr. Moody coined the phrase *Near-Death Experience* for this phenomenon. However, in 1979 right after my NDE, I did not think my experience was an NDE at all, because I had not been clinically dead during the accident and because my mystical experience began before the plane had crashed, while the plane was still plummeting towards the ground. Therefore, I continued to label it a mystical experience.

However, my opinion changed in 1990 when I met the prominent NDE researcher, Dr. Kenneth Ring, at a medical meeting. I discussed my 1979 plane crash mystical experience with him, and he confirmed what I had come to think by that time, that this experience was indeed a type of NDE.

Research had now shown that an NDE could occur when a person was psychologically facing death, not just when they were clinically dead or physically close to death. With this expanded definition, Dr. Ring and I agreed that my plane crash experience was definitely a type of NDE. This confirmation finally gave me a vocabulary, a precise term to describe the mystical experience that had happened to me during the airplane crash, a type of Near-Death Experience.

My "Calling" Mystical Experience – Coming Out of the Closet

As I will describe later, for the first almost twelve years that I researched Spiritually Transformative Experiences, I kept my personal 1979 Near-Death Experience quite private. However, in 1990, a few days before my first meeting with Dr. Kenneth Ring, I had another powerful STE. I had a strong "calling" mystical experience in which I felt called by Spirit to publicly share what I had learned about NDEs and other STEs. After this 1990 "calling" mystical experience, I came out of the closet. I began to speak publicly about my 1979 NDE and my STE research and to publicly advocate for other STE and NDE experiencers.

I felt it was my moral obligation to speak out about what I had learned about Spiritually Transformative Experiences in the past twelve years, to both the general public and the medical profession. I needed to spread awareness as a medical doctor, that Near-Death Experiences and other mystical experiences were real, they were peak human experiences, and they were not symptoms of mental illness, as far too often was thought.

Over those years, I had met many people who reported to me that their NDEs or other STEs had been mislabeled by doctors, clergy, and/or friends as being hallucinations, delusions, or a sign of mental illness. I saw that harm was being done to experiencers by this mislabeling and pathologizing of healthy STEs. I felt called to strive to reduce this harm to others.

In 1990, when I first came out of the closet and began to speak publicly about my plane crash mystical NDE, and other STEs, I had to deal with much professional resistance and many challenges. At the time, I was the first Canadian medical doctor to speak about having had an NDE themselves. I also was the first Canadian doctor to specialize in research and counseling of patients who had experienced STEs. I managed to successfully navigate my way through these challenges. Throughout my medical career, I have spoken with close to 1,000 people who have had diverse types of STEs. This led me to coin the term "Spiritually Transformative Experiences" in 1994.

NDEs Become More Widely Known

Over the years after my 1979 plane-crash NDE, there was a dramatic increase in public awareness of Near-Death Experiences, mainly through the media. For example, in George Lucas' blockbuster 1980 film, re-released in 1997, *Star Wars Episode V: The Empire Strikes Back,* the hero Luke had a Near-Death Experience while freezing to death.

In Luke's quite accurately depicted NDE, he had a mystical vision of a being of light, the spirit of his deceased mentor Obi Wan. As sometimes occurs in NDEs, Obi Wan gave Luke an important life message during it. Director Joel Schumacher's 1990 film *Flatliners* also depicted NDEs, with a group of young people experimenting with trying to induce a Near-Death Experience.

Several documentaries and films have now re-enacted various NDE experiencers' stories. In fact, my own 1979 NDE has now been re-enacted on *Sightings* and in two television documentaries. The popular film *Heaven is for Real,* based on the 2010 best-selling book by Todd Burpo and Lynn Vincent, recounts the dramatic story of the childhood NDE of Burpo's then three-year-old son. All this media attention vastly increased public awareness of Near-Death Experiences.

More NDE experiencers have come forward in recent years and written vivid best-selling books recounting the stories of their Near-Death Experiences. The American orthopedic surgeon Dr. Mary C. Neal, recounted her life-changing NDE in her 2011 bestselling book, *To Heaven and Back.* In 2012, Anita Moorjani, a cancer survivor who lives in Hong

Kong, described the deeply moving and inspiring account of her NDE in her best-selling international book, *Dying to be Me*.

Doctors, psychologists, and theologians from around the world have also increasingly described similar reports made by their patients, and other professional books have since been written on the subject of NDEs. Various groups and organizations began to research and focus on one specific type of STE. Some focused on NDEs, others on Kundalini Awakenings, and yet others on psychic phenomena. This did much to raise awareness of Near-Death Experiences and other Spiritually Transformative Experiences among professionals as well as the public.

I have Multiple Near-Death Experiences

Much to my surprise, on February 27, 1995, a year after I published my first book on Spiritually Transformative Experiences, *A Farther Shore*, I had another profound mystical experience, another Near-Death Experience, in a near-miss airplane incident. This 1995 NDE gave me a life review of peak life experiences, and I encountered a loving blue being of light. The transformational impact of this NDE on my consciousness was far greater than any previous STE. It propelled me into a state of mystical communion afterwards.

For about twenty years, I felt uncomfortable talking publicly about my 1995 NDE and the communion afterwards because it felt very private and sacred. I, therefore, kept it in the closet. Fortunately, in February of 1995, I immediately realized that my mystical experience was a type of NDE, without any external validation being required.

The mystical communion lasted for two months following it. It showed me the reality of higher states of consciousness, God-communion, or illumination, as is described in the mystical treatises of all the world's major faiths, including in great detail in the yogic tradition. However, the after-effects of my 1995 NDE were again a mixture of positive and challenging ones.

To my further amazement, on November 8, 2003, I had yet another life-changing STE, another Near-Death Experience related to a serious accident where I sustained a traumatic brain injury. This 2003 NDE was again different from my other NDEs, with a deeper, and more profound impact on me as compared to my previous NDEs.

During the 2003 head injury NDE, I died completely for a period of time. I found my spirit immediately moving out-of-body at the moment of death, up through a dark space, into the realm of loving light of the Higher Power. I was greeted into the light by two saintly beings of light. In the heavenly light realm, much was revealed to me all at once, in a revelation or *download*.

Suddenly I remembered all of my past lives, and this made the events of my life make deeper sense. It was an aha experience. After a period of time in ecstasy, I was given the choice of whether or not to return to my body. I then abruptly re-awoke in my ice-cold previously dead body, with a deep gasp of breath.

This 2003 NDE was similar yet different in many ways from the other NDEs I had earlier in my life. To me, this was a *Death Experience* NDE rather than a *Near-Death* NDE like my previous ones. The impact of this 2003 Near-Death Experience on my life has been profound. Some of the after-effects of this NDE were wonderfully positive, yet others were very challenging. "I don't care if nobody believes me. I know what I saw," I once confided to a monk about my 2003 head injury NDE.

Following a powerful brain-healing STE in 2016, I resumed my calling of raising awareness about all types of STEs. In 2019, I had a powerful download experience that prompted me to found a new global online organization to further fulfill this mission, *Spiritual Awakenings International,* www.spiritualawakeningsinternational.org.

I am delighted that my life-long spiritual awakening journey gradually led me to feel confident enough to clearly state "There is nothing to fear in death. We are all loved by the profoundly loving Higher Power behind the universe!" However, it took me many years, and many STEs, to fully come to this realization.

Chapter 4

KUNDALINI AWAKENING AND MYSTICAL EXPERIENCE IN 1976

My first adult Spiritually Transformative Experience happened in 1976, during my final year in medical school. That fall, I took a course teaching meditation techniques that claimed to improve the meditator's memory and help university students study more effectively and perform better on exams. Due to a combination of my desires to excel in my medical school final examinations, and to explore spiritually, I began to do regular daily meditations using these techniques.

I found that meditation came easily to me, almost like second nature. I started meditating for an hour each morning and each evening. In December 1976, at the age of twenty-three, and after three months of regular daily meditation practice, while intensely meditating one evening I had a profoundly beautiful meditation experience, that I now realize was a kundalini awakening/spiritual energy awakening that culminated in my first mystical experience.

My Kundalini Awakening

It occurred when I participated in a two to three-hour group meditation session in an auditorium. I was using the meditation technique I had been taught, imagining energy flowing up from the base of the spine towards my head, where I imagined a beautiful white lotus flower was blooming at my crown. At the time the experience began, I was focusing my attention on the lotus on the top of my head. While in this deep meditative state, I also had the impulse to send love and light out from my heart to the others in the auditorium.

About twenty minutes into my meditation, suddenly I heard a loud inner sound, like the roar of a large waterfall. At the same time, I felt a strong wave of energy rush up my spine. As the energy reached the top of my head I felt my consciousness rise up out of my body.

My consciousness expanded in size. I no longer felt that I was the size of my body or my head. I felt I had expanded to the size of the large auditorium where I was seated. My consciousness became filled with light. In this expansive state, I became filled with exquisite feelings of love and bliss. It was as if I had become pure love itself. I remained in this state of expansion, light, and bliss until the meditation ended. After the meditation period ended an hour or so later, my consciousness contracted to its regular state, but I felt an afterglow of inner peace, radiance, deep joy, and love.

I recall thinking, *No wonder people like to meditate. This feels great!* In my naiveté, I thought this beautiful experience probably happened regularly to all the more experienced meditators. Because I knew no better, I assumed that my expansive experience occurred because I had finally managed to meditate using the technique correctly.

Struggling to Find a Name for my Experience

Afterward, I did not talk to others about what had happened, because I was embarrassed to reveal to others that it had taken me a few months to *finally* figure out how to meditate properly. It was only several weeks later, after I discovered that I was not able to reproduce the blissful episode during subsequent daily meditations, that I quietly asked an experienced meditator what I was doing wrong in my technique that I was not having the ecstatic experience again. Only then did I discover from him that these experiences did not occur regularly to others.

I asked the meditation group leaders what it was that I had experienced. As they contemplated, they seemed quite puzzled. One told me that my experience sounded in many ways like a *kundalini awakening*. However, from their training, it was considered impossible that I could possibly have a kundalini awakening as such a young and inexperienced meditator. They believed a person had to practice meditation for many years before a kundalini awakening was possible, and/or that a student needed to be initiated by a guru in order to have a kundalini awakening.

Further, my meditation group leaders had the impression (which I now know is not correct), that following a kundalini awakening, a person would immediately become enlightened, and would be in an ongoing mystical state of higher consciousness, in ongoing cosmic consciousness. My experience was clearly temporary which they could not explain.

My meditation group leaders, therefore, dismissed the possibility that I had indeed had a kundalini awakening. They offered me no other explanation or words to describe or help me understand my meditation-induced experience.

Recurrent Energy Rushes

Interestingly, in the days, weeks, and months following this powerful meditation experience that I now know was indeed a kundalini awakening, I noticed that I continued to have intermittent energy sensations similar to those of the initial awakening experience. I noticed I began to feel frequent episodes of rushes of energy going up my spine.

The energy rushes usually felt like a clear upward movement of energy, starting at the base of my spine and rapidly running up my spine to my head. Sometimes the intensity of the energy rushes would make my body shudder or jolt briefly. Other times the energy would feel hot, like a hot force was trying to push up my back from the base of my spine.

I often felt the rushes of energy while I was meditating, or while contemplating a spiritual concept. Other times I felt the rushes of energy while I was active in the world in normal day-to-day activities.

When the spinal energy rushes came during worldly activities, I quickly learned they had an inner wisdom. The energy rushes would give me a confirmation of "yes," indicating this was the correct choice, or "yes" that the person speaking was speaking the truth.

Yvonne Kason, M.D.

New Inner Sounds

Immediately following my kundalini awakening I also noticed another new unusual physical symptom. I started hearing inner sounds most of the time. The inner sounds varied. Sometimes I would hear an inner rumbling sound, similar to the sound of a heavy truck rumbling down a street. Other times I would hear a chirping sound, similar to the sound of crickets chirping. Yet other times I would hear fine high-pitched tinkling sounds, like the soft clinging of distant wind chimes, or the high-pitched buzzing of bees. Other times I would hear distant roaring sounds, like to roar of the ocean, or the OM sound. Yet other times I would hear a distant gong ring.

I now know that these inner sounds are described in yogic literature as the inner sounds of the chakras. After a kundalini awakening, the chakras or energy centers in the astral body/subtle body's spine become activated. These inner sounds become perceptible after a kundalini awakening. However in 1976, I did not know this, and I therefore observed and made mental notes of these new inner sounds.

Chakra Sensations

Another interesting phenomenon I started noticing within myself was unusual energy sensations at specific points in my body. Through my readings about Yoga, I learned about the chakras or energy centers located at various points of the body. The main chakras are held to be seven centers located along the spine of the astral body, which is interpenetrating the physical body. The first chakra is said to be located at the base of the spine in the coccyx region, the second chakra a few inches higher in the sacral region, while the third chakra is in the lumbar region.

The fourth or heart-chakra, is found around the heart region, the fifth is at the throat level, the sixth chakra (sometimes called the third-eye chakra) is on the forehead, and the seventh or crown chakra, is located at the top of the head. I soon realized that, somehow related to my meditation practice or the extraordinary meditation experience I had, I had now started being able to perceive energy movements at several of my chakras.

I began to have recurrent experiences of feeling energy movements, pressures, or swirls of energy, at my third-eye chakra on my forehead.

Other times I would feel energy swirls at the solar plexus region of my abdomen at the third chakra region, or my heart region in the center of my chest at the fourth chakra.

Sometimes I would feel there was an energy field protruding from one or more of my chakras, especially frequently from my third or solar plexus chakra. Other times I was intensely aware of the crown chakra on my head. I would feel as if my head had expanded, or was being pressured to expand by energy pushing from within my brain. At times it felt as if my skull were too small for the energy pushing outwards from my brain.

As intriguing as these new inner sensations were immediately following my 1976 kundalini awakening, I strove to ignore them. At the time, I had no idea what was causing these sensations. However, I was very busy with my medical studies and examinations near the end of my final year in medical school. I could not permit myself to be distracted. I, therefore, put these experiences out of my mind, for the time being.

Chapter 5

AFTER-EFFECTS OF MY KUNDALINI AWAKENING

My kundalini awakening had definite strong after-effects on me. Looking back, I now see that my 1976 kundalini awakening marked the beginning of a profound long-term spiritual transformation process in my life.

This meditation-related experience stimulated my spiritual drive. I longed to once again experience the state of profound bliss and love that I had glimpsed that wonderful day. However, for several years I had no idea how to label my meditation experience, or the energy rushes up my spine, inner sounds, and chakra sensations that I felt repeatedly afterward.

Called to go to India to meet Gopi Krishna

It was no coincidence that about six months after my kundalini awakening, I had the opportunity to travel to India to meet the renowned kundalini experiencer, researcher, and author, Gopi Krishna. He was going to be talking to my then meditation group about kundalini awakenings. At the time, I was a young newly graduated medical doctor, beginning my internship. Due to the high expectations and long work hours of being a new intern, I did not plan to join this group on the trip to India that year.

However, that changed one evening while watching a homemade video of Gopi Krishna speaking, when I felt strongly called to go to India.

I remember sitting in a small meeting room with several other meditation group students to watch this video. It was being shown by organizers of the trip to India to encourage people to join the adventure to India to meet Gopi Krishna.

As soon as Gopi Krishna's face appeared on the small movie screen, my consciousness was mesmerized. My body seemed to freeze, with my eyes glued to staring at his eyes. I then started to feel very strong pulses of energy repeatedly rush up my spine. The pulses were so strong that my body physically rocked and jerked with each upward pulse. The energy pulsed up my spine so vigorously that my body shook repeatedly, out of my control. I could not divert my gaze which was frozen with my eyes glued to looking at Gopi Krishna's face.

Finally, after several minutes of powerful energy pulses repeatedly rushing up my body and spine, physically rocking me, I turned inwardly to God, and mentally surrendered, *Ok Lord, I will go to India and meet Gopi Krishna*. Intuitively I knew that these powerful energy pulses were a clear spiritual signal to me, that I was supposed to travel to India to meet Gopi Krishna. The energy pulses and resulting body jerks stopped immediately when I made that promise to Spirit.

Therefore, in the summer of 1977, I traveled to India together with others from my meditation group, and I met Gopi Krishna in Srinagar, Kashmir, India. I listened to him talk about kundalini awakening and the yogic model of consciousness during a week of daily seminars. This was all new information to me at that time, which I absorbed enthusiastically. It felt right to me, accurate and true.

I also had the good fortune of being invited to have private meetings with Gopi Krishna while in India in the summer of 1977. In later years when he traveled to the USA and Canada, I also met with him several times. He became a mentor to me.

We also corresponded by mail from 1977 until he died in 1984. He repeatedly urged me to do kundalini research. Little did I know at that time that I had already experienced a kundalini awakening. Perhaps his repeated urging that I do kundalini research was his thinly veiled way of helping me realize that I too had experienced a kundalini awakening.

Due to our close correspondence, I had the opportunity over the years to read all of Gopi Krishna's 17 books about kundalini awakening. I read these avidly. Gradually, as I read all of his descriptions of signs of a kundalini awakening as well as other authors' descriptions of the experience, several years after Gopi Krishna died I finally realized that I had myself had a kundalini awakening in December 1976. I also realized that I was having ongoing signs of continued kundalini activity.

Later, when reading other books that Gopi Krishna had suggested, including William James, *The Varieties of Mystical Experience*, and Evelyn Underhill's *Mysticism*, I discovered the term "mystical experience" accurately described the love-bliss-filled state of consciousness I had also experienced during my kundalini awakening.

Misunderstood by Others

Discovering the names for my profound 1976 meditation experience and its after-effects, kundalini awakening and mystical experience, created new problems, however. Unfortunately, other meditators scoffed at my belief that I had experienced a kundalini/spiritual energy awakening, as they considered me too young, (I was 23 at the time of the initial awakening), and that I was not a sufficiently advanced meditator to have such an experience. I was also told that if I had indeed had a kundalini/ spiritual energy awakening as I thought, I would now be in ongoing cosmic consciousness and fully illuminated. Clearly, I was not in a state of ongoing cosmic consciousness.

My inner perception and conclusion from my reading were very different from this view. I felt that the kundalini/spiritual energy awakening which I had experienced had started an ongoing transformation process within me. It was not that it had instantly completed a massive transformation of my consciousness all at once.

Others scoffed at my interpretations and told me that mystical experiences simply did not happen to ordinary people like me, just to great saints and mystics. Still others cruelly accused me of having an inflated ego, and that I was selfishly trying to gain attention by falsely claiming to have had this meditation experience. Misunderstanding surrounded me.

I received no help at all from those around me in the 1970s in understanding my unusual consciousness experiences. I quickly learned to remain silent about this profound 1976 meditation experience. I, therefore, was forced to seek out books on mystical experiences and kundalini/spiritual energy awakenings to further my understanding of my own experiences.

Now, after my many years of professional research into diverse Spiritually Transformative Experiences, I can confidently state that my 1976 meditation experience was indeed a kundalini awakening/spiritual energy awakening associated with a mystical experience. As I describe in great detail in my book, *Touched by the Light,* the kundalini awakening/spiritual energy awakening does indeed start a long-term process of spiritual transformation of my body, mind, and spirit, as had happened to me. However, it took many years of research until I could confidently label my kundalini awakening and long-term transformation process correctly.

My struggle to understand and give an accurate name to my 1976 meditation experience made me realize firsthand how important it is to correctly label all types of STEs. Giving my unusual consciousness experience a positive, non-pathological name, and learning that it has been described in many cultures and spiritual traditions, helped me integrate this experience into my daily life and understand the ongoing spiritual transformation after-effects.

My struggle to understand my 1976 kundalini awakening and later my powerful 1979 Near-Death Experience, is what propelled me as a doctor, to ultimately specialize in researching and counseling patients who had experienced NDEs and other STEs.

Was my Kundalini Awakening an After-Effect of my Childhood NDEs?

As I reflect on the features of my two childhood NDEs, and the features of my kundalini awakening and first mystical experience in 1976, it is clear that they all included out-of-body experiences. I now wonder if it is possible that the out-of-body experiences in my childhood NDEs somehow made me more open to having other out-of-body experiences as an adult, in 1976, this time brought on by my intense meditation practice.

Yvonne Kason, M.D.

However, my 1976 meditation-induced kundalini awakening experience had additional features that my earlier childhood out-of-body NDEs did not include. It had the dramatic and clear additional features of a kundalini/spiritual energy awakening: the marked sensation of energy rushing up my spine; inner light; a loud inner roaring sound; plus my mystical experience of a dramatic expansion of my consciousness and dissolving into the intense feeling of unconditional love.

This makes me wonder if my childhood NDEs might have in some way prepared my body and consciousness, making it easier for me twelve years later to have a kundalini/spiritual energy awakening culminating in a mystical experience, as compared to someone who had never had an earlier NDE. These are questions for which I have no definite answer. However, on balance, I now think that my childhood NDEs may indeed have somehow been the first steps in preparing my body and consciousness for a kundalini awakening many years later.

Overall, as I look back upon the years of my youth following my childhood NDEs, I think it is quite possible that the childhood NDEs had spiritual after-effects on me. Whatever contribution my personality traits may have had, as compared to the spiritual after-effects of my childhood NDEs, one thing is clear. I certainly had an unusually high interest in spiritual themes outside the box as a teenager and in my early adult years.

I think my childhood NDEs began to open the doors of my consciousness, by giving me glimpses, tiny peeks at the psychic/paranormal realm of out-of-body experiences. My meditation practice when I was a university student seemed to open the doors of my consciousness much further, triggering my first mystical experience and my kundalini awakening occurring during a deep meditation in 1976.

Did my Kundalini Awakening Open Me to Multiple STEs/NDEs?

According to yogic theory and as Gopi Krishna, Paramahansa Yogananda and other yogis state, having an awakened kundalini causes a gradual expansion of consciousness to include STEs – mystical experiences, psychic phenomena, and inspired creativity. Thus I think that my kundalini awakening at age 23 was a major factor in opening my consciousness, resulting in me becoming a multiple STE experiencer over the course of my life.

I think many other people who are multiple STE experiencers may also have an active kundalini. I discuss the yogic perspective on the spiritual awakening of consciousness and the relationship between kundalini awakening and STEs in greater detail in my books *Touched by the Light* and *Farther Shores.*

I think my active kundalini following the initial awakening in 1976 made me more susceptible to mystical experiences, including the mystical experiences I had during my adult NDEs. Further, some NDE researchers, specifically Dr. Kenneth Ring, Dr. Bruce Greyson, and I, have observed that NDEs seem to stimulate a kundalini awakening in some individuals.

Thus, in my case, it seems my kundalini awakening in 1976 may have predisposed me or made me more open and susceptible to my NDEs in 1979, 1995, and 2003. In addition, each of my NDEs may have further stimulated my kundalini to a higher level of activity. This is exactly how it felt to me throughout my life.

Was I Born Predisposed to STEs?

From a spiritual perspective, I wonder if perhaps I was born into this life with an openness to Spiritually Transformative Experiences due to my past lives. During my 2003 NDE, I regained memory of my many past lives and saw that I had also had powerful STEs in many of them, including NDEs, kundalini awakenings, and mystical experiences. Perhaps I came into this lifetime with an openness to spiritual awakenings and STEs. This would be why I started having STEs as a child, a spontaneous kundalini awakening at age 23, and multiple NDEs and STEs throughout this life. I know that this is not the first lifetime I have been having a kundalini awakening and multiple STEs.

My spiritual exploration and practice of meditation continued after my 1976 kundalini awakening, as I grew into adult life, but I chose to keep my outside-the box-interests in the background of my life. Instead, I consciously focused on the intense studies that were required in my continuing training as a medical doctor. Little did I know as I graduated medical school and began my medical residency, that the Higher Power, in its Divine plan for my life, had no intention for me to lose sight or ignore the spiritual experiences of my youth. Many more spiritual experiences lay in store for me and would happen much sooner than I could possibly imagine.

Chapter 6

MY FIRST ADULT NDE – THE 1979 MEDEVAC PLANE CRASH

My first adult Near-Death Experience happened on March 27, 1979, when I was in a medevac plane crash in northern Ontario, Canada. I first described this Near-Death Experience in my earlier books, but here in my personal story, I will expand upon, and share more details of it, and the events surrounding the plane crash. Later, I will reflect in much greater depth than before on the after-effects of this NDE and the impacts on my life, both the positive that uplifted and inspired me and some quite challenging and difficult ones.

I graduated from McMaster University medical school in 1977, and then as a young doctor continued my medical specialty training with an internship at the University of Ottawa, Ottawa Civic Hospital, followed by a Family Practice residency at the University of Toronto, at Women's College Hospital. I had turned 26 years old in February of 1979. In March 1979, as part of my final year of Family Practice residency, I was assigned to work for one month as a doctor in a small, rural hospital in Sioux Lookout, a town in northwestern Ontario. The small hospital provided medical care for several isolated First Nations communities and reservations that lay even further north, in remote, poorly accessible areas of northern Ontario.

I traveled to Sioux Lookout at the beginning of March 1979. For a few weeks, I attended to patients in the Sioux Lookout hospital. In my third week, I was assigned to travel to a nursing station outpost at a remote and isolated First Nations community north of Sioux Lookout, to care for patients there. Because this and other remote Ontario First Nations communities were not accessible by road, access by doctors was usually provided by small seaplanes, which took off and landed on the water of the many lakes in the area.

Although spring had arrived, March was still effectively a winter month in northern Ontario, and the lakes in the area were all frozen solid, covered with a thick layer of ice. Therefore my transportation to my assigned remote community was by a small ski plane, which took off and landed on the ice of a frozen lake using skis instead of wheels or pontoons. I found the experience of flying north on a tiny ski plane and the immersion for a week into the culture of an isolated First Nations community to be fascinating and very enjoyable.

On March 27, 1979, I was back working in my base hospital in Sioux Lookout again. My supervising physician assigned me that day to accompany a patient, a critically ill Native American woman, Jean Marie Peters, on a medical air evacuation, a "medevac," traveling by small airplane from Sioux Lookout to the closest large city, Winnipeg, Manitoba. Jean needed the more specialized and advanced medical facilities available in a Winnipeg hospital Intensive Care Unit to treat her rapidly deteriorating medical condition.

I clearly recall preparing to go on this medevac plane trip. My supervisor had told me to go to the doctor's lounge and put on one of the warm, government-issued arctic parkas that were hung there provided for our use. I was also told to wear warm clothes and put on thick arctic boots or mukluks. As I was donning this arctic gear in the doctor's lounge, I saw a plate of cookies that had been placed out for doctors to snack on.

As a young single woman at the time, I was extremely weight and figure conscious and therefore virtually never ate sweets or desserts of any kind, and I definitely did not eat snacks of cookies. However, that day, I had a very strong unusual inner thought that I still remember to this day. *I better eat a couple of cookies. I am going to need the energy later.* This inner impulse was so strong that I ate two cookies, something totally out of character for me at the time. As it turned out, later that day as I struggled to swim to shore after the plane crash, I really did need all the energy I could muster.

I was assigned to supervise the patient Jean's care during the medevac flight. I would need to supervise her intravenous drugs and fluids being used to stabilize her condition en route. Jean was unconscious and intubated, with an airway tube inserted through her mouth. She was not breathing well on her own, so I was also required to pump her breathing bag, the Ambu bag, by hand at regular intervals, so that air with supplemental oxygen would be pumped down the plastic airway into her lungs.

We loaded the patient Jean and all the medical equipment into the small propeller plane, a six-seated, twin-engine Piper Aztec. Jean was strapped onto a stretcher with IVs running into both of her arms, and had been loaded through the plane's rear cargo hatch. The aircraft was packed full. Her stretcher was placed on the left side, directly behind the pilot's seat where the seats in the second and third row had been removed to make room.

The foot of her stretcher reached the back of the tiny plane. I sat in the second-row seat on the right side beside the head of Jean's stretcher, so that I could easily reach the Ambu bag I was squeezing to ventilate my patient. The oxygen tank was wedged in front of me, behind the right front seat normally used by a copilot.

Sally Irwin, the nurse who had also been assigned to this medevac flight with me, was seated behind me in the right third-row seat where she could easily tend to the intravenous lines in Jean's arms. Her two intravenous bags were fastened up high by the window tops so that the fluids would drip down the IV tubing into her arms. The tiny plane was very crowded.

Because this medevac flight took off from the ground at the local airport and was scheduled to land on solid ground again in Winnipeg, the aircraft had normal wheel-based landing gear, rather than ski landing gear.

The Plane Crash

When the plane lifted off the runway, I was so busy tending to Jean, that I didn't notice a heavy snowstorm had begun. By the time we had flown for thirty or forty minutes and were about twenty miles from

Kenora, a town on Lake of the Woods, the storm worsened and had become a blizzard. The flight was very turbulent, as the plane was buffeted by the strong winds and heavy blowing snow.

Suddenly, I noticed a change in the loud roaring sound of the twin-propeller engines. I looked up and saw through the window beside me that the right propeller was sputtering to a stop, and it then stopped moving. The pilot, Gerald Kruschenske, was vigorously pushing control panel buttons and pulling levers. Something was obviously wrong. Shouting over the roar of the single functioning left engine, I anxiously asked "What's going on?"

Gerry quickly shouted back, "Everything's all right," as he continued to focus intently on piloting the faltering plane, vigorously pushing buttons and levers. About ten seconds later, I was reassured when the right propeller started spinning again. *Hurray,* I thought. Thankfully, Gerry had managed to restart the right engine. Everything seemed to be back to normal, with both engines working, so I returned my full attention to my patient.

A few minutes later I again heard a change in the engine noise, this time from the other side of the plane. It was the left propeller sputtering loudly. Looking up, I saw that the right propeller was now working fine, but the left propeller was now sputtering to a stop. With only one propeller working, the plane's turbulence as it was buffeted by the strong winds, was even worse than before. Alarmed, I shouted again to the pilot Gerry "What's going on?"

He didn't answer. Gerry was intensely focused on flying the distressed plane, desperately pushing buttons, pulling levers, and pumping handles in what seemed to me to be an attempt to restart the left engine. I looked down out my window and noticed we were not flying as high up in the air as we had been previously. Gerry had lowered our altitude over the last few minutes. We were now flying quite low over the trees, hills, and frozen lakes.

I later learned from our pilot, Gerry Kruschenske, that unknown to the nurse and me, he had been in radio contact with nearby Kenora airport for some time already, and was trying to make an emergency landing there due to the very bad weather and our engine problems. He had already made one attempt to land there, but flying with only one engine in the strong howling winds, he had not been able to maneuver the plane into the proper landing position.

The airport then tried to direct him to a landing strip on a nearby frozen lake. With very limited visibility due to the raging snow, Gerry had spotted what he thought was the landing strip on a frozen lake and made an attempt to come down. But once again, he couldn't get the struggling plane into proper landing position.

As he fought to pull the sluggish plane up again to circle around and make another attempt at the landing, he saw there was a large hill in front of us, near the edge of the lake. He realized instantly that in the strong winds, the limping plane with only one engine running would not have the power to clear the hill. We were going to crash into the trees.

Thinking it his only option to avoid the trees, in order to save our lives, he turned off the remaining right engine. He attempted an emergency belly landing on the ice, with the landing gear wheels pulled up. The plane headed down towards the ice. Gerry heroically tried to steer the free-falling plane into a guided emergency belly-landing on the ice, praying that the ice would hold. Unfortunately, the ice did not hold.

When this drama began to unfold, although Sally and I both realized something was wrong, with my attention focused on my patient, I had no idea how desperate the situation was until I saw the second propeller die. Now I could see through the windows that both engines were not working. From my perspective, the plane was crashing towards the ground. We had no working engines. The plane violently jerked and bumped repeatedly in severe air turbulence as we plunged downwards, buffeted by the blizzard-strength winds, as Gerry wrested desperately with the steering controls. This was the most severe air turbulence I had ever experienced in an airplane.

A wave of intense fear and panic instantly overtook me. I faced what I thought was certain impending death. *Oh my God, we're going to crash,* burst through my mind. *God, help me. I'm going to die,* I mentally cried out.

Feeling of Peace and Calm

An instant after I desperately prayed for help in my profound fear of imminent death, my Near-Death Experience began. Immediately after my mental cry for help, I suddenly felt a wave of profound peace and calm begin to descend upon me. It felt as if a huge wave of Divine peace somehow flowed down upon me from above, in a powerful force-field of peace that slowly pushed away all my fear. I now felt calm, at peace, and no longer afraid of death.

Together with the descending profound feeling of peace and calm, I heard a strong clear, inner voice comforting me. Before the event, I had never heard an inner voice. Verses from the Bible—verses that I didn't know by heart and wasn't consciously trying to remember—were somehow clearly spoken to my inner mind by some external source: "Be still, and know that I am God. I am with you, now and always." I heard. "God is your refuge and your strength, of what shall you be afraid?"

As the words penetrated my soul, I was overwhelmed with an awareness of the presence of God. I was no longer afraid. My mind was still. In my state of profound peace, I knew that God was there. And somehow, I knew with absolute certainty, something I had never known before: There was absolutely nothing to fear in death. I felt enveloped and protected by God's peace.

The plane continued to tumble towards the ground. Remaining in my powerful paranormal state of peace, I turned again to tend my patient. She had regained consciousness now and was frightened by the terrible air turbulence and the atmosphere of tension in the plane. Her beautiful dark eyes looked into mine, frightened, pleading for help. Filled with the peace, calm, and bliss that had somehow come upon me, I was able to reassure her with conviction. Gazing into her eyes, I tried to comfort her. "Everything will be all right," I assured her, somehow knowing this to be true whether we lived or died.

Just then nurse Sally suggested that I turn off the oxygen tank before we crashed. Agreeing, I turned off the tank and freed Jean so she could breathe on her own since she was breathing well now. I then continued to calmly comfort and reassure her with absolute conviction. Somehow I knew in that extraordinary state of Divine peace that I was experiencing, that no matter what happened, whether we lived or died in the crash, everything was proceeding according to some Divine plan and there was nothing to fear.

Gerry managed to wrestle with the controls of the engineless falling plane and steer a wheels up belly-landing onto the ice of the frozen lake below us, avoiding a deadly crash onto the fully forested hill in front of us. Miraculously, we had survived the crash landing. But just as the plane belly-landed on the ice, Gerry saw that on this particular lake, the ice was only partially frozen. The plane was skidding and sliding rapidly forward across the ice surface towards a huge stretch of dark open water.

Seeing that the plane would never stop in time, he tried to force its nose down into the ice, to try to brake our skid. The nose dug in, and again by some miracle, the plane stopped moving just at the edge of the ice, right beside the black open water. We all would have been okay, thanks to Gerry's quick thinking and heroic emergency belly-landing, if the ice on the lake had been thicker.

But as soon as the plane stopped moving forward, the full weight of the plane settled on the ice and the ice began to break. The plane started sinking rapidly into the deep freezing water of the lake. Gerry quickly opened the front left plane door beside him, stood on the left wing just outside his doorway, and started radioing out an emergency "mayday" message.

Meanwhile, icy water quickly started filling the floor of the plane. I reached forward towards the right front door by the empty copilot's seat and struggled without success to open that door so that the rest of us could exit the sinking plane. The door handle seemed to be jammed, frozen shut. The freezing water kept rising in the plane. I shouted to the pilot Gerry, "Help me open the door. It's stuck." But Gerry was busy, as he frantically tried to radio for help.

The water was pouring deeper and deeper into the plane. Although I was still in a mystical, peaceful state, I knew we urgently needed to get out of the plane if we were going to survive. Again I shouted to Gerry, "Help me open the door." Dropping the radio, he grabbed the right door handle, found it was jammed, and banged with his fist and later his foot until he finally managed to force the door open. I turned to Sally, "Help me lift the stretcher and we'll float it out."

I stepped out through the doorway onto the right wing of the sinking plane and found myself up to the groin in freezing lake water. Though I pulled with all my might at patient Jean's stretcher, while nurse Sally pushed from the rear, I could not get the stretcher out of the door. I called Gerry for help. But just as I did, he shouted "Step back, the plane is going down." I quickly grabbed Sally and pulled her out from behind the stretcher in the plane.

Standing together outside on the underwater right plane wing, we desperately tried to pull Jean, out of the copilot's door. I imagined we could float her out, still strapped to her stretcher. But it was impossible. The stretcher simply would not fit. Then I remembered that the stretcher had been loaded through the cargo hatch at the back of the plane and there was simply no way to get it out of the front copilot door. Before we could try to unstrap Jean from her stretcher, the plane suddenly tilted radically, took a sharp nose-dive, and sank. There was no way to dive for Jean on the stretcher. The plane had sunk without a trace into the deep, pitch-black, freezing cold lake water.

The Inner Voice of Higher Guidance

I quickly looked around me and assessed our situation. The plane had disappeared completely into the deep dark water. Gerry, Sally, and I were floating in freezing water in a lake, about 200 yards from an island. Dark open water with a strong, swiftly moving current separated us from the shore. Behind us, the rest of the lake appeared to be frozen solid with ice, but we had no way of judging the thickness of the ice.

Later, I learned that we had landed on Lake of the Woods at a place called Devil's Gap, so named due to the strong treacherous current. The lake water never freezes over completely at Devil's Gap in winter because of the strong current there. The howling winds and pelting snow swirled above us.

As I kicked and struggled to keep my head above water, my body quickly began to tire. My bulky arctic parka was dragging me down, and my heavy insulated boots were starting to feel like lead weights pulling me down into the frigid water. I tried to take off the parka so that I could float better, but I discovered that by that time my hands were already so close to frozen that I had lost my sense of touch and couldn't manipulate the zipper. I knew we had to get out of the freezing water and fast. I looked across the black, frigid water and heard a strong clear inner voice say, "Swim to shore." Fortunately, I was an excellent swimmer.

Being new to intuitive experiences and higher guidance, I did not listen to the inner voice at first, and in my mind argued with it. My rational mind remembered what I had been taught about water safety in childhood swimming lessons and lifeguard training as a teenager: *Never try to swim to shore. It's always further than it seems. You'll drown if you try.* Meanwhile, Gerry repeatedly shouted, "Try to get on the ice." In the urgency of the moment, I ignored my inner voice's instructions and instead turned away from shore and swam towards the ice. I then tried to climb on.

Each time I tried to pull myself up onto the ice, kicking my feet and reaching out onto the ice with my arms, the ice beneath my arms would break off in large chunks and sink. Again and again, I tried, struggling and kicking my feet vigorously, becoming more exhausted with each unsuccessful attempt to pull myself up. The inner voice in my head repeated, "Swim to shore." Sally was clinging tightly to Gerry. I later learned that she could not swim. Together they persisted in desperately trying to get onto the ice. But the ice was too thin to support anyone's weight. "Swim to Shore" the inner voice repeated strongly in my mind, for the third time.

Finally, I surrendered to the inner voice's guidance. I now think this inner voice was Higher Guidance, which ultimately saved me from drowning that day. Thank goodness I finally listened it. "The ice is too thin. We have to swim to shore," I shouted to Gerry and Sally. They were still struggling, trying to get onto the ice. I then turned away from the ice, Gerry, and Sally, and began swimming through the fast-moving open water towards the island. It was a long and very difficult swim.

Going Out-of-Body

Thankfully I was a very strong swimmer at that time and swam several times a week as one of my preferred forms of physical exercise. Despite my swimming strength, I struggled to stay afloat as I swam through the fast-moving frigid water. The heavy weight of my waterlogged parka and soaked boots slowed me and pulled me downwards into the deep water. The howling winds churned the choppy surface of the water, splashing icy water on my face and into my mouth. The strong current was pulling me strongly towards the right.

I had managed to swim about halfway to shore the first time my body went underwater in sheer exhaustion. I went completely underwater, sinking below the surface for a few moments. My throat filled immediately with icy lake water. Instinctively, I struggled desperately, with all my strength and willpower, to kick my way back up to the surface. I coughed, sputtered, and gratefully gasped a big breath of air into my lungs as I reached the surface again. Then I continued swimming, desperately striving, stroke by stroke, inching my way slowly closer to shore.

As I continued my struggle to stay afloat and swim through the fast-moving frigid water, I suddenly heard a strange low-pitched whooshing noise, something like the rushing of a large bird's wings in flight, or the roar of a waterfall. At the same time, I felt my consciousness and my point of perception abruptly rise up out of my body, and I found myself looking down at my body struggling through the water below.

It seemed as if my awareness, or what I perceive as me, had expanded to fill a much larger space than it had before, and my main point of perception had risen twenty feet or so above my physical body. My body was still very much alive, and desperately striving to swim to shore through the fast-moving water. My physical body was still a long distance from shore, as I watched from above.

Consciousness Two Place at Once

From above, in my expanded state of consciousness, I watched as my physical body struggled to swim to shore. But somehow my awareness seemed to be in two places at once. A small part of my awareness was still in my physical body, struggling to swim to shore, but most of my awareness – say 95 percent – was out of my body, floating above my body and looking down, watching the drama unfold below me.

I sometimes compare this experience to feeling as if I were perceiving my life as two images at the same time on a split-screen TV. In the bigger picture, 95 percent of my awareness, was the out-of-body perception. The smaller picture, as in the upper corner of a split-screen TV, was the tiny portion of my awareness that was still in my body. I was aware of both realities at the same time. However, most of my awareness was above my physical body, in the peace of the other side.

The Loving White Light

My spirit and main point of perception then moved further upwards, to a space filled with bright white light and a powerful feeling of unconditional love. The sense of peace and calm I had been feeling intensified, and now powerful unconditional love also poured through me and enveloped me. As I basked in this love, the space around me was bright, filled with light. Despite the heavy snow and the dark, heavy clouds in the sky that day, the world around me now seemed bright and filled with white light, as if the sun were brightly shining through a very light mist.

The light of this white light realm was not brilliant and blinding, but was soft and diffused, glowing beautifully. The closest thing I have found on earth that resembles the appearance of this realm of white light is the bright yet soft sparkling luminescent daylight inside the very top of clouds. I have seen this several times during airplane flights, just before a rising plane breaks through the top of thick clouds into bright sunshine above. In the last few moments in the top edge of the clouds, the beautiful soft sparkling light you can see glowing all around reflecting through the clouds is very similar to what I saw in the white light realm.

I briefly saw a luminous face of light in this light realm, gazing at me gently from the soft cloud-like perimeter, then the face faded from view. I did not recognize this benevolent-appearing face and still wonder about it to this day. This masculine face appeared kind, emanating gentleness and love. I did not disclose that I saw this face in the light for many years because it felt so extraordinary and sacred to me.

This space glowing with white light emanated an incredibly powerful feeling of universal unconditional love. I felt that I was being permeated, embraced, and cradled by a vast, profoundly loving, intelligent force. I immediately knew somehow in my soul, that this omnipotent intelligent force was the power behind the universe, what I call God. I also knew, somehow, that this loving Higher Power was infinitely intelligent, underlying and interpenetrating all of creation – past, present, and future.

This was not intellectual knowledge; it was a soul knowing, a certainty that went to the very core of my being. The profound unconditional love of this immense intelligence enveloped and permeated me. I felt like I was *Home*, where I belonged. The magnitude of the Higher Power I was glimpsing is far beyond my ability to express in words. My soul was in ecstasy. This was the most profoundly beautiful, blissful experience that I had ever had in my life.

How I was experiencing God, the Higher Power, was not at all like what I had been taught in my religion of childhood. I did not see an old man, with a long white beard, sitting on a throne and judging me as good or bad, as I had been taught. Instead, what I was actually experiencing was that our Higher Power, what I call God, was like an immense infinitely intelligent, all-powerful, forcefield of love that was interpenetrating and underlying all of creation, and everyone/everything in creation.

In my mystical state of ecstasy in the light realm, it did not matter to me whether my physical body lived or died in the worldly drama unfolding below me. I felt certain in my soul that there was nothing to fear in death because I was already basking in the love of the other side. I knew somehow that I would live on, even if my body died.

I also somehow knew in my soul that the intelligent Higher Power behind the universe which was embracing and enveloping me already knew the outcome of the drama unfolding below. My soul sensed that the Divine Higher Power was totally aware of the past, present, and future. I felt like a spectator watching a play that had a predetermined ending unfolding in front of me. I was curious to see the ending, but I did not really care whether the play ended with me continuing to live in my physical body below, or dying and staying in the wonderful loving light. I knew I would live on either way.

Swimming to Shore

As my physical body continued to struggle to swim to the island shore, I again sank below the water's surface from sheer exhaustion and the heavy weight of my waterlogged clothes. Again, I choked as icy lake water filled my throat and went into my lungs. As I watched from above, and to some degree also experienced below, I struggled intensely to swim back up to the surface, then sputtered, and coughed water out of my airway to breathe. Summoning all my strength and with fierce determination, I then continued desperately to strive to swim towards shore.

A few minutes later, when my physical body became completely exhausted, about to go under for the third and final time, the split screen images of my awareness flipped, and my consciousness seemed to slip mainly back into my body for a while. Still in a blissful, mystical state of consciousness, I found most of my awareness in my near-drowning body in the icy water, looking towards the shore with my physical eyes. The shore was about twenty feet away, but I could swim no further. My body was physically exhausted, and my energy was completely depleted. A strong current was pulling me to the right, and my heavy wet clothes were pulling me down into the deep water.

In the beautiful, mystical state of mind that I was in, I knew with absolute certainty that death held nothing to fear. I knew that I would live on whether my body lived or died. I felt only intellectual curiosity and I can clearly remember calmly thinking, *Oh, I see. I guess I am going to die here*, and *It is true, you do drown the third time you go down.*

Fearlessly and blissfully I surrendered to the Divine and the thought of death. But just at that moment, as I was about to slip underwater and go down for the third and final time, I saw – once again, through my physical eyes – that a tall, fallen pine tree lay in the water, extending out from the shore. The tree was to my right, and the current was rapidly carrying me towards it.

Suddenly I realized that if I could swim just two more strokes, the current would carry me right to the tip of that tree. In my paranormal expanded state of consciousness, the tree looked to me like it was overshadowed by a rescuing spiritual hand of light, that an etheric rescuing hand was superimposed on the tree, a hand that beckoned and reached out to help save me.

Somehow I was given the strength to swim those last two strokes. The current carried me right to the fallen tree. When my frozen hand struck the fallen tree, I felt nothing, no sensation at all. I looked down at my completely numb hand holding the tree, saw that it was bright red, and felt surprised.

My rational, medically trained mind pierced my blissful state of consciousness, telling me my hand should be white if it was frozen since blood vessels constrict to save body heat. Later I learned that, in the latter stages of freezing, the body loses the ability to constrict blood vessels and white freezing hands then become red. Death usually comes fairly quickly after this if the body isn't rewarmed.

Slowly and mechanically I pulled myself along the fallen tree towards the island shore. A few feet from shore my feet were finally able to touch the ground in the water. Mustering all my strength, I climbed up over some piles of shore ice onto the snow-covered island. On land, I immediately turned to face the lake and shouted out to Gerry and Sally, "Swim to shore. Swim to shore. You can make it." I urged them.

Gerry by that time had helped Sally grab a floating piece of frozen wood and ice that was keeping her afloat. It wouldn't support them both, so Gerry turned towards me and started swimming to shore. He eventually made it in, the current carrying him to the same fallen tree that had saved my life, and he crawled to my side on the heavily forested island. We stood there soaking wet, in sub-zero weather, with a strong wind chilling our bodies even further, on a remote unpopulated island. The lake was silent. The nurse Sally had stopped crying for help. I believed that she, like our patient Jean, must have drowned.

Still in both paranormal and worldly consciousness, I spoke briefly with Gerry "We are freezing to death," I said, "Do you have any matches to start a fire?" I asked.

"No," he said, muttering something about the emergency kit in the sunken plane.

"Do you know how to light a fire without matches?" I asked him.

"No."

Deathly cold, I started vomiting repeatedly, perhaps because my body was trying to get rid of the dirty lake water I had swallowed. A strong desire to sleep came over me, almost overwhelmingly, but my inner voice screamed "*No!*"

Somehow I knew that even though my consciousness was floating out of my body, I must not let my physical body fall asleep. If I went to sleep, I knew I wouldn't wake up again. Instinctively, I crouched into a full squat position to try to maintain some body heat and tucked my frozen fingers into my armpits to try to warm them. I told Gerry to do the same. The bitter, freezing cold was beyond description.

Then I felt my consciousness start to move more and more away from my physical body again. I knew that we could not survive long in the snowstorm and subzero weather, in our wet, nearly frozen clothes. We were freezing to death. My consciousness hovered above my freezing body in light and love.

The Rescue

We almost certainly wouldn't have been rescued in time if it hadn't been for an amazing series of coincidences (if you believe in coincidences). Where we crashed, the snowstorm was so severe and the terrain so hilly that our final distress signal could only have been picked up by a plane flying almost directly overhead. Just at the critical moment, one was. An Air Canada flight, on its way from Edmonton to Ottawa, picked up our distress signal and radioed our crash location to the airport in nearby Kenora.

Still, we were a long way from rescue. We had crashed in a remote region. The island was not accessible by road. Because of the mix of ice and open water, the island was also not accessible by either boat or snowmobile. Nothing but a helicopter could reach us, and normally none was located in the region.

But, on that day, and at that time, one was being ferried from Edmonton, Alberta, to Val d'Or, Quebec, by a pilot named Brian Clegg. Concerned by the snowstorm, Brian had hoped to land at Kenora Airport, but the bad weather had forced him to come down instead at a small Ontario Ministry of Natural Resources base about five miles from where our plane had crashed.

When Brian had first landed, he had gone into the base and met a Ministry staff pilot, Bob Grant, who had also been grounded by the storm. As they were talking, the phone rang: Kenora Airport was relaying a distress message from the pilot of a twin-engine Piper Aztec that was flying in the area and having serious engine trouble.

Brian Clegg sensed that his helicopter might be needed. He rushed out, began removing its protective weather covering, and turned on his radio. He then heard the emergency crash message relayed from the Air Canada jet flying high above our crash site, and immediately started his engines. He called to Bob Grant and without any thought for their own safety, the two headed into the snowstorm in the helicopter, to search for us.

As they flew, Kenora Airport directed them to the general area of the crash. The two pilots searched frantically for the large pieces of wreckage they thought would be visible on the ice or among the trees, but could see none. Hampered by the snowstorm, they could not see Gerry and me huddled under the trees on the island or Sally floating like a human icicle clinging to a piece of ice-caked wood in the patch of open water on the semi-frozen lake.

After making a rapid sweep of the area and finding no wreckage, they decided to take a closer look at the open water of Devil's Gap, where they thought they might have seen something floating in the open water. Coming down low, they spied a seat cushion – then they spotted Sally, who was unconscious.

Brian hovered the helicopter a few feet above her in the icy water, while Bob climbed out and, standing on a skid, tried to pull her rigid, ice-covered form out of the water. She was like a human icicle, completely ice-coated. Again and again, she slid from his grasp.

When all else failed, Brian tried to balance the helicopter right on the water, a dangerous maneuver since the least shift in weight could cause the helicopter to crash. Fearlessly Bob—a non-swimmer—straddled the skid, dangled his legs in the icy water, managed to grasp Sally, and, eventually, get one of her hands around the skid. With Sally hanging and Bob pressing her hand onto the skid, the helicopter dragged Sally's unconscious body along the surface of the ice to a spot where the ice was thick enough to hold Sally's weight. As the helicopter hovered a few feet above the ice, Bob balanced on the skid and tried in vain to push all of Sally's rigid, frozen body through the doorway and onto the seat. Finally, he managed to wedge in all but her legs. Using his body to brace her in, Bob stood outside the helicopter on the ice-caked skid while they flew to nearby Kenora Hospital.

From the shore of the island 200 yards away, Gerry and I watched Sally's rescue intently. We waved our arms above our heads and tried to shout to the helicopter pilots, in the hope that they would spot us too. Unfortunately, they did not seem to see us. When Sally was finally loaded into the helicopter, the helicopter flew away, going away from the island. The lake became deadly silent again, except for the sound of the howling winds. There was no indication that the helicopter crew had spotted us. I was very discouraged. "Do you think they will come back to look for us?" I said.

"I don't know," Gerry mumbled, as he shrugged uncertainly. We both huddled there silently, waiting glumly while the bitter cold became increasingly unbearable. We hoped desperately that the rescue helicopter would return and then find us, too.

Thankfully, about twenty minutes later the two men did return to Devil's Gap in the helicopter, to search for any other possible survivors of the crash. As Gerry and I desperately waved to the helicopter from the heavily treed shore of the island, Brian and Bob finally spotted us there. But Brian could not find a place to land the helicopter, to get us. The island was covered with trees and bordered by fast-moving open water.

They were on the verge of despair when they spied a small inlet or bay on the island's shore, maybe fifty feet to the right of where Gerry and I huddled. The water in the tiny inlet was protected from the strong current and appeared to have frozen solid. Brian managed to land the skids of the helicopter on this small piece of ice, but the inlet was so small that the rear propeller was dangling over open water.

Our rescuers gestured to us to walk from where we were, over a small rise, to reach the helicopter. Gerry was able to stumble to the helicopter, but I was only semi-conscious and did not have the strength to walk that distance. Without hesitation, Bob jumped out and—not knowing if the ice could support his weight—walked over the inlet's ice onto shore and came to get me. He carried and pulled me over the hill, across the inlet's ice, and into the helicopter.

Once in the helicopter, Brian and Bob asked, "Is there anyone else?"

"One. But for her, it's too late," I said.

I then lost consciousness and floated in the loving white light above my body.

Yvonne Kason, M.D.

Resuscitation in Hospital – Returning to my Body

When we arrived at Kenora Hospital, the helicopter landed on the hospital's driveway. While my consciousness hovered above my body, I watched as my body was taken out of the helicopter, placed on a stretcher, and wheeled into the hospital emergency department. I still felt completely at peace and had no fear of what seemed to be my impending death.

As I watched from above, a nurse covered me and my wet, frozen clothes with a thin, loosely woven cotton hospital blanket. This light blanket over my ice-encrusted clothes did nothing to warm me up. Another nurse tried to take my temperature and was puzzled that she couldn't get a temperature reading. My body temperature was so low that day that a standard hospital thermometer could not measure it. My body temperature was lower than the bottom reading on the thermometer.

As I watched from above I felt myself start to float further and further away from my body. I knew that I was dying, and I was at peace.

Suddenly, I heard a voice say, "Boy, could I use a hot bath." Hovering above, I was surprised to realize the voice had come from my own physical body. I had not thought of saying these words, but somehow they came out of my mouth. Later I learned that rewarming the body by submersion in hot water had come to be considered an excellent emergency treatment for advanced hypothermia. However, I hadn't been taught this in medical school—and I have no idea why or how my body uttered these words.

Thinking I was regaining consciousness and making a brave attempt at humor, the nurses laughed. But then one nurse grew serious and suggested that hot water might help revive us. The nurses then wheeled our stretchers to the physiotherapy department, pulled off our ice-encrusted clothes, and slid our frozen bodies into the hot whirlpool baths.

It was soon after I was put into the hot whirlpool bath that I finally felt my consciousness reenter my body. As my body was submerged in the hot water, I suddenly heard a loud whoosh and I felt pulled down, abruptly shrinking from my expanded state above, and pulled down into the small confines of my body.

I felt like my consciousness was abruptly sucked back into my body through the top of my head. The sensation was similar to what I imagine a genie might feel like when, as is depicted in movies and on TV, it is forcibly sucked back into its tiny bottle. I heard a whoosh, felt a downward pulling sensation, and was suddenly aware of being totally back in my body again.

I then rubbed my numb hands along my legs and my arms in the hot water, and exclaimed with joy, "I'm back. I'm back. I'm going to live. I'm going to live." And I knew that it was true.

Even though I was quite ill—with severe frostbite on my face, neck, and hands and a wrenching cough from the dirty lake water I had aspirated—I felt wonderful emotionally. I was overwhelmed with joy at being given another chance at life and awed by the spiritual impact of my experience. Peace and joy flowed over me.

The Aftermath

That night, Sally and I were put in the same hospital room. I had a nasty wrenching cough and kept coughing up foul-tasting liquid, what I assumed was dirty lake water. Dear Sally, despite her own ordeal, insisted on helping me deal with my cough. Once a nurse, always a nurse. "Let me give you some chest physio," she insisted.

She climbed out of her hospital bed, and dressed in her hospital gown became my nurse. She told me to turn on my stomach and lie on top of a pillow. She then rapidly banged my back with cupped hands for several minutes. This pummeling helped loosen the unwanted fluids in my lungs, so I could cough them out better. Sally was an angel to me that day, and I remain deeply grateful for her loving care.

Resting comfortably in a state of bliss, I noticed that Sally also seemed to be strangely blissful and at peace that evening we shared a hospital room. At one point Sally turned to me and said, "I don't know why it happened, Yvonne, but we have both been saved. Maybe we are going to do something important in our lives one day." I just smiled in agreement. I too felt that we had been saved by some miracle of events, or perhaps the grace of God. I also suspected that Sally must have had some sort of intense spiritual experience that day as well.

The next day, Sally and I were discharged from the hospital and picked up by a staff driver who drove us back to Sioux Lookout. My supervising physicians at Sioux Lookout Hospital who had assigned me to the medevac flight were openly relieved to see me upon my return. I learned that they had been informed about the crash of my medevac plane immediately after it happened. They had no idea if there were any survivors of the crash for several hours.

Suspecting that we probably crashed somewhere in the bush in the heavily forested surrounding area, they thought our survival very unlikely. Unfortunately, they did not receive news about our rescue until hours later. Similarly, my supervising physician at Women's College Hospital who had assigned me to work in Sioux Lookout that month anxiously waited for hours after hearing of the crash, hoping that there were survivors. Finally, later in the day, she learned that I and two others had miraculously survived the plane crash.

The news of our plane crash traveled quickly. Articles describing our crash and the heroic, dramatic rescue appeared in newspapers all across Canada. I have seen newspaper clippings with news of the crash that were printed the day of the crash and shortly thereafter in The Globe and Mail, the Toronto Star, the Dryden Observer, The Times News, and the Daily Miner and News. Later even Readers Digest became interested in the story, and printed a recap of the incident entitled "Down in Devils Gap" in their "Drama in Real Life Section" February 1981 Readers Digest issue.

A few days after the accident, the body of Jean Marie Peters, the patient who drowned when the plane sank, was recovered by Kenora police and Ontario Provincial Police divers during an underwater search. The police found the sunken airplane with Jean's stretcher and body wedged in the doorway about 85 feet underwater at the edge of Devils Gap. They, too, had difficulty removing Jean's body from the sunken plane. The OPP diver later told me that he had to cut both the IV lines, and cut through the stretcher straps, in order to free Jean's body from the stretcher to recover it out of the plane. Special equipment and barges had to be used to later surface the plane.

The Heroes are Recognized

An inquest into the accident was held. Our pilot, Gerald Kruschenske, received a commendation for his quick thinking and skill in the emergency belly-landing that undoubtedly kept us from all dying by crashing into the trees when our plane first went down.

In May of that year, 1979, I was invited to Queen's Park, the Ontario Government buildings in Toronto, to attend an award ceremony honoring the helicopter rescue pilots Brian Clegg and Bob Grant. The then Ontario Premier William Davis and Lieutenant Governor Pauline McGibbon presided over the award ceremony, which was also attended by several other high-ranking government officials. At the ceremony, Brian Clegg and Bob Grant were publicly acknowledged by the government of Ontario for their courage. They received medallions and framed plaques acknowledging their bravery and heroism in our dramatic rescue.

This event was the first time that I saw Brian and Bob following the day they rescued us. They had not lingered around the hospital the day of the crash, so I had never yet been able to speak to them and thank them. I had tears in my eyes as I watched Brian and Bob humbly receive their awards. When I first had a moment alone with them, I felt a strong need to thank them for saving my life.

With tears of gratitude in my eyes, I said "How can I ever thank you enough for saving my life? Thank you. Thank you. Thank you." Brian and Bob were extraordinarily humble about the whole affair. They both stated in a rather matter-of-fact manner, that it was an immediate reflex, like an instinct to go and search for us, as soon as they heard the news of our crash sent out by Kenora airport.

Gerry and Sally were also invited to attend this award ceremony for Brian Clegg and Bob Grant. That award ceremony was also the first time that I saw Gerry and Sally after our discharge from Kenora hospital. It was a very moving event for us all. I still treasure the photograph of us taken together that day. We all chatted over refreshments after the ceremony. It was there that I heard for the first time from Gerry, Brian, and Bob, the details surrounding our plane crash, and the details of our heroic rescue.

In September of 1979, the Governor General of Canada awarded both Brian Clegg and Bob Grant the Star of Courage, one of Canada's highest awards for civilian valor. Two months later they both received an international award for outstanding valor—a Silver Medal from the Andrew Carnegie Hero Fund Commission. The inscription on a Carnegie Medal reads, "Greater Love Hath No Man Than This, That a Man Lay Down His Life for His Friends." I am eternally grateful for the heroism and courage of these outstanding men who selflessly risked their lives to save my life, and the lives of Sally and Gerry, that fateful day.

Chapter 7

PROFOUND AFTER-EFFECTS OF THE PLANE CRASH NDE

The mystical Near-Death Experience I had during the 1979 medevac plane crash transformed me and forever changed the course of my life. This NDE combined with my kundalini awakening experience in 1976 launched me personally on a quest to research and understand diverse Spiritually Transformative Experiences and started a process of long-term spiritual transformation of my consciousness.

Together, these STEs and their after-effects propelled me professionally as a medical doctor to later specialize in the research and counseling of patients who had diverse STEs. However, this career transition and deepening understanding of spiritual transformation of consciousness evolved over many years. Immediately following my 1979 mystical NDE, I was just a young 26-year-old doctor with traditional Western medical training who wondered, *What on earth just happened to me?*

The day after the 1979 plane crash, I was released from Kenora Hospital. I was scheduled to fly back home to Toronto a day later, but due to the traumatic plane crash, my supervisors offered that I could travel by train instead if I preferred.

Something deep within me said, *No. I am not going to be afraid of flying*, and I insisted on flying back to Toronto. I decided to face this fear head-on, determined to overcome it. As I sat in the small commercial plane taking off for Toronto the next day, I started to tremble involuntarily with waves of fear. I asked the woman sitting next to me, a complete stranger, if I could please hold her hand during the take-off. She kindly agreed. I prayed intently during the take-off. Once we were airborne, I released the kind woman's hand and thanked her. She replied, "That's ok. Lots of people are afraid of flying."

"No. I am NOT afraid of flying. I'm just nervous because I was in a plane crash 2 days ago," I said firmly.

Her jaw dropped in incredulity.

Upon my return to Toronto, I was unable to work as a doctor for about four weeks as I recovered from my injuries of frostbite and near-drowning. At first, the frostbite on my hands was so severe that I had absolutely no feeling in my fingertips. My completely numb fingers were incredibly clumsy, and due to the lack of feeling, I couldn't even hold a pen or grasp a fork properly. This meant I couldn't use my hands to examine patients or write medical records at work.

The front of my neck that had been exposed to the icy lake water was also severely frostbitten, and I had no feeling there for weeks. For a while, I also coughed and was feverish, while my lungs cleared the residue and lake water I had inhaled. Eventually, my cough subsided and my lungs healed.

The month I had off work helped me recuperate physically but, more importantly, gave me time to begin to integrate the overwhelming emotional and spiritual impact of the experience into my daily life. I focused even more deeply on my twice-daily meditations, which I had been doing regularly since 1976.

As I contemplated my plane-crash experience, using terms from my Christian upbringing I could have said that I had been blessed with a miracle, or had experienced the grace of God because I had survived. I had no vocabulary, no precise words to describe the spiritual experience that had happened to me in the plane crash.

Now, after my many years of research on NDEs and other STEs, I can confidently say that what I experienced during the 1979 plane crash was a Near-Death Experience with an out-of-body and mystical experience.

Yvonne Kason, M.D.

Immediate Spiritual Impact – Love Intoxicated

For some time after the NDE, I was "love intoxicated," drunk with love, blissfully bubbling love constantly. It was as if I had brought back with me a little bit of the powerful unconditional love that I had experienced on the other side in the white light realm. When I looked at the world, a wave of love flooded out of me toward everyone and everything.

My heart swelled with love when I looked at squirrels running in my yard. Watching neighborhood children playing would make a wave of intense love pour out of my heart toward them. Any song that mentioned God, romance, children, parents, animals, or righting any type of social injustice made me weep tears of joy and triggered feelings of intense bliss and love. I remained in a state of awe. I wept with joy at the thought of being alive and at having been given a second chance at life.

During the first few weeks after my NDE, I found one particular song that touched me very deeply and helped me process my deep feelings surrounding the experience. I recall listening over and over to the then recently released song by John Denver, "I Want to Live." It felt to me like the words of this song spoke to my soul. "I Want to Live" became like a theme song for me in the early weeks after my NDE, as I reflected on my intense brush with death, the blessing and love of the white light realm of the Higher Power, and the heroic rescue. I remember playing this song over and over, and singing along, choked with emotion. The chorus would often make me sob with tears. The chorus' words are:

> *I want to live, I want to grow,*
> *I want to see, I want to know,*
> *I want to share what I can give,*
> *I want to be…*
> *I want to live.*   John Denver, 1977.

These words and this song still move me deeply to this day.

In the early days after my NDE, I felt a very powerful, personal connection to the totally loving Higher Power, the intelligent loving force behind the universe, what I call God. I somehow knew in my soul that every other person on the planet was connected to our one loving God in the same way, whether they knew it or not.

I also had a new strong inner conviction, a new knowing, that the God that I had glimpsed was the same one loving mother/father Creator God of all religions. I experienced a newfound sense of the ultimate unity of all religions, under the umbrella of the same one God.

My NDE had awakened an intense spiritual hunger in me. I developed a new, strong yearning to read from the Bible daily, as well as to study other religions' holy books. I developed the urge to "talk to God" regularly, to pray earnestly to my God, who now felt very real and very close to me. My desire to meditate regularly intensified.

I absolutely lost my fear of death after this Near-Death Experience. I emerged with a new conviction based on my own experience, an inner knowing, that I was not just the physical body, but I was a soul living in a physical body, a soul that will live on after the death of the body.

I had a deep intuitive understanding of the sanctity of life and knew life to be a precious opportunity. Somehow I knew intuitively that it was spiritually incorrect to end one's life prematurely, by suicide. Many years later, I learned through my clinical research, that as an after-effect of white-light type of NDEs, many experiencers emerge with similar spiritual convictions.

Misunderstood and Mislabeled by Others

I returned to work one month after the plane crash and my profound spiritual experience. The news of the crash had spread throughout my coworkers – the doctors, nurses, and secretaries I worked with every day in Women's College Hospital. I later learned that my supervising physician has instructed the nurses and secretaries not to talk to me about the plane crash because talking about it might be too upsetting for me and re-traumatize me. But I felt exactly the opposite. When I returned to work I was eager to talk about my extraordinary experience with my coworkers. I broke the code of silence and talked excitedly with them about what I had experienced in the crash.

I recall one day during my lunch break, I sat in the hospital cafeteria's doctors' dining room talking openly with several other medical doctors eating lunch there. Physicians with diverse medical specialties, many of them highly experienced teaching physicians who were my teachers, were seated huddled beside me at the long lunch table, eating and listening.

I told them about my experiences during the plane crash: floating out of my body; being in the white light; feeling permeated and surrounded by profound unconditional love and peace; feeling as if I had been in the presence of the loving Higher Power behind the universe— glimpsing God; and, abruptly being sucked back into my body when my body was rewarmed. I asked my medical colleagues if they had ever heard of such an experience and if they had an accurate name for such an experience.

No one could offer me an acceptable explanation. I recall my supervisors and medical colleagues thoughtfully contemplating what I had said. They all knew me to be a high-functioning medical doctor, who was mentally sound. One of my physician colleagues suggested that I had merely had a hallucination brought on by extremely low blood sugar. Another physician colleague speculated that perhaps I had been delirious and confused due to an electrolyte imbalance. Yet another physician thought I had been hallucinating due to the effect of severe cold on the brain.

These biochemical explanations of hallucinations or delirium did not ring true to me. As a young doctor, I had already seen many patients with low blood sugars and electrolyte imbalances, and none had described a profoundly positive, uplifting spiritual experience such as I had. The theory of an effect of cold on the brain also did not ring true, because my profound spiritual experience began before the plane crashed, while I was still warm inside the plane. I was certain in my heart that this experience was not just a hallucination.

As I searched further striving to understand my experience, I spoke with a senior person in my then meditation group, who claimed to have some knowledge about Near-Death Experiences. I described my experience to him, and he pointedly asked, "Were you completely dead?"

"No," I said.

"Did you see a dark tunnel with a white light at the end?"

"No."

"Then you did NOT have a Near-Death Experience. Just forget about it, and get on with your life," he said firmly.

Because I knew no better at the time, I assumed that my experience was not an NDE. However, I was absolutely unable to forget about it, because the experience was etched in my mind, and continued to have a powerful effect on me. I continued searching for a name for my experience.

Weeks later, one person, a physician who was also a devout Christian, finally gave me an acceptable explanation. He called it, simply, a mystical experience. After hearing the story of my out-of-body and loving white light experience during the plane crash, he slowly responded, "Yvonne, I think you have had a *Mystical Experience.*"

I felt relieved and validated on hearing his words. I had finally found an explanation that rang true and a term that accurately described what I had experienced.

"Yes," I said to myself, "I had a mystical experience."

When I spoke of my experience for many years from that day on, I would use that phrase to describe my experience while I was near death in the plane crash.

Unfortunately, as I continued to search for a deeper understanding of the extraordinary mystical experience I had during the plane crash, I lost several friends due to their misunderstanding. A few people openly turned against me and ridiculed me. I recall one individual accusing me of having an "inflated ego," claiming that I was exaggerating what had happened to me in order to seek attention from others.

Another opinionated person went even further and accused me of "turning to the dark side," alleging that I had fabricated the story of my mystical experience and was deeply misguided in my new spiritual convictions.

Despite this criticism and rejection, I remained convinced of the reality of my mystical experience during the plane crash, and I remained certain in my soul about the spiritual truths that were revealed to me while I was in the extraordinary realm of loving white light. The memory of the experience was etched clearly in my mind. I knew in my heart that I was not exaggerating.

I remained absolutely certain in my soul that it had been a positive spiritual experience, not some sort of dark experience. Surrounded by much blatant criticism and misunderstanding, I nonetheless continued in my search for a deeper understanding, albeit with a smaller circle of friends.

Yvonne Kason, M.D.

Transformational Impact on my Life

Soon after the 1979 NDE and airplane crash, I became aware that the experience was affecting other areas of my life, and having a profound transformational effect on me psychologically. The experience seemed to have a "time to grow up" impact on me. I spontaneously realized it was time to come to grips with and heal some of the unresolved psychological issues in my life. At the same time, suppressed childhood memories began to surface spontaneously. One involved my father.

Dad and I had been feuding since I was a child, and we hadn't spoken for some time before my NDE. In a moment of clarity shortly after the NDE, a childhood memory spontaneously surfaced to my consciousness during one of my meditations.

I recalled witnessing a heated argument between my mother and father when I was a young child. As the memory resurfaced, I realized how traumatic the experience had been for me as a child, how I had sided with my mother, and that I had been angry at my father from that moment on. The awareness came to me that much of the anger I had directed towards Dad over the years stemmed from my unresolved feelings related to this childhood incident.

In my state of mental and emotional clarity following the NDE, I immediately wished to resolve this issue between me and my father. I telephoned him, and for the first time ever told him that I loved him.

"Dad, I love you. Let's be friends," I said.

I asked him if we could meet to talk. When we met, we had a truly meaningful discussion about how my parents' marital difficulties had negatively influenced our father-daughter relationship. I shared my traumatic childhood memory with him, and we discussed it openly.

Now that I understood the root source of my anger, somehow the intense love and clarity that stayed with me in the weeks following my near-death mystical experience enabled me to effortlessly let go of my anger and resentment. I forgave my father. The anger, hurt feelings, and misunderstanding I had harbored towards my father for 20 years evaporated quickly. Dad and I made peace and warmly embraced each other.

I now consider this emotional healing between me and my father to be one of the blessings, or gifts of grace, that I was blessed with, as an after-effect of my 1979 Near-Death Experience. Dad had not changed in character from before my NDE to afterward. He still had the character quirks that I previously considered intolerable. I was the one who had changed after the NDE. Those quirks no longer bothered me.

My previously repressed anger no longer gripped me. It seemed I had grown up psychologically after the NDE, and I was eager to let go of my emotional baggage. A willingness to forgive and unconditional love were pouring out from me after the experience, enabling me to quickly resolve and let go of this emotional baggage from the past.

I am grateful to this day for the Divine gift of this emotional healing and reconciliation between me and my father. Dad and I then shared seven wonderful years of a close, loving, father-daughter relationship, until Dad died in 1986. I am eternally grateful for the Divine blessing of having had those seven precious years of a close relationship with my father.

A definite psychological transformation was occurring in my emotional maturity and inner strength after this NDE. With newfound self-awareness and maturity, I seemed to be able to see things more clearly than before. I soon became aware of another piece of psychological business that needed to be resolved.

As I mentioned previously, at the time of the plane crash I belonged to a small meditation group. But after the crash, I realized that for many reasons this particular meditation group was not my correct spiritual path. Despite much peer pressure to remain there, filled with my new strength, clarity, and intensified spiritual convictions after the NDE, I left this meditation group, feeling clearer emotionally than I ever had in my life.

The months of transformation that occurred after my 1979 NDE left me feeling psychologically strong, clear, and centered. I felt a tremendous inner strength and the courage to speak honestly and lovingly. This NDE still remains a source of tremendous inspiration forty years later.

More importantly, the process of psychological transformation that it began has continued to this day. My urge to embrace my psychospiritual housecleaning is now permanent. However, the psychological healing and recovery work I have done over many years after my NDE has required time, honest self-reflection, and depth psychotherapy, just as it does for all people focusing on their personal growth and emotional healing.

Yvonne Kason, M.D.

My Psychic Awakening

When I returned to work, I still didn't know that I had undergone a Near-Death Experience, and I certainly didn't know such an event could leave one's mind open to psychic input. I was shocked when, about a month or so after the plane wreck, I had a startling and vivid psychic experience.

After work one evening, I was driving to visit a friend whom I will call Susan. As I was stopped at a red light, a vivid, bright, and almost glowing image popped into my mind's eye: a brain coated in pus. The image was so clear I was stunned. I was somehow certain the picture I saw represented meningitis—an infection of the surface lining of the brain. Additionally, I was also sure that it was Susan's brain.

Initially surprised and shocked by the vision, I decided not to mention it to anyone. But to be safe, when I arrived at Susan's house I cautiously asked her how she was feeling, and specifically asked about symptoms of meningitis. Susan told me she had been suffering for several hours that day from a severe, unusual headache.

I knew severe headache could sometimes, albeit rarely, be a symptom of meningitis. I didn't want to alarm her, but, just to make sure, I asked her about other symptoms. The image of the pus-covered brain haunted me, and I felt I had to say something. Hesitantly, I told Susan in confidence about the vision I had seen and what I thought it represented.

She thought for a moment and then asked how she could tell if her headache did indicate early meningitis. I explained meningitis symptoms to her, and we agreed that, if these symptoms indeed developed, she would go to the local hospital emergency department and explain that a friend who was a doctor had suggested she be tested for meningitis.

Later that evening, Susan did become increasingly ill. When she went to the emergency department, the doctors tested her thoroughly and confirmed that she had developed a rare, often-fatal type of meningitis. Although she needed hospitalization for two weeks of high-powered antibiotic treatment, the early diagnosis allowed the doctors to treat her successfully.

Although I didn't realize it at the time, I now know that the image I saw in my mind's eye that day was a type of psychic experience known as a clairvoyant vision. It was a symbol that represented a physical reality that I could not possibly have known about. I had never had a clairvoyant vision before that day, beyond the year that I could see ghosts immediately after my childhood NDE at age eleven. After this 1979 psychic awakening, however, I found myself open to other clairvoyant visions repeatedly over the years.

As amazed as I was by the first and later clairvoyant visions, I was reluctant to mention them to others, especially other doctors. I was afraid that I would be disbelieved or ridiculed, even though I knew in my heart how real and powerful the visions were.

Much to my surprise, over the months and years that followed my 1979 NDE, I discovered that I also developed a second psychic ability. I became clairsentient, an empath, able to pick up and feel other person's emotions and mental states by feeling physical sensations in my body. I laughingly started secretly referring to this new ability in me as my "Truth-o-Meter," as my intuition would reveal to me the truth of what others were feeling or thinking.

When somebody in front of me was sad or upset, I would instantly begin to feel a heaviness and pressure in my heart region. When someone in front of me was angry or agitated, I would feel an uncomfortable heavy pressure on the center of my forehead.

Most dramatic, however, was my body's response when somebody would tell a lie. If someone told me an untruth, I would feel nauseated, sick to my stomach, with heavy pressure in my stomach. This Truth-o-Meter would also react very strongly if I inadvertently exaggerated or spoke an untruth.

If I inadvertently said anything untruthful for some reason, perhaps a slip of the tongue, I would feel immediate nausea and stomach pressure. I learned quickly that I needed to correct my error and state the exact accurate truth, in order for my stomach discomfort to finally go away.

Basically, I became a person who was unable to speak a lie. I have always striven to be an honest person, but after the development of my Truth-o-Meter, I became unable to tell a lie.

Over the years, I learned a great deal more about psychic experiences, but only in 1990, when I met Dr. Kenneth Ring, the eminent NDE researcher and author, did I learn that scientific research existed to show that many people who have NDEs have similar psychic awakenings afterward. Additionally, I have had many STE experiencers share with me over the years that they became clairvoyant and clairsentient after their NDE or other peak STE. Many have also told me that they also developed a Truth-o-Meter and have been physically unable to tell a lie after their STE.

NDE Features of my 1979 Plane Crash NDE

Comparing the features of my experience in the plane crash with the NDE features first defined by Dr. Raymond Moody, (listed in Chapter 2), it is clear that my experience included twelve of the fifteen classic NDE features. These were:

1. *Ineffability*: The experience had aspects that were beyond words, and are difficult for me to describe to others

2. *Auditory awareness*: *Clairaudience.* While I was unconscious, floating above my frozen body in the Kenora hospital emergency room, I could both see and overhear the nurses talking around my body. I clearly recall hearing the nurses discuss taking me to the hot whirlpool baths of the physiotherapy department to reheat my frozen body… "Perhaps that would help them," one nurse said.

3. *Strong feelings of peace*: A strong feeling of peace came over me right at the beginning of my NDE, and before the plane had crashed, as I faced what I thought was imminent death. While we tumbled in severe turbulence towards the ground in the engineless plane, buffeted by the strong winds, I was intensely afraid, and had cried out a desperate prayer, "God, help me, I'm going to die." The profound experience of peace began immediately afterward. A sudden a wave of profound peace and calm descended upon me and pushed away all my fear. I felt permeated with calm, bathed in a cloak of serenity, accompanied by an intense sense of peace that told me all was right with the universe. A strong sense of peace remained with me throughout the duration of my NDE.

4. *Unusual inner sounds:* While I was struggling to swim to shore, I suddenly heard a low-pitched whooshing noise, somewhat like the sound of the rush of a large bird's wings. At the same time as

I heard this deep whooshing sound, my spirit slipped out of my body. Later in my NDE, while in the white light realm, I could hear a different sound, a very soft, difficult to describe, musical sound. I would describe it now as the music of the spheres, or celestial music. I also heard an inner whooshing sound when my spirit re-entered my body while rewarming in the hot whirlpool bath.

5. *Floating out-of-body:* My spirit and point of perception floated up out of my physical body, allowing me to view my physical body struggling to swim to shore. I could then view myself huddled freezing on the shore of the island, and later I observed my unconscious body being tended to by nurses in the emergency room of the hospital. Before I became unconscious, much of the time it felt as if my consciousness were in two places at the same time, mainly out of my body, but partially still in my physical body.

6. *White Light Experience.* My out-of-body spirit moved into a realm of profoundly loving white light. The white light realm emanated unconditional love, infinite intelligence, and infinite size. I intuitively recognized this universal intelligent loving force to be what I call God.

   While in this white light realm, I instantly knew certain truths, without words being heard or spoken, perhaps in a type of revelation. I somehow knew with certainty that all souls live on after the death of the physical body and that there was nothing to fear in death. I knew that this Higher Power unconditionally loved all humans equally, regardless of age, sex, race, or religion.

   I also somehow knew that past, present, and future were all known to the infinitely intelligent Higher Power, and therefore the outcome of the plane crash drama happening to my body below was already lovingly known to God.

7. *Meeting spirits.* When I first entered the white light realm, I perceived a luminous face, the face of a benevolent spirit of some sort. This masculine face smiled and radiated love at me briefly, then softly faded from view.

8. *Abrupt return to the body:* I clearly recall my spirit being abruptly pulled back into my physical body, seemingly through the top of my head. This occurred suddenly when my frozen body was reheated in the hot whirlpool bath. The instant my spirit returned into my body, I knew that I had survived the ordeal. "I'm back. I'm back." I exclaimed.

9. *Conviction of the reality of the experience:* I have always had a clear memory of my Near-Death Experience in the plane crash, and this memory has remained extraordinarily clear in my mind despite the passage of over forty years. Further, whenever I remember and think about my NDE, I start re-experiencing the extraordinary feelings of bliss, peace, and unconditional love that I originally felt during the experience. Despite many people dismissing or invalidating my experience at first, I was absolutely certain that this experience was real, and positive in nature.

10. *Transformational impact:* This 1979 NDE transformed me profoundly on many levels.

    a *Psychologically,* the NDE had a *time to grow up* after-effect on me. I very quickly resolved and healed my relationship with my father, and quickly left the meditation group which no longer met my needs.

    b *Spiritually,* I was transformed dramatically by the experience, with a marked increase in my spiritual urge to read Holy Scriptures and to meditate deeply – after-effects that have persisted lifelong. The spiritual transformation propelled me to deeply embrace my personal spiritual path, to deepen my process of self-realization. The NDE also propelled me to research NDEs, mystical experiences, kundalini awakening, and psychic experiences.

    c *Psychically,* I had a psychic awakening shortly after the NDE, when I saw a clairvoyant image of my friend's brain covered in puss. I also developed clairsentience, the ability to accurately perceive others' feelings as physical sensations in my body.

11. *New Views of Death:* I lost my fear of death in this NDE. I became absolutely certain that the soul lives on after the death of the physical body.

12. *Independent corroboration:* I observed from above many events that were independently confirmed as true afterward, a.k.a., veridical perceptions. I watched as my body struggled and swam to shore.

Later I observed my frozen body being pushed on a stretcher from the helicopter on the hospital driveway to the emergency department inside. I observed as my unconscious body was tended to by nurses in the ER, and later wheeled to the physiotherapy department and placed in the hot whirlpool baths there.

When my spirit re-entered my body, I was still in the whirlpool bath, thus confirming what I had viewed from above. Also, details that I observed, while floating above my body before our helicopter rescue, were later corroborated for me in discussions with the pilot Gerry.

As I learned more about Near-Death Experiences in the years following my plane crash, I slowly became convinced that my mystical experience during the crash was indeed an NDE, even though I had never been clinically dead at any time during it. In my case, the NDE began when I was psychologically facing imminent death, and continued as I became physically closer to death: nearly drowning; and profoundly hypothermic.

My conclusion was that the definition of NDE triggers needed to be expanded, to include out-of-body and mystical experiences that occur when individuals are facing possible imminent death. It was only when I met Dr. Kenneth Ring in 1990, that I learned that he and some other NDE researchers had also now concluded that NDEs could be triggered by psychologically facing death, as mine had. From that day forward, I have confidently labeled my 1979 medevac plane crash experience as a Near-Death Experience.

Premonition of the NDE?

As I reflect upon the 1979 event, I wonder whether or not I had a premonition about the plane crash and NDE, before it happened. I clearly recall the unusual incident that occurred in the hospital doctor's lounge in Sioux Lookout on March 27, 1979, the day of my plane crash, as I was donning the heavy arctic parka prior to boarding the plane for the medevac.

I spied a plate of cookies in the doctor's lounge that day, placed there for us to snack on. I would normally not consider eating any of those cookies, because of my efforts to remain thin. I can still clearly recall that on that day I had a very strong inner impulse, an unusual but strong inner thought, *I better eat a couple of cookies. I am going to need the energy later.*

I recall being puzzled by the strangeness of this impulse, but I obeyed the strong inner prompt and ate a couple of the cookies. This was very out of character behavior for me at that time. It is also very odd that I still remember this incident so clearly, over thirty years later.

Had the medevac flight to Winnipeg gone smoothly as planned, it would have been a relatively short trip, perhaps a one-hour flight. Before a short flight like that, there would be no need for me to eat extra calories. However, as it later turned out, due to the plane crash into the open freezing water, my body truly did need the energy of those two cookies. In fact, I desperately needed all the energy I could possibly muster, in order to survive the icy water and the arduous swim to shore.

This subtle premonition of the plane crash haunts me. How was it possible that my spirit could have known that I would desperately need the extra energy of those cookies later that day? My thoughts about this NDE premonition relate to one of my revelations in the white light – my intuitive realization that the past, present, and future are all known to the Higher Power – that they are all connected in consciousness.

From this perspective of the interconnectedness of time, it would be possible in some extraordinary circumstances for information from the future to somehow travel backward in time through consciousness, in the form of a premonition. I think that this occurred on March 27, 1979, when I received the premonition or precognition of the need to eat a couple of cookies. The knowledge somehow traveled backward in time through consciousness, to inform me that I would need the energy from those two cookies later that day.

Starting Research on Spiritually Transformative Experiences

First labelling my spiritual experience in the 1979 plane crash as a mystical experience, propelled me later in the year to personally research mystical experiences. This was similar to how my struggle to understand my 1976 meditation experience prompted me to learn more about kundalini awakenings. Propelled by my quest to understand my own personal experiences, in my private time I began to read numerous books from diverse spiritual traditions about both types of experiences,

As I began to deepen my personal understanding, I also developed a strong desire as a doctor, to professionally research mystical experiences and kundalini awakening, and to discover what was known about these topics from a Western medical and psychological perspective. I wanted to discover what was known to doctors and scholars about mystical experiences, Near-Death Experiences, kundalini awakenings, and, due to my psychic awakening, psychic experiences.

My personal and professional search led me to the writings of great Western scholars and scientists, as well as to the writings of Spiritual Masters of diverse spiritual traditions. I began my search by studying several of Gopi Krishna's books on Kundalini Awakening. As I mentioned in Chapter 5, I had first met him during a trip to India in 1977, and several times later when he visited Canada or the USA.

I privately corresponded with him, and I read every book he wrote up to the time of his death in 1984. He had become a mentor to me, encouraging me to do kundalini research. At the time, I had no idea how I could possibly do kundalini research related to my medical practice, and I imagined that any such research would have to continue to be a private interest, outside of my medical career.

I began my personal research into mystical experiences by reading two Western doctors' books that Gopi Krishna had recommended, Dr. William James' classic *The Varieties of Religious Experience*, and Dr. Richard Maurice Bucke's *Cosmic Consciousness*. When I added Near-Death Experiences to the range of topics I was researching, I began by reading Dr. Raymond Moody's book *Life after Life*.

For more than ten years after the airplane crash, I kept my quest almost completely private. I was in the closet. Having met with a great deal of skepticism and misunderstanding in the early days after the experience, I had learned to keep quiet about my extraordinary experiences and my quest for a deeper understanding of them. I kept my STEs private and rarely spoke to others about them. During work hours, I focused on my professional work as a traditional Western-trained Family Physician.

After completion of my Family Practice residency in June 1979, I opened my Family Practice in Toronto, Canada. In 1980, I became a full-time teaching physician at Women's College Hospital, part of the University of Toronto, Faculty of Medicine. I excelled in my professional work, and I thoroughly enjoyed being a Family Doctor and a teaching physician.

In the 1980s I trained to specialize in MD Psychotherapy, earning an MEd, Masters in Education degree, in Applied Psychology. I essentially led a double life during those first years. By day I was a highly respected Family Physician on the full-time teaching faculty at the University. In my private time, I was secretly a spiritual seeker, meditating daily, praying deeply, studying scriptures, and researching diverse spiritual and paranormal states of consciousness. I led this double life for over ten years.

I rarely spoke publicly about my plane crash experience during those years. I would agree to speak to small groups occasionally when a supportive relative or friend would ask me to speak about my plane crash mystical experience to their community group or church group. I recall talking to my uncle's local Kiwanis club, and two small church groups. Otherwise, I kept my STEs private.

Despite my relative anonymity, my few small public talks started to attract people to me. People who had experienced NDEs, mystical experiences, psychic experiences, past-life recall, and/or kundalini awakenings began to seek me out, and book appointments to see me in my office as a medical doctor. Somehow, by word of mouth, it became increasingly widely known that I was a doctor who had experienced some paranormal experiences, and that I was receptive to hearing the stories from others who had experienced similar things.

Thus, people who had experienced STEs increasingly began to book appointments to see me at my medical office. I discovered that these patients wanted to share the stories of their extraordinary spiritual experiences with me as a medical doctor, and hoped that I would believe their stories and validate them.

Many told me heart-breaking accounts of being mislabeled by other doctors or by clergy. Many had been misunderstood and critically judged by others, just as I had been. Some had even been labeled as mentally ill, and incorrectly institutionalized for a time, because they insisted to closed-minded family members and/or psychiatrists, on the reality of a powerful spiritual experience.

These patients were deeply grateful to be validated by me as a doctor, rather than immediately judged as "crazy" or "imagining." They took great comfort when I could provide them with a non-pathological name for their specific experience, whether it was a mystical experience, a kundalini awakening, a psychic experience, or an NDE. Slowly over the years my clinical expertise in counseling people who had STEs increased, and my understanding of diverse STEs continued to deepen through my study of scholarly books on the topic.

My Soul Lesson – A Profoundly Loving Higher Power Exists.

As I look back and reflect upon the core soul lesson I learned during the 1979 plane crash Near-Death Experience, I see that I realized firsthand that the Higher Power truly exists. Before the NDE, I had been told by my parents, and by my church, that God existed, but I had no firsthand proof. After this NDE, I absolutely knew that a Higher Power exists, because I had experienced it. I had been immersed in the Higher Power's loving light while I was out-of-body during my NDE.

My awareness of being permeated by the loving presence of the Higher Power, what I call God, did not come to me through intellectual analysis, or a verbal explanation, but through direct perception – soul-level recognition at the core of my being. While I was in the realm of heavenly light, I understood and knew, somehow, that I was in the presence of the Divine Source, God. I experienced an indescribable, profound, unconditional love, emanating from a massive and incredibly powerful PRESENCE, from a universal intelligent force.

Somehow I knew, perhaps through a type of revelation, intuitive knowing, or soul-recognition, that this profoundly loving PRESENCE was our Higher Power God. I also somehow knew that this PRESENCE was omnipresent—permeating and underlying all of creation, omnipotent—all-powerful, and infinitely intelligent—the omniscient intelligent force underlying all creation.

Nobody had to tell me or explain to me what I was experiencing. I knew to the depths of my being that I was being blessed with a glimpse of the Higher Power underlying the universe. The profound unconditional love radiating from the Higher Power penetrated my soul deeply, suffusing my being with love. This was a lived experience of the reality of the Higher Power behind the universe.

Because of the experience, I knew without a doubt, to the core of my being, that the Higher Power or God exists, and that our Higher Power God is profoundly loving in nature.

Long-Term After-Effects – The Spiritual Quest

As I reflect upon the long-term transformational after-effects of the 1979 event, I see that this NDE changed the course of my life. Immediately after it, I had a spiritual transformation in my personality, a psychological transformation of character with a growing-up impact, and a psychic transformation opening me to new psychic experiences.

In the long-term, this NDE launched me onto a new spiritual life-stage, a stage of intense spiritual searching. I meditated and prayed devotedly, and eagerly researched the literature, both professional and spiritual, relating to mystical and paranormal states of consciousness. I learned from many different perspectives, medical, psychological, and diverse spiritual traditions.

Overall, as I reflect back on my 1979 NDE, I am struck by the profundity of the long-term after-effects upon me and the course of my life. I see that it changed the course of my life forever.

However, unbeknownst to me, the Divine sculptor had only begun to shape the course of my life with powerful spiritual experiences. My life's course would be changed dramatically once again by another powerful mystical experience, several years later.

Chapter 8

MY 1990 "CALLING"
MYSTICAL EXPERIENCE

The Divine sculptor touched my life again, with a powerful mystical experience in 1990 that dramatically changed the course of my life. It permanently altered the course of my professional career and ultimately led me to become the first Canadian medical doctor to specialize my practice in the counseling and research of people with Spiritually Transformative Experiences.

This life-changing experience happened to me eleven years after my 1979 NDE, while I was attending the 1990 conference by the Spiritual Emergence Network (SEN) and Institute for Transpersonal Psychology (ITP) in Asilomar, close to Monterrey, California. I refer to this powerful STE as my "calling" mystical experience.

By 1989, I finally felt confident enough from my 10 years of research and clinical experience counseling people with STEs, to speak professionally to some supportive colleagues about this. In 1989, I presented my first professional talk about counseling patients with STEs at a small conference in Philadelphia, USA. A small group of pioneering professionals, doctors, clergy, and psychologists, who were also researching and counseling people with spiritual experiences, were in attendance. I presented material about kundalini awakening. It was through this conference that I first met Dr. Bonnie Greenwell, who later became a close friend and colleague of mine.

Dr. Bonnie Greenwell PhD, a California-based Transpersonal Psychologist, had also had a kundalini awakening and had done her PhD research thesis on kundalini awakening. She was fascinated by my knowledge of kundalini awakenings based on my deep study of the writings and mentorship by Gopi Krishna. She invited me to speak the following year, at the 1990 SEN and ITP conference that was focused on kundalini awakenings. My private research into STEs had now taken its first baby steps out of the closet, towards becoming public knowledge.

While at this 1990 kundalini conference, I had my calling mystical experience. Here is how it happened.

Deeply Moved by Mistreatment of STE Experiencers

I was walking on the sand-dunes in Monterrey, California when this calling mystical experience occurred. I was contemplating what I had experienced that evening and over the last three days while attending this conference. Dr. Bonnie Greenwell had asked me, and I had agreed, to be one of the facilitators that evening for an impromptu meeting, a supportive sharing circle for any conference participants who thought they were experiencing kundalini and wished to share their stories in a supportive small group. She and I did not know how many, or even if any, conference participants would come to this informal gathering.

To my amazement and much to my surprise, a large group of people came to this informal meeting. The room was packed. The large group was divided into 2 smaller groups where each participant would have a chance to share their stories, with the support of a professional facilitator, either Dr. Greenwell or me.

I was randomly assigned a group of 20 or so participants who had shown up. I started my group's sharing session by sharing my own story. I told them that I was a Canadian medical doctor and that I had personally experienced a kundalini awakening in 1976, as well as a Near-Death Experience in 1979. My personal sharing had the effect of opening a flood gate.

One after another, the participants in my group shared their moving personal stories of the intense challenges they had endured after their kundalini awakening experiences. Many told of horrible, traumatic reactions from others, of being falsely labeled as mentally ill, and even sometimes committed to a hospital psychiatric ward by doctors and psychologists who knew nothing about kundalini and other Spiritually Transformative Experiences.

Other participants shared other tragic experiences, such as being labeled by clergy, family members, and/or friends as delusional, imagining it, or self-inflated. A couple of people even recounted being told by their pastor that their kundalini awakening experiences were the work of the devil.

Many of those present openly wept tears of relief, and expressed deep heartfelt gratitude to me, that I, as a practicing medical doctor, had disclosed my own kundalini awakening and NDE experiences to them. Many exclaimed that this sharing group was the first time, after perhaps five, ten, or even twenty years of being ridiculed or pathologized for their STE, that they could share the story of STEs with a doctor who believed them, validated their lived experience, and did not automatically label them as crazy. Everyone in my group wanted to hug me in gratitude at the end of this moving sharing circle.

I was deeply moved to the core of my being by this sharing event, and the outpouring of gratitude towards me as a supportive medical doctor knowledgeable about kundalini awakening. I decided to go for a walk after the circle ended, at the nearby ocean-front sand dunes trail, to contemplate this deeply moving event.

My Calling Mystical Experience

After a few minutes of walking in the clear starlit evening, I suddenly felt as if the heavens opened, and a brilliant white light descended upon me from above. I felt that my head had cracked open like a flower bud opens when it blossoms. I felt like I no longer had a top to my head, and the open top of my head had become a brilliant beacon of light – radiating light in all directions.

I felt as if the Light of the Higher Power had cracked me open in body, mind, and spirit, and I was now completely exposed to the Divine above. My soul felt naked before God—completely open, completely exposed.

I felt an indescribable, luminous, divine nectar, exquisitely beautiful, dripping into the back of my throat.

While basking in the infinitude, the ecstasy and wonder of this exalted experience and savoring the Divine ambrosia, it seemed that my consciousness opened and expanded. In this luminous, expanded state of consciousness, I somehow instantly knew something that I had not known before. In an aha experience or revelation, I suddenly knew what I must now do with my life.

Without any words having been heard or spoken, I suddenly knew this as if it had been revealed by the Light somehow. I knew that I must now come out of the closet and begin to talk publicly to doctors, patients, the public, the media—anyone who will listen, to declare that STEs were real. This included mystical experiences, kundalini awakenings, NDEs, and psychic experiences. I was to proclaim that these were healthy human experiences, NOT mental illnesses. I needed to advocate for STE Experiencers who were being mislabeled and mistreated.

I knew this awareness about kundalini and other STEs that I had been shown experientially and through my research was sacred knowledge, and a Truth, a Truth that I had glimpsed and experienced within my own being by Divine grace, and by God's Divine plan for my life.

I felt deeply humbled by the realization that I had been shown holy knowledge—the reality of our true spiritual nature, and the potential within all of us to awaken spiritually, to have more expanded states of consciousness. I further understood to the core of my soul, that the knowledge about kundalini awakening that the Divine had revealed to me, directly through my own experience and deepened through what I had learned from Gopi Krishna, was sacred.

Indeed, I felt like I had been given a very precious and sacred gift from the Divine, like a sacred "spiritual baby," that I must now care for and nurture, spreading this knowledge to truth-seeking souls craving this information.

I knew that Spirit/the Higher Power was now calling me to action. It was time for me to openly speak my Truth about kundalini awakening, STEs, and human consciousness potential, to share what I had learned, and to advocate for STE Experiencers.

Called to Action – Come Out of the Closet

The Light and profound expansion of consciousness slowly faded after several more minutes. I then returned to my normal state of awareness. I was trembling inside.

I realized that with the sacred gift the Divine had given me, was a responsibility—a clear calling for my life. It was time to come out of the closet. It was my moral and sacred obligation to share with others what I had learned and experienced.

This calling mystical experience changed the course of the rest of my life. It launched me onto a new stage in my life, focused on helping others by sharing what I had learned. I was to publicly tell the story of my 1979 NDE, and soon officially specialize my medical practice in counseling and researching patients who had experienced NDEs and other STEs.

At the time of my calling mystical experience, I did not know how this could be done, but I would soon discover that Spirit would open surprisingly many doors for me, enabling me to follow my calling, to start sharing what I had learned about Spiritually Transformative Experiences.

Chapter 9

LIFE-CHANGING AFTER-EFFECTS OF MY "CALLING" MYSTICAL EXPERIENCE

My 1990 "calling" mystical experience changed the course of the rest of my life. From that day forward, I began to speak openly and publicly about my 1979 Near-Death Experience and my research into all types of Spiritually Transformative Experiences. I knew it was time to come out of the closet, and do what was needed.

Founding the Kundalini Research Network

The day after the 1990 SEN/ITP kundalini-themed conference ended, I went to a professional networking meeting held in Dr. Bonne Greenwell's home in California. Following a lively discussion, the other doctors and psychologists at this meeting, and I, collectively decided to found the *Kundalini Research Network*, to promote research and spread awareness of kundalini awakening both to the public and to professionals internationally.

I served on the Board of the Kundalini Research Network from that founding meeting in 1990 until 2004. I also became the chair of the Kundalini Research Network's questionnaire research project for almost a decade.

It was also at this 1990 networking meeting where I first met the eminent NDE researcher and co-founder of the International Association of Near-Death Studies, Dr. Kenneth Ring. It was during a private discussion there that Dr. Ring confirmed that my 1979 plane crash mystical experience was indeed a type of NDE.

Coming Out of the Closet

Emboldened by Dr. Ring's confirmation that my plane-crash experience was indeed a Near-Death Experience, and propelled inwardly by my intense calling mystical experience, when I returned to Toronto a few days later I immediately started talking publicly about my NDE and research into STEs. [In 1990 I called them collectively "Spiritual Emergence Syndrome." I later coined the phrase which I now use, *Spiritually Transformative Experiences* (STEs)].

In the remainder of 1990, it felt to me that by amazing synchronicities, life started opening doors for me, giving me opportunities to speak at medical conferences, to public groups, on radio, on television, and to newspapers and magazines. The doors opening began my first day back at work after the conference, when I answered a medical colleague's question, "How was that conference in California?"

I told him briefly about the theme and my decision to specialize in STEs, and he immediately invited me to speak the following week at a doctors' rounds, a regular educational meeting for physicians, at his local hospital. A medical media journalist attended this rounds and wrote an article about my NDE and current interest in counseling patients with NDEs and STEs.

This article created a cascade effect, with other medical media requesting to interview me, followed by several mainstream media interviewing me… magazines, newspapers, then radio, and later television.

I intuitively knew that my spiritual work was to heed my strong calling and to have the courage to walk through the doors that Spirit was opening for me. I needed to have the bravery to speak my truth about Spiritually Transformative Experiences publicly, even before somewhat skeptical audiences.

Yvonne Kason, M.D.

Launching my Career Specialty –
Spiritually Transformative Experiences

More and more people who had had diverse types of Spiritually Transformative Experiences began to seek me out as a doctor, for counseling and psychotherapy. I continued to increase my expertise in STEs by joining and attending meetings held by many professional organizations pioneering this new and emerging field. In addition to the Kundalini Research Network (KRN), of which I was a Board member and Chair of the KRN Questionnaire research project, I soon joined the International Association of Near-Death Studies as a Professional Member, the Spiritual Emergence Network, of which I became the Canadian Coordinator, and the GP-Psychotherapy Association of Canada, of which I later became a Mentor.

Wishing to follow my calling and specialize my medical practice in STEs, I scheduled a meeting with the Chairman of my department at the University of Toronto, the Department of Family and Community Medicine. I frankly and openly discussed with him my interest in STEs which had been propelled by my own NDE in the 1979 medevac plane crash. I told him about my deep commitment to speak publicly about my NDE and to increasingly specialize my medical practice in counseling and researching patients who had STEs. I had come up with the idea of opening a clinic for people having STEs.

My department Chairman thoughtfully gave me sound and sage advice. "Focus on research," he said. He went on to tell me that as long as I was doing research in my area of clinical interest, he considered my proposed clinic and research acceptable to the university department.

Following my university Department Chairman's advice, and with his blessings for which I remain ever grateful, in 1992 I founded the *Spiritual Emergence Research and Referral Clinic* (SERRC) in Toronto. I advertised it widely within the Ontario medical community. Together with a few like-minded therapists, I invited referrals of patients with STEs from other doctors and healthcare providers.

Referrals indeed began to flow, and gradually more and more of my medical practice became specialized in counseling people who were undergoing STEs. I strived to accurately diagnose these patients. I would give them an accurate name for their STEs, help them understand their experiences, and help them use their spiritual experiences to enhance their psychological healing and deepen on their spiritual journeys.

My growing body of knowledge and experience plus numerous requests from patients and other doctors, inspired me to start writing my first book on STEs, sharing the story of my 1979 NDE and my research and many case studies of Spiritually Transformative Experiences. My first STE book, *A Farther Shore*, was published in 1994.

After *A Farther Shore* was released, my publisher, HarperCollins Canada, sent me on a cross-Canada promotional tour, with radio shows, TV interviews, and book-store signings. Afterward, my invitations to do media interviews and speaking engagements increased dramatically. Although I was not paid for these many interviews or speaking engagements, I spoke at these many venues eagerly and pro bono – due to my strong inner sense of calling.

The strong public profile I developed as a Canadian media resource and professional expert relating to NDEs and other STEs, was a permanent long-term change in my life. Thus with the publication of *A Farther Shore*, my response to my 1990 calling to go public to try and help others with STEs, had now come into full expression.

Misunderstood by Others

Coming out of the closet, divulging my stories, opening the Spiritual Emergence Research and Referral Clinic, and publishing *A Farther Shore* were not smooth sailing, however. I had to deal with criticism and misunderstanding from professional governing bodies, critics in the medical profession, critics in the general public, and some friends.

On two separate occasions, my professional work focused on patients with STEs was challenged by governing bodies within the medical profession. They posed the question to me, "What does this have to do with the practice of medicine?" I was required to respond to the challenge. I drew on my department Chairman's advice to help stave off the challenges from the medical profession's governing body.

"I am doing clinical research in a new and emerging field in medicine," I said.

Fortunately, I had additional evidence to back up my argument to the medical governing bodies that research into STEs was relevant and valid. I was also able to inform them that "Religious or Spiritual Problem" [V62.89] was slated by the American Psychiatric Association for inclusion as a new diagnostic category, to be published in the upcoming DSM-IV, a diagnostic standard for medical practice.

By synchronicity, I had met the pioneering California psychiatrist, Dr. Robert Turner, at the Kundalini Research Network's annual conference in 1992. He had informed me that he, together with California psychiatrist Dr. Francis Lu, and California psychologist Dr. David Lukoff PhD, had submitted a proposal to the American Psychiatric Association (APA) for a new diagnostic category relating to STEs.

Dr. Turner also informed me that this proposal had just been accepted by the APA. I was, therefore, able to inform my medical governing bodies about this new recognition by the APA of "Religious or Spiritual Problem," before this was public knowledge. I argued to them that this new diagnostic code, V62.89 - Religious or Spiritual Problem, put my pioneering clinical work and research on STEs on the cutting edge of medical research in Canada. I was the first medical doctor in Canada to specialize in this newly defined area. Thankfully, my explanations seemed to satisfy my medical critics.

I also had to deal with some harsh public criticism after the publication of my 1994 book, *A Farther Shore*. A few public critics challenged my authority and credentials to write the book. Some challenged me claiming that because I was not fully illuminated or a Spiritual Master or guru, I had no authority to write a book talking about kundalini awakening and mystical experiences or to express my own opinions on these topics. Others simply did not believe my account of my NDE and kundalini awakening mystical experience.

One medical critic stated that I had made an error in assuming that because I had a specific unusual experience, (probably a hallucination in his mind), that others were having similar experiences. Some former friends also openly criticized me, saying that I was "full of myself," implying that I was somehow exaggerating or falsely claiming to have had a Near-Death Experience and a kundalini awakening. Some religious types criticized my work and research, saying that mystical experiences were "not supposed to be talked about" according to their spiritual tradition.

I rebuffed the accusations of these critics because I knew in my heart and soul that I had been strongly and clearly called to share what I had learned about NDEs, kundalini, and mystical experiences. I knew my experiences were real. I knew the truth, that as a doctor I had done much scholarly research into NDEs and other STEs, and I had had by this time many years of clinical experience counseling hundreds of STE patients.

I also knew that hundreds and perhaps thousands of people or more, were experiencing STEs and that many wanted somebody supportive and knowledgeable about STEs to talk to about their experiences. Although I was clearly not a guru or a fully enlightened Spiritual Master, I knew that I had much to share, and my Higher Power had clearly called me to share what I had learned, to try to help others. I, therefore, continued to heed my calling despite the criticism, sharing what I had learned with others, and continuing to counsel STE experiencers.

Long-Term After-Effects

As I reflect upon an overview of the numerous long-term transformational after-effects of my 1990 calling mystical experience upon my life, I see that this experience shifted me into a new, different, life-stage. Having completed almost twelve years from 1979 to 1990 of a life-stage of spiritual searching, privately researching STEs, my 1990 calling mystical experience propelled me into a new life-stage, one of publicly sharing what I had learned, to try to help others. I was to be of service to others.

Although I continued my quest to learn more about STEs after my calling in 1990, and I continue to learn more to this day, my primary inner commitment became to serve others, advocate for STE experiencers, and share what I had learned about STEs. I was determined to heed my calling, despite the professional obstacles I faced, and the personal criticism that I had to endure.

This desire to share publicly what I had learned, and to try to help others having STEs, became a permanent, long-term after-effect of the 1990 experience. In 1990, after I came out of the closet, my professional life became very focused on spreading awareness about STEs. I did many media interviews on radio and television, for newspapers, and magazines, and was increasingly invited to speak at professional conferences and to community groups.

The number of STE experiencers coming to see me as patients grew year by year, especially after I opened SERRC in 1992, and again after my book, *A Farther Shore,* was published in 1994. The calling mystical experience thus transformed me into the first Canadian medical doctor to publicly specialize in counseling and researching patients who had diverse types of STEs.

As I look back, I realize that another interesting after-effect of the 1990 experience was that my intuition and psychic openness increased. Around 1992, I suddenly developed the intermittent ability to perceive my past lives. These vivid memories would usually be triggered by meeting someone whom my memories showed me I had known in a past life. This new ability to see my past lives helped me greatly in understanding the complexity of human relationships.

Finally, as I reflect, I also wonder whether or not this experience was in fact in some ways a long-term after-effect of my 1979 NDE. I wonder if perhaps my mystical experience in the 1979 NDE somehow made my consciousness more open or more receptive to subsequent mystical experiences.

Certainly, the fact that I meditated regularly twice a day, and sincerely embraced my spiritual life all those years also contributed to my openness to a mystical experience. But in addition, did my 1979 NDE perhaps make me more receptive, or prepare me in some way for my powerful calling mystical experience in 1990? I cannot be certain, but I think perhaps it did.

Honored by Indigenous Elders

In the years following the 1990 calling experience, when I spoke publicly about my 1979 medevac plane crash NDE, I had several opportunities to meet elders from various Canadian and U.S. Native American communities. I always felt a strong connection between my 1979 NDE and the Native American communities, because the plane crash occurred during my time working in Northern Ontario with Native communities. My patient who died during the crash was a Native American woman, Jean Marie Peters.

It is striking to me that my 1979 NDE was always deeply respected, and I was always honored and treated with respect, by the Native American elders whom I met. Over the years I have been given several sacred gifts by Native elders, including a sacred feather and a medicine bundle. Although I have only a partial understanding of the sacred meaning of these gifts in the Native American spiritual traditions, I feel honored at being given such gifts.

Two of my encounters with Native American elders stand out in my mind. Both impacted me deeply. The first occurred around 1995, when I had the opportunity to meet a Native American elder from Manitoulin Island, Ontario. After I shared the story of my 1979 plane crash and NDE with him, he reflected upon my story, and then slowly responded with a comment that moved me greatly:

> "Elders of our people realize that it is the Creator who reveals to us who the shamans and elders of our society are to be. The people cannot determine who is a shaman or elder themselves. It is the Creator who reveals this to the people. Had you been born to my people, Yvonne, you would have been recognized as a shaman because of the Near-Death Experience the Creator gave you. The Creator has revealed that you are a shaman, one who has walked on both sides. Those who have eyes to see will realize that."

I felt deeply honored and respected by these comments. How different this respectful spiritual reflection on my 1979 NDE was, compared to the skepticism, criticism, and misunderstanding I had to face repeatedly from the traditional Western community.

In 2002, I met another Native American elder whose comments touched me deeply again. This elder came from the Sioux Lookout, Kenora area, the region in which my 1979 plane crash occurred. He had heard me describe my 1979 NDE in a presentation at the University of Toronto, Spirituality and Health-Care conference, that I chaired in 2002. At the

Yvonne Kason, M.D.

end of the conference, the elder quietly waited until the crowd of people wishing to talk to me had dispersed. The elder then humbly stepped forward. I had not met him or spoken with him before that moment. He said to me "Many eyes were watching you that day."

I stopped moving immediately, struck by the deep spiritual vibration of his words. I looked deeply into his eyes and said, "I do not understand what you mean." He went on to explain as follows:

> "You swam to The Island [he used the native name for the island] after your plane crash. This island is sacred ground to my people. There were many invisible eyes watching you from The Island, that day."
>
> "Many eyes watched as the Creator took one of our family, Jean Peters. And they watched as the Creator saved your life that day, as you swam to safety to our sacred ground."

As the elder spoke these words, I felt chills and rushes of energy running up my spine. I was riveted by his words. I felt deeply moved, touched to my soul to learn that I had swum to Native American holy ground. I was deeply humbled by the sacred meaning behind these words, to realize the beautiful synchronicity that the Island that had offered me safe harbor, that had saved my life, was holy ground to the Native American people.

I felt doubly humbled by the grace of God, that not only was my life spared on that fateful day of my 1979 plane crash, but also that it was holy ground, a sacred island, that saved my life. I was deeply moved.

Reflecting on this elder's comments about the invisible eyes of Spirit watching me from the ethers above The Island's sacred ground, I thought about the etheric hand that I had seen outstretched towards me from The Island, superimposed upon the fallen tall pine tree in the water. It all made sense to me in some mysterious yet beautiful way.

Etheric eyes had been watching the plane crash drama unfold, and an etheric hand truly reached out from the other side, guiding me to the fallen pine tree, to help save my life that day. The sanctity of this synchronicity still moves me deeply, and brings tears of gratitude and devotion to my eyes, to this day. I feel heartfelt gratitude for having been repeatedly honored and respected this way by elders of the Native American communities.

However, unbeknownst to me in 1979 after my NDE, and in 1990 after my calling mystical experience, the Divine hand would continue to beckon me later in my life, during two more Near-Death Experiences and other powerful STEs that I was yet to have.

Chapter 10

COINING "SPIRITUALLY TRANSFORMATIVE EXPERIENCES"

I think it important, as I share my spiritual awakening story with you, that I also share how I came to coin the phrase *Spiritually Transformative Experiences* and give you a brief summary and description of the types of Spiritually Transformative Experiences, as I define them. As my professional, clinical, and personal research continued in the early 1990s, I realized that there was no precise term to describe the cluster of peak spiritual and paranormal experiences I was researching and counseling patients about.

Some people were using various terms such as "Exceptional Human Experiences," "Extraordinary Experiences," "Experienced Anomalous Trauma," "Ascension Experiences," "paranormal experiences," and more. "Spiritual Emergence Syndrome," a term coined by Dr. Stan Grof and Christina Grof, was being used by psychologists associated with the Spiritual Emergence Network at that time.

However, in my mind, "Spiritual Emergence Syndrome" was also not an exact fit for what I was researching. Spiritual Emergence Syndrome included many psychological phenomena in addition to some peak Spiritually Transformative Experiences. Further, the word "syndrome" in the name seemed to me to imply that there was something unhealthy about these experiences.

This need for a precise, positive term inspired me to coin the phrase "Spiritually Transformative Experiences," (STEs) in 1994. I first published this phrase in my book *A Farther Shore*, and in the article "Near-Death Experiences and Kundalini Awakening: Exploring the Links" which appeared in the *Journal of Near-Death Studies,* that same year.

My Greatest Inspirations for Coining "Spiritually Transformative Experiences"

Three major sources influenced how I defined "Spiritually Transformative Experiences" in the manner in which I did. The first major influence on me came from the views and writings of Gopi Krishna. He first introduced me to the yogic model of consciousness back in 1977.

It was the best and most comprehensive model I was able to find to explain STEs and the spiritual transformation of consciousness I was observing. This model helped me understand both the STEs I and others had been experiencing, and their powerful after-effects. Gopi Krishna thought spiritual awakening of human consciousness was an evolutionary process occurring in humanity, and may lead to a kundalini awakening, mystical experiences, and inspired creativity and genius, occurring in increasing numbers of people.

The second major influence on my thinking throughout the 1980s and 1990s emanated from my further readings into the yogic model of consciousness, especially in Patanjali's *Yoga Sutras*, an ancient, but classic, yogic text. In one chapter of the *Yoga-Sutras*, Patanjali describes in detail many states of consciousness that may occur during a soul's spiritual awakening process.

As I read the *Yoga-Sutras*, I quickly identified with many of the states of consciousness Patanjali described, because I had experienced them myself. Using classic yogic terminology, STEs are grouped and differentiated into "samadhis," or mystical experiences, and "siddhis," or psychic phenomena.

The writings and teachings of Paramahansa Yogananda were the third major influence upon me, helping me come to a yet deeper experiential understanding of the spiritual awakening process. I first read *The Autobiography of a Yogi*, Paramahansa Yogananda's best-selling classic, in 1988.

I found this book gave the most complete and understandable

Yvonne Kason, M.D.

explanation of the yogic model of consciousness, for the modern-day Western mind. He included descriptions of samadhis and siddhis, some of the STEs one might experience along the path of spiritual awakening and deepening.

Subsequently, I read all of Yogananda's 17 books, and I continue to study his writings to this day. In retrospect, these were the three major contributors, Gopi Krishna, Patanjali, and Paramahansa Yogananda, who helped me conceptualize, define, and organize Spiritually Transformative Experiences in the manner I present in my books.

Types of Spiritually Transformative Experiences

In 1993, while I was writing *A Farther Shore,* after considering several other possible terms and discussing options with friends, I coined the phrase *Spiritually Transformative Experiences* (STEs). I intended the term to be positive in meaning and to reflect how STEs all tend to change people's lives, transforming them, and causing a spiritual awakening.

I intended Spiritually Transformative Experiences to be a contemporary umbrella term, easily understood, which would encompass the broad range of spiritual and paranormal experiences I had been studying and experiencing. Finally, by creating an umbrella term, I wanted to indicate that I thought all these STE experiences of consciousness were related in some way, all part of a gradual expansion of the range of normal human consciousness.

I categorize STEs into six main types, each with many subtypes. I describe all types of Spiritually Transformative Experiences in great detail, and give many case examples, in my books *A Farther Shore, Farther Shores,* and in the most up-to-date detail in my latest book *Touched by the Light.* I would encourage readers who wish to learn more about STEs to read *Touched by the Light.*

I define types of Spiritually Transformative Experiences into the following six categories:

1. Mystical experiences (samadhis)
2. Psychic/intuitive experiences (siddhis)
3. Kundalini awakenings

4. Near-Death Experiences
5. Other death-related STEs
6. Inspired creativity and genius

Types of Mystical Experiences

Mystical experiences are the most profoundly impactful of all types of Spiritually Transformative Experiences. Mystical experiences by their very nature are beyond words, completely experiential, beyond one's capacity to describe in words. They are a first-hand, lived experience of the greater spiritual reality underlying creation. All types of mystical experiences give one an experiential glimpse of some aspect of the vast and multi-faceted nature of the greater reality behind the universe, the Higher Power, the Source.

I divide mystical experiences into the following 7 main sub-types, based on what feature of the mystical experience is most pronounced. Many mystical experiences may have features from several of these categories.

1. Unitive or communion experiences
   These are mystical experiences where the most pronounced feature is a sense of oneness or unity. This may vary in degree, from a sense of oneness with a lover, to a sense of oneness with a scene in nature, to an even more expansive sense of unity and connection with the entire planet. Or, it may be an even vaster experience of communion with the Higher Power underlying the universe. Duality disappears.
2. Ecstatic or bliss episodes
   These are mystical experiences where the most marked feature is the joy, the love, the bliss, the ecstasy.
3. Mystical visions
   Mystical visions are inspiring and awe-provoking mystical experiences that have a very strong visual aspect. This could include visions and uplifting spiritual communication with angels, saints, spiritual teachers, and/or Spiritual Masters such as Jesus, or Buddha.
4. Expansive episodes
   These are mystical experiences that include a strong sense of expansion, as if one's consciousness has expanded from the normal

size of the head, to much larger, perhaps expanding to enfold a country. Or, consciousness may expand further to enfold the cosmos, or even to a sense of infinity.

5. Spiritual rebirth, conversion, or healing mystical experiences
The spiritual rebirth type of mystical experience includes a profound and dramatic spiritual conversion/or a dramatic spiritual healing. This may begin with a powerful purification or soul-cleansing experience. Perhaps it may even include hitting bottom, an extreme low point of despair, which then changes into a spiritual rebirth or spiritual renewal experience.

6. Revelations or illumination
These are mystical experiences whose most profound feature is the revelation of new knowledge, new information, new understandings of the nature of life, or the nature of the universe, or of one's life purpose.

7. Dissolution experiences
Dissolution mystical experiences are very difficult to describe in words. They are profound mystical experiences that include a sense of complete dissolving or disappearance of the ego self and personality, sometimes into nothingness, sometimes into the infinite oneness.

Kundalini Awakening/ Spiritual Energy Awakening

Kundalini awakening, or the awakening of a spiritual energy, is described in the mystical traditions of most religions, with varying names, such as: Holy Spirit awakening; Holy Spirit quickening; Holy wind; Dumo fire activation; Chi movement; and other terms. According to Gopi Krishna, a kundalini awakening can happen to anyone of any religious or cultural background. The classic features of a kundalini awakening are 2 or more of the following:

1. Sensations of energy movement, usually up the spine and/or up the entire body
2. Inner sounds, often an inner roaring sound, or a rushing of wind sound, sometimes a ringing sound, or other times sounding like "OM"

3. Light perceptions, such as a perception of inner liquid light flowing up the body or spine, or a sense of luminosity surrounding you, or even a sense that you are radiating light

4. They may sometimes be accompanied by sexual sensations or spontaneous sexual arousal

5. Lastly, depending on the degree of awakening, they may culminate in a mystical, psychic, or inspired creative experience

Once awakened, kundalini remains active to some degree, leading to the experiencer feeling repeated rushes of energy up the spine, chakra sensations, inner sounds, light perceptions, and STEs. A kundalini awakening is not an isolated incident. It is an awakening, a beginning of a long-term process of spiritual transformation of consciousness and psychological/ego cleansing. It gradually or abruptly expands the experiencer's range of consciousness to include STEs.

The long-term goal of a kundalini awakening is ongoing unitive consciousness, a.k.a. cosmic consciousness, nirvana, God-consciousness, nirbikalpa samadhi.

Types of Psychic/Intuitive Experiences

There are many types of psychic and intuitive experiences, more than I could possibly define and summarize. Here are the definitions of some of the more common psychic or intuitive experiences, extracted from how I describe them in my book, *Touched by the Light*.

1. Abstract intuition.
   Automatically knowing the answer to a problem without having to go through the logical steps of thinking and learning.
2. Astral travel.
   Episodes in which the spirit (sometimes called the astral body, soul, or spirit personality) seems to leave the physical body and travel to another place, time, or dimension.
3. Automatic writing.
   Writing or some other creative endeavor such as art or musical composition done without conscious thought by the experiencer.

It is often assumed that a spirit guide connects in some way to the experiencer's hand or arm and uses it to write messages, paint, draw, or play a musical instrument.

4. Bilocation.

The ability of an individual to appear in physical form at two distinct places at once.

5. Channeling.

A phenomenon in which the experiencer's own personality or spirit seems to step aside, and another personality or spirit seems to use the experiencer's physical body to communicate, write, or draw.

"Trance Channeling" is most common, where the experiencer goes into a trance during the channeling episode and has no awareness or memory of the information being channeled through them.

"Conscious Channeling" is less common. It's where the experiencer has full awareness of the information being channeled through them as it occurs, and they retain the memory of the experience and information afterward.

6. Clairaudience.

Mentally perceiving or actually hearing sounds or voices that are beyond the range of natural hearing.

7. Clairsentience.

The ability to physically feel and know the true feelings and mental state of another, including the ability to locate pain in another by sensing it in one's own body. Also, it may be an ability to intuitively know correct information or details about another person, facilitated by: touching the person; looking at the person, looking at a photo of the person, and/or touching an object the person has touched.

8. Clairvoyance.

The ability to visually perceive things beyond the normal range of vision, including: (1) The ability to see auras, subtle energy fields, or chakras; (2) the ability to see meaningful colors, patterns, or symbols that are not normally visible; (3) the ability to see objects, beings, or events that are concealed or beyond the natural range of sight (one type is called "remote viewing").

9. Communication with spirit guides.

   The ability to communicate with a spirit helper, guardian angel, or guide by seeing, hearing, feeling, knowing, or smelling their presence.

10. Higher Guidance and "Downloads."

    The ability to spontaneously receive intuitive guidance or warnings about life events, or to suddenly become aware of helpful previously unknown information, by guidance which seems to come from Spirit or a Higher Source. It may be heard, seen, intuitively known, or sensed. This higher guidance may suddenly pop into the experiencer's awareness, like a computer download of new information.

11. Materializations.

    The ability to make solid objects or people appear out of thin air. Includes Stigmata.

12. Mediumship.

    The ability to hear, see, and/or feel spirits of what seem to be disembodied deceased persons, and to communicate with these spirits.

13. Out-of-Body Experiences. (OBEs)

    Episodes in which the spirit or soul seems to leave the physical body, but remains within sight of or in the general location of the physical body. Out-of-body experiences where the spirit travels away from the location of the physical body are called "astral travel" type of OBEs.

14. Past-life recall.

    The ability to know, see, or clearly sense what seems to be previous incarnations. Past-life memories are often stimulated to surface spontaneously when one travels to a physical location on the planet where it seems the experiencer lived a past life, or when one meets a person with whom it seems the experiencer lived a past life. Past-life memories may also surface during meditations or in dreams.

15. Precognition.

    The ability to see, know, or emotionally sense the future; this includes having premonitions, prophetic dreams, and premonitory visions.

16. Psychic or spiritual healing.
    The ability to heal others by touch (also called "the laying on of hands"), by one's energy field, by prayers, or by focused mental thought; the related experience of being healed by the touch, energy field, prayers, or focused thoughts of another. Of course, no matter what modality achieves a healing, it's not the practitioner doing it. The practitioner realizes that they are but a humble vehicle for God/Spirit.

17. Psychometry.
    The ability to receive intuitive information about a person or object by touching either the person or the object with one's hands.

18. Stigmata.
    A type of materialization experience, with the spontaneous appearance of wounds, often discharging blood, which appear in locations that generally replicate the wounds of Jesus Christ on the cross. Many stigmatics enter a mystical state of consciousness during the stigmata materialization episode.

19. Synchronicities and Meaningful Coincidences.
    A type of intuitive experience when events occur that appear to be significantly related, with no outward causal connection.

20. Telekinesis.
    The ability to move objects by thought or mental influence.

21. Telepyrokinesis.
    The ability to start fires by thought or mental influence (also called pyrokinesis).

22. Telepathy.
    The ability to send and/or receive thoughts or mental images to or from another person.

23. Trans-dimensional Experiences.
    a) Episodes in which the experiencer temporarily enters what seems to be another dimension, or
    b) Seeing beings or encountering entities that seem to originate from another dimension.
    Trans-dimensional experiences may be associated with a discontinuity or an incongruence in the passage of time, such as

missing time, or a lengthy experience occurring in a very short earthly time frame.

24. UFO Encounters.

Many perceived UFOE contact or abduction experiences seem to be trans-dimensional psychic experiences, with the experiencer being moved to other places or dimensions, seemingly by beings living in another space/time dimension, or beings from other dimensions entering ours. (See Trans-dimensional Experiences above). UFO encounters are sometimes perceived as an abduction during which the experiencer is medically examined. At other times, they may be seen as a contact when the experiencer is taught spiritual lessons. NOTE: UFO sightings of lights or strange spacecraft in the sky may or may not fall into this trans-dimensional category.

It is important to note that psychic or intuitive experiences are not always uplifting and positive to the experiencer. In yoga, it is understood that psychic experiences may sometimes access lower astral planes, rather than the higher astral planes and causal planes of consciousness that are glimpsed during mystical experiences. Therefore psychic experiences may sometimes feel frightening or intrusive. For more information on this point, please refer to *Touched by the Light*.

Near-Death Experiences

As I have previously described in this book, NDEs are an out-of-body and/or white light, mystical experience that occurs when a person is close to death, clinically dead, or facing imminent death or severe trauma. Classically an NDE has at least five of the fifteen features first defined by Dr. Moody.

Based on my research, I divide Near-Death Experiences into three major sub-types. Each sub-type of NDE has somewhat different after-effects on the experiencer. These three types are:

1. The out-of-body type NDE: a psychic experience, when you are able to view the dead or unconscious body from outside the body;

2. The mystical/white light type NDE: a mystical experience, when you move past the out-of-body experience and continue to move into a loving realm of white light, where you may be met by loving beings of light, have a life-review, learn spiritual lessons, and/or feel yourself in the presence of the Higher Power; and

3. Distressing NDEs, with three sub-types:

   a) Fighting the NDE pull to the Light – in which the distress is due to the intensity of the struggle, as the experiencer resists the strong NDE pull out of body

   b) Low astral NDEs – including encounters with dark or tormenting entities

   c) Nightmare-like distortions

Other Death-Related STEs

There are three main types of other death-related STEs. I divide them according to when they occur, and to whom they occur.

1. Deathbed Visions, also known as End-of-Life Experiences, Nearing-Death Awareness, and Terminal Lucidity
   These are STEs that occur to people shortly before they actually die.

2. Death-Watch Experiences, also known as Shared-Death Experiences, and Shared Crossings
   These are STEs that happen to a living person at the time that another person dies, most commonly at the time that a loved one dies.

3. After-Death Communications, also known as mediumship experiences.
   These are STEs that occur days, weeks, or months after another person dies, when it seems their spirit is trying to communicate with the living experiencer.

Inspired Creativity and Genius

Gopi Krishna wrote extensively about the relationship he saw between inspired creativity and genius, and kundalini awakening. Inspired Creativity is an STE marked by a profound creative experience that seems mixed with a mystical experience.

"Spiritually Transformative Experiences" Becomes Widely Used

I am absolutely humbled and delighted that over twenty years after I first coined the phrase, now the term "Spiritually Transformative Experiences" has become recognized and is being used regularly in the field, both by researchers and especially by STE experiencers. It now seems that the term that I coined so long ago now feels like a "fit" to so many experiencers.

I chuckled silently with contentment when I recently heard an experiencer describe Spiritually Transformative Experiences saying, "These experiences change you, and they transform you for the rest of your life, in a more spiritual direction. This is why they are called spiritually TRANSFORMATIVE experiences."

Yes, I contentedly thought to myself. Others are now understanding and agree with what I observed both within myself and in others that led me to coin this phrase. All types of Spiritually Transformative Experiences change you in a spiritual direction and confirm that we are much more than just our physical bodies. We are truly spiritual beings.

Chapter 11

MY FOURTH NDE IN 1995 – "IT IS NOT YOUR TIME"

My fourth Near-Death Experience happened on February 27, 1995. I was flying home to Toronto from Edmonton, Alberta that day. I had just finished a weekend speaking engagement with an open-minded church group, whose minister had invited me as a guest speaker on Near-Death Experiences and Spiritually Transformative Experiences. By this time my book, *A Farther Shore,* had been published in 1994.

Over the year since the publication of *A Farther Shore*, I had been very active doing book promotion and spreading awareness about NDEs and other STEs. Over that year, I had done many media interviews for radio, television talk shows, TV documentaries, newspapers, and magazines. I'd also been invited to be a guest speaker at numerous professional conferences and to many community groups across Canada and in the USA. My invitation to speak about my NDE to this church congregation in Edmonton arose from this book promotion and increasing awareness in Canada about my NDE, and research into STEs.

My presentation at the small Edmonton church's "Sunday Celebration" had gone extremely well. The church congregation was very welcoming and clearly excited to hear the story of my 1979 NDE. The minister was delightful, a highly intelligent and deeply spiritual woman, with whom I felt a spiritual kinship. We later became very good friends.

The following day, as I was preparing to return home, I felt content, inspired by the beautiful weekend I had just spent in Edmonton. I felt spiritually uplifted by the high level of spiritual awareness evident in the discussions there. As I boarded a large Toronto-bound Air Canada jet, I had no idea that my life was about to dramatically change once again during that flight.

February is a deep winter month in Canada, perhaps the coldest month of the year. During the winter, commercial airlines like Air Canada routinely de-ice planes with some sort of ice-melting liquid before take-off. Seated next to the window just over the front of the large jet's wings, I watched calmly as the airport staff sprayed the de-icing mixture over the entire aircraft. Our departure was slightly delayed because of this precautionary step, but this did not concern me.

I had been told many years earlier that the engine trouble the airplane had in my plane crash of 1979 was thought to be due to the freezing over of some engine component, perhaps the air filters, due to the freezing cold and heavy snow that day. Well, now in Edmonton sixteen years later, it was definitely freezing cold, and it was also snowing quite heavily. I was reassured by Air Canada taking the precaution of de-icing the plane.

Reminders of my 1979 Crash and NDE

The jet took off with a bit of a struggle, due to high winds and a winter storm starting. However, soon we were airborne, and I began to relax into my seat. I napped for a short while, then after I awoke I decided to read the newspaper that the flight attendant had given me earlier. As I read the paper, I looked out the window to my right and saw that it was still snowing heavily, and ice was starting to form on the wing of the plane beside me.

I remember thinking, *Huh, interesting... Ice forming on the plane is what caused the plane crash back in 1979.* Still unalarmed, I curiously watched the patch of ice forming on the right wing grow larger and larger. *I wonder if this is a concern for a big jet like this?* I thought. Not really alarmed, I continued to read the newspaper.

The flight abruptly became increasingly turbulent. The captain put on the "fasten your seatbelt" sign, then the flight attendant quickly walked through the cabin to her seat and strapped herself in. She spoke briefly with the captain through her service phone, then she announced on the loudspeaker, "The captain has turned on the "fasten your seatbelts" sign. For your safety please keep your seatbelt fastened at all times. The captain is expecting to have turbulence for much of the remainder of the flight. A winter storm has moved into the Toronto area, but the captain thinks we can still land safely in Toronto. We will keep you updated if any change of plans is required."

Although my seatbelt was already fastened, I pulled my seatbelt tighter after this announcement. *Interesting,* I thought. *On the day of my plane crash, we also flew into bad weather, into a winter storm.* As the air turbulence continued, I remember thinking, *This is almost like the air turbulence we had before the plane crashed in 1979.*

Because we were now only about one hour flying time from Toronto, I wondered where we were on the map, and thought, *I wonder if we might possibly be flying right over Devil's Gap, where my 1979 plane crash occurred?* After all, it had been an Air Canada flight from Edmonton that had been flying high directly overhead on the day of my plane crash in Devil's Gap, (close to Kenora, Ontario), that heard pilot Gerry's mayday radio message that we had crashed.

I thought it odd that I was thinking so much about my 1979 plane crash, and that this turbulent flight had many similarities to that ill-fated flight. However, I attempted to shrug this off, and I returned to reading my newspaper, the best I could amid the jostling of the air turbulence.

As we drew closer to Toronto International Airport, slowly, the pilot began to make the long descent. Looking out the window to my right, I noticed that the area of ice buildup on the wing had grown significantly in size. We were flying through a heavy snowstorm, with strong blowing winds. It was very dark outside.

Just like the day of my crash, I thought.

To distract myself, I returned my attention to reading the newspaper. I suddenly glanced at the date printed on the top corner of the newspaper page. March 27, 1995, it clearly read. *What!* I inwardly exclaimed in alarm. *What am I doing flying on March 27 again!*

March 27, 1979, had been the date of my plane crash and NDE. Alarmed, and not believing my eyes, I blinked repeatedly and stared at the date printed on the newspaper page. It still clearly read March 27, 1995.

The turbulence that was bouncing the plane continued to worsen as the plane began its final descent to land at Toronto airport. I looked again at the newspaper date with concern. The date still clearly read March 27, 1995. Then, the letters slowly started shifting in front of my eyes. They slowly swirled and corrected themselves to read, February 27, 1995, the correct date. I breathed a sigh of relief and wondered why my eyes had played this trick on me.

I stared out the plane window, nervously glancing at the large area of ice on the wing, at the darkness. and the heavy blowing snow surrounding us, as we continued our bumpy descent. Because of a severe ice storm in the Toronto area, we felt severe turbulence all the time as our plane descended. *I will be relieved when I can finally see the ground,* I thought.

The airplane descended lower and lower, but I was still not able to see the lights of the city below due to the low-lying clouds and the heavy winter storm. Finally, after what seemed like an eternity, the plane broke through the bottom of the low-lying clouds and I could see the ground below us. We were already flying very low, perhaps a couple of hundred feet above the ground, just seconds away from landing on an illuminated runway which I could see below, just in front of us.

The Near-Miss Accident

Suddenly, the plane jerked back violently. The pilot had slammed the wing flaps into the reverse position, out of the landing position. Within view of the runway below us, the pilot had abruptly aborted our landing. The jet engines of the large aircraft were now screaming, revving at high speed, as the captain was clearly trying to get up enough airspeed to keep the plane in the air and to ascend again.

But in preparation for landing, the pilot had slowed the plane tremendously over the last many minutes as we descended. It was obvious that the pilot was desperately struggling to pull the nose of the plane up, away from the ground, but the screaming jet plane was not cooperating.

We did not have enough airspeed. The plane shook violently with air turbulence as the engines screamed.

Passengers in the plane started crying out in alarm. Instantly, I thought, *Oh, now I see why I thought about my 1979 plane crash. Today is the day that I am going to die in a plane crash.* Instantly, I inferred that by Divine design, I was meant to survive the 1979 plane crash so that I could do my clinical work researching NDEs and STEs, but now that I'd done that work and published my book as a permanent testimonial, I was going to die today in this plane crash.

The plane continued to shake and jerk with severe turbulence as we continued to be buffeted by extremely strong winds, while the jet engines continued to scream, revving at high speed. The captain was pushing the engines' limits in an unsuccessful attempt to gain enough airspeed to lift the still descending plane. The other passengers became hysterical and vocally upset. Some passengers were screaming. Others were crying. Somebody beside me started vomiting into a vomit bag.

Despite the mood of terror on the plane, I was unafraid. I had lost my fear of death in my NDE in 1979. Instead, I faced what appeared to be my impending death head-on. I had learned over my years of research into NDEs and STEs, that according to many religious traditions, especially according to the yogic and Buddhist models of consciousness, the most auspicious way to die is consciously. I had learned that ideally one should embrace impending death, and strive at the moment of death to move as high as possible in consciousness, to go as quickly as possible and as high as possible into the Light. I chose to consciously die.

Amid the turbulence of the plane which I thought was about to crash, facing what I believed to be certain imminent death, I closed my eyes and quickly went into deep meditation. My only attachment keeping me bound to my earthly life was my then seven-year-old son. I prayed deeply for my son and asked God to please look after him after I died, then I let go of my life.

Convinced that I was about to die, I consciously strived in my intense meditation to move my consciousness upwards, going as deep and as high as I possibly could. This was in the hope to reach the realm of heavenly Divine Light on the other side that I had glimpsed in my 1979 NDE.

Dark Tunnel and Life-Review

Instantly, I felt my spirit, my consciousness, leave my body. I lost all awareness of my physical body seated in the crashing plane. I then found myself moving rapidly upwards through a dark but calm and peaceful space. I felt a deep peace and inner stillness. I was being lifted upwards somehow, and I was also mentally striving to push myself upwards through this dark space, towards the light realm.

As I traveled upwards through this dark space, I experienced a type of life-review. I was not trying to remember these life events. They spontaneously came to my awareness, as I was striving to move higher and higher towards the Light.

During my life-review, I re-experienced three peak spiritual experiences, powerful mystical STEs that I had in my life. I did not just remember these events, I fully re-experienced them, as if I had traveled back in time somehow, and was skipping through time experiencing these life highlights again. As I experienced each event, I felt that the STE was actually happening to me right now.

First, I found myself back in my 1979 NDE, at the point of time when I was swimming to shore and my spirit had risen out of my body into the heavenly realm of the profoundly loving white light. It felt as if I had time-traveled somehow, and I was now in 1979, with the crash and NDE events happening to me at the present moment.

I felt my spirit being embraced in the realm of the loving white light of the Higher Power, just as it had in 1979. I felt myself permeated once again with the powerful unconditional love I had felt during the NDE. I could see the white light surrounding me again. I could feel the strong sense of being safe, of being home. I re-experienced my knowing that there is nothing to fear in death, that "I" would live on even if my physical body died in the worldly drama unfolding in the lake below me. I fully re-experienced every aspect of that blessed time in the Light, along with the ecstasy, peace, and profound unconditional love of the heavenly white light realm.

Then, suddenly, I jumped through time to another peak mystical experience I had, my 1990 "calling" mystical experience. I seemed to have jumped in time to the exact moment that I was at the highest peak of this mystical experience. I relived it completely. I re-experienced the profound expansion of my consciousness. I perceived the brilliant white light radiating from my head in all directions, seeming to illuminate my surroundings with light. I once again felt the ecstasy, the joy, tasted the divine amrita nectar, and re-experienced my calling revelations.

After several moments, my spirit/consciousness once again jumped in time. I instantly found myself shifted to about 1994. Once again, it felt as if somehow I had traveled in time. I vividly re-experienced a strong mystical vision experience that I had while meditating one day in 1994. This mystical experience had been very significant to me at that time.

My husband and I had separated in December 1993, and I was deeply heartbroken about this. The 1994 mystical vision came to me at a time that I was grieving this breakup and was deeply distraught, yearning for spiritual comfort. The love, beauty, and symbology in this deeply personal mystical vision had uplifted me and given me much spiritual strength at that difficult time, as I adjusted to the end of my marriage. I fully experienced the bliss of this powerful mystical vision experience for several seconds. I again saw and felt all the images, joy, and bliss.

This life-review was not an intellectual process. It was totally experiential. Then, as quickly and mysteriously as it had begun, my life review suddenly ended.

The Being of Light

After the life review ended, I found my spirit back in the expanse of dark space, continuing to move upwards. The darkness around me had now developed a very deep royal blue color, and it had started to become brighter, more filled with light. The powerful feeling of peace and calm continued to pervade me in this deep royal blue realm.

Suddenly, descending from above, a luminous being of light appeared in front of me, blocking my path upwards towards the Light. My spirit's upwards movement stopped instantly. The body of this being of light seemed to be made of translucent, luminescent, royal blue light, rather than matter. Its color was the same royal blue color as the surrounding space.

This radiant blue being of light was striking, as it stood profiled against and also reflected the background of deep blue-colored space. I did not recognize this being. It had a most extraordinary form. It appeared to me that it was half male and half female, female on the left side and male on the right side of its body. He/she also appeared to have four arms, like some yogic and Buddhist icons I have seen. The four arms were held positioned in unusual positions, like a pose, and one leg was held raised in a dancing posture. The total position was somewhat similar to what I have subsequently seen in sculptures and portraits of the dancing Shiva.

The being of light radiated a Divine aura of gentleness and love. I did not know who or what he/she was, but it felt to me that he/she was a heavenly messenger, a saint, or an angel sent to meet me. He/she then spoke to me mentally, through telepathy or thought transference. "It is not your time," he/she lovingly but firmly said.

Abrupt Return to my Body

Instantly, in the blink of an eye, I found my spirit back in my physical body again, onboard the Air Canada plane. The plane was still in peril, with the pilot still struggling to gain altitude after the aborted landing. The air turbulence remained severe, as strong winds and heavy blowing snow buffeted the struggling plane.

At first, my inner intuitive vision seemed to remain wide open. As I gazed out at the worldly drama unfolding around me, in addition to clearly viewing the physical reality surrounding me, I could also see etheric hands of light cradling the struggling aircraft.

Tears of awe and raw emotion started streaming down my face. With my eyes open, I continued to see the hands of light holding the endangered plane, as the jet engines continued to scream loudly beside me on the violently shaking plane. Other passengers continued to cry and pray out loud, as the captain wrestled with the struggling aircraft.

A few minutes later, the captain finally managed to get up enough airspeed to bring the airplane into a controlled ascent. The plane then began to slowly rise upwards, flying up, away from the ground. Finally, the turbulence began to decrease. The hands of light slowly faded from my view. In another few moments, the engines stopped their horrible screaming and settled into the roar of a normal jet sound. The plane gradually rose up, away from Toronto International Airport, and began to circle high overhead.

The passengers in the plane slowly calmed down, reassured that the plane now seemed to be out of danger. It was several minutes before the pilot finally made an announcement over the plane's loudspeaker system, about the close call. The pilot spoke in an exaggeratedly calm tone of voice, a tone that seemed to me to be rehearsed and intentionally extremely calm. He said, (approximately), "You may have noticed that I needed to abort our landing at the last minute."

A brief roar broke out from the passengers. *He must be joking,* I thought. *How could anyone possibly not have noticed that we almost crashed?*

The pilot then went on with his announcement in his exaggeratedly calm voice, "Just as we were about to land, I saw that there was a pack of coyotes on our runway. It was not safe to land, because we would have hit them. I had no choice but to abort our landing. The airport has been notified and the runway is being cleared. We will be circling the airport until Toronto air traffic control gives us the all-clear to land."

Instantly the plane was buzzing with chatter. *Coyotes?* I thought to myself. Other passengers were talking loudly with each other, relieved that the pilot had regained control of the plane, and that we were no longer in peril. Some people made loud comments about coyotes and other animals that sometimes dangerously wander onto airport runways.

I sat quietly in my seat, in an extraordinary state of consciousness. The state I was in immediately after this NDE is very difficult to describe. I felt completely open psychologically and spiritually. I felt as if I did not have any skin, as if no boundary separated me from the world around me.

The pilot finally landed the plane safely at Toronto International Airport about ten minutes later. We all disembarked. I was deeply grateful to be safely back on the ground. Still in a profoundly altered state of consciousness, I carefully walked out of the plane and picked up my luggage in the airport. As I made my way home, little did I realize, that the profound Near-Death Experience that I had during this close-call incident would have a far greater transformative impact upon me than my 1979 plane crash NDE.

Chapter 12

MYSTICAL COMMUNION: AFTER-EFFECTS OF MY 1995 NDE

When I returned home on the evening of the fateful day of February 27, 1995, I did not think about what to call the extraordinary out-of-body and mystical experience I had earlier that day in the near-miss plane incident. I suspected what I now know to be true, that it was a type of Near-Death Experience. I did not pause to think analytically about what I experienced, because all evening I remained in an extraordinary and unusual state of consciousness. I was in an expansive state of consciousness, that was unlike anything I had ever previously experienced. To put it simply, I felt completely open.

Normally, my sense of self is similar to what other people presumably feel. I normally experience myself, what I call "I" or "me," to be the size of my body. I have a clear mental perception of my physical size, and I can perceive a boundary where "I" end. Where my external skin encases my physical body, is where I usually perceive that "I" end. My normal perception is that the rest of the world exists separate from me, outside that perimeter.

However, on that day, after the extraordinary mystical NDE, I no longer had any sense of a boundary separating me from the rest of creation. I felt like I had no skin. My state of consciousness that evening is very difficult to describe in words.

I felt completely open, as if nothing separated me from the rest of the universe. I felt emotionally exposed, and vulnerable, and yet somehow I also felt completely safe. I felt like I was emotionally and energetically naked, that the clothes that normally cover my soul's nakedness were now stripped from me, and I was fully exposed.

I went to sleep that evening in this extraordinary, open state of consciousness. I slept very deeply and soundly that night. When I awoke the next morning, I found myself in a profound, exquisitely beautiful, expansive state of ongoing mystical union.

Immediate Spiritual After-Effect – Ongoing Communion

The state of ongoing mystical union in which I found myself the morning after my 1995 NDE is extremely difficult, if not impossible, to describe in words. Physically, it felt as if I no longer had a top to my head. I felt as if my consciousness had expanded overnight, and that through the open top of my head my expanded consciousness was now directly connected to the vast ocean of cosmic consciousness which underlies all of creation.

The sense of the perimeter of my body had returned to normal overnight, except for the top of my head. The profound expansive state of consciousness and communion that I was experiencing, together with the small boundary of my physical body which I perceived, gave me a feeling something like being a small wave of an immense ocean, or one of a trillion tiny legs on a huge millipede.

I experienced ongoing mystical communion 24 hours a day, while I was awake, alert, and actively functioning in the world, and while asleep. Nobody had to tell me or explain to me what I was experiencing. I knew to the core of my soul what I was experiencing. I was experiencing Divine Communion.

My soul realized, understood by direct perception, that I was communing with, and in direct connection with, the profoundly loving, super-intelligent, vast Higher Power that underlies the universe. My communing consciousness was connected to and a minuscule small part of this vast, omnipotent, and omniscient intelligent force.

In this state of ongoing communion, I knew many things to be true through direct knowing, without words being heard or spoken. In some inexplicable way, I also experienced truths within my being, because I could feel them within myself. For example, I both knew and experienced in my being that I was one small emanation of the vast intelligent ocean of consciousness, that I call God.

I knew with certainty, and also experienced within my expanded being, that every person and every speck of creation, were all emanations of the same vast one Divine ocean of consciousness. I experienced and knew that all human beings are just as directly connected to the one loving ocean of God consciousness, as I now experienced myself to be.

I clearly realized that the only difference between me in this unitive state of consciousness, and other people who were not in this unitive state, was that I had now become aware of my direct connection. I had realized my oneness with the Higher Power, which all of us actually share in spirit.

I felt that the veil that normally blinds us as human beings from seeing and feeling our direct connection to the Higher Power had been removed from my consciousness. It was as if I, as one wave of the vast Pacific Ocean of God, had suddenly been gifted with the development of true self-awareness by an obscuring veil being removed. Thus, I now realized and could feel within myself that I was a small part of the vast living ocean.

Other persons, the other waves without the gift of self-realization, still had their perceptions obscured by the veil and could not see or feel this bigger picture. They were only aware that they were small individual waves. This revelation was a very humbling experience.

In this state of communion, it seemed that all information necessary to me would be immediately known to me. I did not have to think to remember things. Necessary information for my daily activities inexplicably was there in my awareness when I needed it. My state of knowing was no longer governed by my intellect.

It felt as if the vast ocean of consciousness was the source and the storehouse of all knowledge and information in the universe, from the past, in the present, and in the future. When my soul needed some information for my daily activities, the ocean of consciousness instantly brought that information to me, by some form of extraordinarily fast and accurate intuition.

My ego mind and normal intellect had a small subservient role relative to the intuitive wisdom which flowed directly from the ocean of consciousness. It was clear to me in this unitive state of consciousness, that the ego mind and normal intellect were merely tools required by the soul to operationalize into the physical world the insights and direction that flowed to my higher mind from the ocean of cosmic consciousness.

I can compare this somewhat to the pen in the hand of a writer. The pen is a necessary instrument for the writer to be able to write down his inspirations and ideas onto paper in the physical world. However, the pen is not the source of inspiration and ideas. The pen is only the instrument required to manifest the inspiration and ideas into physical written form.

Similarly, the ego and the lower intellectual mind were required by the higher mind of intuitive wisdom, in order to physically operationalize the inspirations of spirit. I was living the experience, which I later found was described in the yogic tradition, as the ultimate subservience of "manas" or the lower or ego mind, to "buddhi" the higher mind of intuitive wisdom.

My ego mind felt totally comfortable and at home in this diminutive role. It felt like previously my ego-mind had been like a young child trying to drive a race car, overstepping its abilities. This task was truly beyond the child's/ego's capability. The child/ego mind was much more comfortable in the passenger seat, following the instructions of the adult driver/Spirit who had now stepped into the driver's seat.

The Divine communion required my lower ego mind to step back, surrender control, and follow Spirit's higher wisdom and instruction. This happened automatically, and felt completely right and completely natural during the state of ongoing mystical communion.

One of the most profound aspects of this unitive state of consciousness was the sense of finally being *Home*. I felt complete, content, and at peace, that I could now rest. I felt I had finally found my way back to my true home, to my creator, my cosmic mother/father, God.

Nonetheless, I sensed that there was still much deeper that I could go into this state of communion, and much more that I could still grow. I felt as if after a long and extremely arduous journey filled with much wandering and confusion, I had finally found my way to the safe harbor of my true home. I was safe. I was with my Divine beloved parent. I felt security greater than that of a young child who is being closely held to a loving mother's chest. I was *Home.*

Revelations while in Ongoing Communion

In this extraordinary unitive state, I understood and realized many things about the nature of life and death, at a deep soul level. I saw clearly that all of life's experiences are part of the divinely perfect plan of creation. From this state of awareness, I could clearly perceive that all of life's experiences, all difficulties, challenges, and hardships, in addition to all joys, adventures, and mysteries, were all facets and contrasts of the great cosmic melodrama. I both experienced within me, and realized, that all of life's experiences were designed in the loving Creator's plan to ultimately prod all of us to once again find our ways back home, to God-communion.

The ongoing state of communion gave me deep emotional equipoise. I realized that it was unnecessary to be caught up in a see-saw of emotionality relating to the events of life. I remained emotionally unruffled by life's ups and downs while in this unitive state. I felt emotionally peaceful and calm.

Somehow, while in the unitive state, I was not emotionally impacted or reacting to the drama of life events around me. I felt emotionally centered, and detached from the emotionality of others around me, although I was fully aware of others' feelings and concerns.

I can compare this feeling of emotional detachment to what one might feel while watching a television show with the volume muted, and observing a young child throwing a temper tantrum when his parent tells him it is his bedtime. As a detached observer, you would understand that the young child is upset, but you are not drawn in by the emotions displayed, especially because the volume is muted. In this unitive state, I somehow remained calm mentally, regardless of how emotional those around me might be.

In the unitive state of consciousness, I also somehow knew reincarnation to be a reality. I both experienced and knew that all souls are immortal, like immortal drops of the immortal ocean of God. However, souls incarnate in physical bodies, lifetime after lifetime, to learn spiritual lessons and grow, just as a child goes to school year after year to continue their book learning and grow emotionally.

While I was in that unitive state, I could easily penetrate consciousness to perceive the past. Memories of many of my past lives were easily accessible to me. When I looked in another person's eyes or thought about someone, I could perceive some of their past lives. I understood karma, the balancing of experiences across incarnations, as being the Divine's loving method of helping us learn and grow as souls. The perpetual learning of souls across many lifetimes was clear and obvious to me.

This state of ongoing mystical communion remained with me for about two months. During those two months, I continued to be fully active in the world, fulfilling my daily activities and responsibilities. I looked after my seven-year-old son and our household as normal, attended to patients in my medical office, and did psychotherapy with my STE patients. I continued my volunteer work on the board of KRN, and continued making professional presentations about my 1979 NDE and STE research when invited to do so. I did all these normal worldly activities while I remained in this most extraordinary state of consciousness, ongoing mystical communion.

I recall that my ability to be a psychotherapist, counseling my patients who had previously had STEs, was particularly impacted by my transformation of consciousness. When a patient would sit before me in my medical office, before they even told me what issues or problems were on their mind that day, the expansive ocean of cosmic consciousness would reveal to me what their emotional block was, and I instantly also knew how to best help them overcome that particular block. The psychological work I was able to help my patients speed through while I was in that unitive state of consciousness was extraordinary.

At the time of my ongoing communion, and for many years afterward, I never spoke to anyone about the ongoing unitive state of consciousness I experienced. I didn't need to. I was absolutely certain, to the core of my being, of the nature of what I was experiencing. This was Divine Communion, a state that I had read about in the lives of saints and mystics.

The profound state of union felt intensely private and sacred. I felt blessed and was deeply grateful to be living in what I felt was a state of grace. I had no need and no desire to talk to anyone about it. I continued with my professional life as normal while in this blessed state. It felt like I was living the old yogic proverb, "Before enlightenment, chopping wood and hauling water. After enlightenment, chopping wood and hauling water."

For the first couple of weeks after my 1995 NDE, the unitive state of consciousness stayed with me constantly, effortlessly, throughout the day and night. When I meditated, the depth of the communion increased, but the lived experience of Divine communion did not leave me after I finished my meditations.

After about two weeks in this blessed state, I began to notice that sometimes as the day progressed, my expanded consciousness would seem to contract somewhat. When this happened, I would need to shut my eyes, fix my gaze at the third eye center on my forehead, and meditate. Meditation would then lift my consciousness up again, and cause it to expand into the fullness of the unitive state.

As more time passed, the shrinking of my consciousness started happening more frequently and to a greater degree, and it increasingly took greater time and effort in meditation to restore the full unitive state. Then, ultimately, after about two months of blessed unitive consciousness, I lost the ability to enter the state of mystical communion. I have been striving to re-experience this divine state of ongoing mystical communion ever since.

NDE Features of my 1995 Near-Miss NDE

At the time of the 1995 near-miss plane incident, I did not pause to seek a vocabulary to describe the profound spiritual experience during the mishap and the ongoing state of mystical union that I experienced afterward. Now, reflecting on the NDE features which occurred during my experience, and the transformational impact of this experience, it is clear that even though I was not dead at any time during this near-miss plane incident, this was still a Near-Death Experience, a facing-death NDE.

Comparing the features of my mystical experience in the 1995 near-miss plane incident with the NDE features first defined by Dr. Raymond Moody, (listed in Chapter 2), it is clear that my experience included eleven of the fifteen classic NDE features. These were:

1. *Ineffability*: The experience had aspects that were beyond words, and are very difficult for me to describe to others

2. *Strong feelings of peace*: A strong feeling of peace came over me right at the beginning of my NDE, taking away all my fear. I felt permeated with calm, an intense sense of peace, that all was right with the universe. The strong sense of peace remained with me throughout the duration of my NDE.

3. *Floating out of the body: An out-of-body experience.* My spirit and point of perception left my physical body and I lost all awareness of what was occurring around my physical body in the distressed plane.

4. *Dark tunnel:* I found my spirit moving upwards, away from the earthly plane, through a dark expanse of space. The darkness around me started to gradually get lighter as I moved further and further upwards.

5. *Life Review:* I rapidly re-experienced three significant peak spiritual events of my life.

6. *Meeting Spirits: Mystical Visions:* I saw a radiant and luminescent being of light, which radiated light and love. I did not recognize this being of light, which had a deep blue color and an unusual and archetypal form. This loving spirit seemed to me intuitively to be a saint or an angelic messenger sent to meet me. The being of light informed me "It is not your time."

7. *Life Barrier:* When the being of light appeared, it blocked me in my upward movement towards the light. It created a physical barrier.

8. *Abrupt return to the body:* When the being of light told me "It is not your time," I suddenly and abruptly found my consciousness returned into my physical body in the distressed airplane, against my conscious will.

9. *Conviction of the reality of the experience:* I have always had a clear memory of my NDE in the near-miss plane incident of 1995, and this memory has remained extraordinarily clear despite the passage of over twenty years.

   The memory of the unitive state of consciousness which I entered immediately afterwards has also remained unusually clear. Whenever I think about the unitive state of consciousness, I start to a small degree re-experiencing some of the extraordinary peace, expansion, and communion that I felt while in that state. I did not require external validation about what I experienced in 1995. I knew with absolute certainty to the depths of my soul, the reality and spiritual nature of what I had experienced.

10. *Transformational impact:* This NDE transformed me profoundly on many levels.

   a. *Spiritually,* the after-effects of this 1995 NDE were profound. For two months after it, I remained in an expanded state of unitive consciousness, a state of mystical communion. After the period of communion ended, I knew that ongoing mystical communion was possible for ordinary persons such as me, and I yearned to once again reach that blessed state of consciousness. My spiritual hunger became even more intense than it was before the 1995 NDE. I now intensely yearned for deepening spiritual communion on a daily basis.

   b. *Psychologically,* the 1995 NDE impacted me tremendously. A major shift happened to my personal goals after this NDE. The two-month-long period of communion after the NDE created a strong yearning in me to once again experience that state. It propelled me to deeply strive spiritually, through regular, deep, and long meditations. I became a deeply devoted spiritual aspirant, deeply committed to my yogic path of personal growth and spiritual deepening through daily meditation and self-purification. My personal focus now became to deepen in my spiritual practice, and deeply embrace my psychological purification process.

   c. *Psychically,* I was also transformed after the 1995 NDE. I found myself increasingly intuitive, and much more open to many types of psychic experiences. I became extraordinarily capable of perceiving my own past lives, and often the past lives of persons close to me.

11. *New Views of Death:* I had previously lost my fear of death in my 1979 NDE. This 1995 NDE confirmed for me with absolute certainty that the spirit lives on after the death of the physical body. It also gave me the additional certainty of the reality of reincarnation.

As I reflect upon these eleven features that formed a part of my mystical experience in the 1995 near-miss plane incident, it is clear that this was indeed another NDE. Even though I was not clinically dead at any time during this brush with death, it was still a full Near-Death Experience.

It is interesting to me that my 1995 NDE, like my 1979 NDE, began when I was facing imminent death, when I psychologically thought I was about to die. In my 1979 plane crash, the NDE also started when I was psychologically facing death, when the powerless plane was plummeting towards the ground. It then continued and deepened when my body later became physically close to death.

My 1995 episode, however, occurred entirely while I was psychologically facing imminent death. My body was not injured physically in any way during the 1995 NDE. Nonetheless, both these NDEs included the majority of Dr. Moody's classic features.

Transformational Impact

The transformational impact of the 1995 NDE was in some ways greater than the after-effects and impact of my 1979 plane crash NDE. My 1995 near-miss plane incident Near-Death Experience transformed me spiritually, psychologically, and psychically.

As I mentioned in Chapter 5, my medevac plane crash NDE as a young doctor launched me into a life-stage of being a spiritual seeker. Propelled by my quest to understand my 1979 NDE, I sought to study and learn about STEs from books, scholars, and teachers from diverse spiritual traditions. My 1979 Near-Death Experience propelled me into a life-stage of spiritual learning.

My 1990 calling mystical experience seemed to transform me spiritually by shifting me into another new life-stage, a stage in which I was committed to my calling to be of service to others. I felt called to share what I had learned about STEs, to strive to help other people who had STEs, and to inform the medical profession and the public that NDEs and other STEs were real, peak human experiences, not signs of mental illness, as was far too frequently thought. I also felt called to disclose publicly the story of my own NDE, to show that a mentally healthy professional such as myself could have an NDE.

My 1995 near-miss plane incident, and the 2 months of ongoing mystical communion afterward, also transformed me spiritually, but in a different way. It shifted me into yet another new life-stage. Although outwardly I continued to serve and help others with STEs through my professional work and volunteer work as I did before this NDE, my focus shifted inwards dramatically, due to my now intense yearning for spiritual deepening.

I yearned to one day re-experience the exquisite and blessed state of ongoing mystical communion that I had after this NDE. In my private time, my personal spiritual practice took on new greater importance in my life. I increased the length and depth of my daily meditations. I started going on long meditation retreats. I became a much more deeply devoted spiritual aspirant, deeply committed to my yogic path of personal growth and spiritual deepening through regular daily meditation and self-purification.

My love for the Divine Higher Power intensified dramatically after my 1995 NDE. My prayer life became much stronger than before. Thinking about the Divine would often bring tears to my eyes, tears of love, gratitude, and devotion. I craved to open myself up to the Divine, to surrender my ego self and ego desires to the Divine, to surrender to the Divine will.

I craved to have my human character impurities washed away by the cleansing waters of the Divine Holy Spirit. My relationship with the Divine had shifted into a spiritual craving to surrender to the Divine in all ways. My inner prayers became "Purify the dross in me," "Make me your purified instrument" and "Thy will be done."

Psychologically, I intensely embraced my psychospiritual housecleaning process, my psychological purification, which I had learned is essential for spiritual deepening on the spiritual path. I embraced my personal depth psychotherapy, to root out my unconscious patterns or tendencies. My emotional recovery work became a much more important aspect of my inner psychological life. I deeply embraced my psychological purification process.

One song resonated very deeply with my soul after my 1995 NDE. This was the Prayer of St. Francis of Assisi. It became my motto and heartfelt prayer. The beautiful words of this prayer encapsulated my inner craving to be purified of my character imperfections, so that I could be a

Yvonne Kason, M.D.

clear instrument of the Higher Power. It also expressed my desire for my ego to die so that I could be reawakened into the blessed state of Divine communion – eternal life. I repeatedly sang the song of this prayer for many years after the 1995 near-miss NDE:

Prayer of St. Francis of Assisi

Lord, make me an instrument of your peace
Where there is hatred... let me sow love,
Where there is injury... pardon,
Where there is discord...unity,
Where there is doubt ... faith,
Where there is error ... truth,
Where there is despair... hope,
Where there is sadness... joy,
Where there is darkness... light.

O Divine Master, grant that I may not so much seek
To be consoled... as to console,
To be understood... as to understand,
To be loved... as to love.

For it is in giving... that we receive,
It is in pardoning, that we are pardoned.
It is in dying... that we are born to eternal life.

My research into STEs also transformed after my 1995 NDE and ongoing communion afterwards. My focus now shifted to learning more about the mystical path and mysticism. I began to read intently about the lives of great saints and mystics. I searched the literature to learn more about the progressive stages on the mystical path.

I now began to identify myself as a mystic, a person who had experienced many mystical experiences. I read *Mysticism: The Nature and Development of Mystical Consciousness*, by Evelyn Underhill, and studied other scholarly texts detailing the lives of great mystics, and the mystical path to spiritual deepening.

The 1995 NDE also transformed me on a psychic level. I found myself much more open to various types of psychic experiences. I found that I had become highly intuitive, especially during the two months of ongoing communion but also to a lesser degree for many years afterwards. I became highly clairsentient, able to perceive information about people and objects by touching them, or by being physically close to them.

Most notably, I became extraordinarily capable of perceiving my own past lives, relating to individuals that I met or knew in this lifetime. I considered my ability to see other people's past lives as an intrusion into their privacy. Because my new psychic openness to perceiving past lives was so strong, I actually felt compelled to make efforts to avoid spontaneously perceiving other people's past lives.

For the first few months after my 1995 NDE, I deliberately avoided making any prolonged eye contact with other people, to try to avoid perceiving any of their past lives. If I started to pick up information about another person's past lives during a conversation with them, I would intentionally try to distract my attention, or interrupt the conversation briefly, to try to block the flow of psychic information to me. Fortunately, my ability to perceive other people's past lives decreased significantly after my period of ongoing communion ended.

Looking for Words to describe the Communion

Immediately after the 1995 event, while I was still in the ongoing state of unitive consciousness, I did not talk to others about what I was experiencing. It all felt far too sacred, and much too personal to discuss with others. However, a few years later, I did confide in two different spiritual teachers about my two-month ongoing unitive state of consciousness after the NDE. Both offered sage advice.

One spiritual teacher commented that in their yogic tradition, it is believed that sometimes God blesses devotees with the gift of a glimpse of a higher state of consciousness, to show them what is possible. Then, the exalted state is taken away, because it is now required for the spiritual seeker to work, through self-effort in meditation and in the purification of character, to be able to once again reach that state of ongoing unitive consciousness.

Yvonne Kason, M.D.

He said this was analogous to giving a dog at a race track a taste of the treat dangling on the end of a pole, before prodding the dog to race with all his might to try to catch the moving treat. I was given a taste of the spiritual goal that I now needed to work hard to attain. This explanation made sense to me.

A teacher from a Buddhist tradition gave me an additional perspective, which I also found helpful. He stated simply that this ongoing unitive state of consciousness sounded like what in his tradition was called the first stage of enlightenment. There are several deeper, more stable stages that very advanced adepts strive to achieve. However, in the first stage of enlightenment, our karma and the pull of worldly events around us, can still pull our consciousness out of the unitive state. This explanation also felt correct to me.

I found further understanding of my two months of ongoing unitive consciousness in the writings of the yogic saint and guru, Paramahansa Yogananda. In his books, he describes two broad categories of mystical states of consciousness or samadhis, "sabikalpa samadhi," and "nirbikalpa samadhi."

He described a "sabikalpa samadhi," as a temporary mystical experience, in which the experiencer is usually focused almost exclusively on their powerful inner experience, and can be almost totally unaware of the world around them. A person in sabikalpa samadhi is inwardly absorbed, and unable to function in the world around them during the samadhi or mystical experience. As I understand it, this type of temporary sabikalpa samadhi experience would correspond with the temporary inner states of mystical consciousness that occur during diverse mystical STEs, including mystical white light Near-Death Experiences.

On the other hand, Yogananda described "nirbikalpa samadhi" as a more advanced state of mystical consciousness, a state of ongoing mystical communion, in which the experiencer remains in a stable mystical state of consciousness while they are also fully aware of the world around them. Experiencers in nirbikalpa samadhi are fully capable of functioning in the outer world while in their ongoing state of mystical communion. This nirbikalpa samadhi state of ongoing unitive communion is held to be much rarer, and a more spiritually advanced state of consciousness, as compared to transient sabikalpa samadhis.

The yogic saint and guru also stated that, according to the ancient yogic tradition, there are progressively more advanced levels of nirbikalpa samadhi states of ongoing mystical consciousness. Translating esoteric Sanskrit yogic terms into an English vocabulary, Yogananda called the first level of exalted nirbikalpa samadhi "Christ Consciousness." The next, more advanced stage of nirbikalpa samadhi, Yogananda called "Cosmic Consciousness." Finally, he called the most advanced state of nirbikalpa samadhi "God Consciousness."

From this perspective, and using Yogananda's yogic vocabulary, I realized that my life had been blessed over the years with several transient mystical experiences or sabikalpa samadhis. This included my 1976 Kundalini awakening and mystical experience, my 1979 NDE in the plane crash, and my 1990 "calling" mystical experience.

But now, after my 1995 near-miss plane incident NDE, I had been blessed with a brief two-month-long glimpse of nirbikalpa samadhi, ongoing mystical communion. I presumed that I had glimpsed the lowest level of nirbikalpa samadhi.

This yogic perspective gave me solace, by providing me with a well-established context within which to understand my personal mystical experiences, including the period of ongoing communion. I now realized that I had become what is defined as a mystic, a person who has had multiple mystical experiences. Additionally, now that I had tasted the exquisite joy and ecstasy of ongoing Divine communion, my heart and soul intensely yearned to experience this blessed state of consciousness again.

Coyotes Crossed my Path – The Wrong Teacher

Another interesting after-effect of my 1995 NDE was that it gave me clarity about my spiritual path and choice of a spiritual teacher. Surprisingly, this clarity came to me through my reflections on the fact that coyotes crossed my airplane's path to cause the near-miss accident. For days following the near-miss incident, the thought, *Coyotes crossed my path,* stuck in my mind for some strange reason.

The repeated nagging thought of, *Coyotes crossed my path,* prompted me to look up the meaning of an encounter with coyotes according to Native Indian traditions. Over the years after my 1979 NDE, my intuition increased, and one thing I discovered was that Native Indian medicine card interpretations of the possible spiritual meaning of various animal encounters seemed to apply to me in certain circumstances. Further, these shamanic interpretations were sometimes very helpful to me in understanding current life challenges at a deeper spiritual level. Therefore, nagged with the thought, *Coyotes crossed my path,* I looked up the shamanic meanings of a coyote encounter.

When I read about the coyote in my *Medicine Cards* book, I intuitively looked at the section for the contrary coyote. Nearly causing my plane to crash was surely a contrary encounter with a coyote, I thought. When I read the possible shamanic meanings for a contrary coyote, my mind, in its state of ongoing communion, immediately jumped to the sentence on the page which stated that a coyote encounter may be a sign or symbol of being deceived by the illusion of the wrong teacher. The words that resonated in my soul were, "the wrong teacher."

At the time of my 1995 NDE, I had been studying yoga quite deeply. Over the previous couple of years, I had met several different yogic teachers, from different yogic lineages. I learned quite a bit about yoga and meditation from two of them, albeit from greatly differing perspectives. Both embraced me as their student, and both wished me to accept them as my guru. (In the yogic tradition the guru is your spiritual teacher, to whom you make a commitment to follow their teachings.)

However, I had been having recurrent visions of a yogic guru appearing in my meditations since 1988, and I intuitively felt certain that this adept had been my guru in a past lifetime, and continued to be my guru now, on the other side. Therefore, in my heart and soul, I knew that neither of the yogic teachers I had met around 1995 was my true guru. Nonetheless, I appreciated what I had learned from both of these individuals.

Following my 1995 NDE, and after I read the shamanic interpretation of coyotes reversed as "the wrong teacher," I instantly knew what I needed to do. I knew that since I was certain that neither of these two yogic teachers was my true guru, I needed to stop studying with both of them. With a clear conscience, I finally informed both of them gently and kindly that their particular lineage was not my heartfelt spiritual path. This break was another significant change in my life path after the 1995 NDE.

Purification of Character

After my 1979 plane-crash NDE, I began to experience psychological "purgation," a process that is described in the scholarly literature on mysticism, notably in Evelyn Underhill's classic book *Mysticism: The Nature and Development of Spiritual Consciousness."* "Purgation" is a psycho-spiritual cleansing process that occurs spontaneously to mystics, i.e., persons having repeated mystical experiences. During purgation, the soul and/or the unconscious mind spontaneously exposes to the conscious mind issues within the self which need to be purified – dealt with, healed, and resolved.

For example, in my case, immediately after my 1979 NDE, I spontaneously unblocked the childhood memory of my parents having a heated argument. I quickly realized that this childhood incident had impacted me tremendously and had been a major unconscious contributor to my deep anger at my father over the years. I then went on to resolve this issue between my father and me.

I found in my clinical practice, counseling many STE experiencers, that purgation, the spontaneous surfacing of previously suppressed traumatic memories, did indeed occur frequently as an after-effect to NDEs and other strong STEs. I have come to understand purgation of unresolved issues to be an integral part of the psychological purification process that is essential on the spiritual path.

In my books, *Farther Shores* and *Touched by the Light,* I refer to "purification" and "purgation" as *psycho-spiritual housecleaning.* The term purification is generally used to describe the voluntary and intentional effort to purify the character and consciousness through self-reflection and conscious efforts to manifest noble traits of character.

As I continued in my regular practice of prayer and meditation in the years after my 1979 NDE, this process of purgation within me continued to occur. I embraced both the spontaneous purgation of unresolved issues, and my conscious efforts at purification of my character.

After my 1995 near-miss NDE, I continued and intensified this character purification process. Additionally, a new focus on character refinement seemed to develop spontaneously within me – the stage of surrender and detachment. I became consciously aware that to attain the equipoise and stillness of mind needed to access deep spiritual states during meditation, I needed to surrender to the Divine will, and strive to let go of my desires and wants, to detach from emotionality and emotional reactions.

The necessity for emotional detachment in a spiritual aspirant is described in detail in yoga, as well as in most mystical traditions. Therefore, after my 1995 NDE, I actively sought to not only heal and resolve my emotional wounds, but I also actively strived to let go, to get rid of my emotional attachments, and surrender to Divine will.

Misunderstood by Others

In my ongoing public and professional talks and media interviews after my 1995 NDE and my two-month period of unitive communion afterwards, I continued to talk only about my 1979 NDE, and about my research into diverse types of STEs. Unknown to others was the fact that my research and understanding of STEs had become enriched, not only by my scholarly research and clinical research, but also by all my more recent experiences.

After my 1995 NDE, I continued to be met with incidents of misunderstanding and criticism even though I only spoke publicly about one of my STEs, my 1979 NDE. Despite the increasing public awareness about Near-Death Experiences during the 1990s, and the publication of my book in 1994, misunderstanding and criticism still occurred repeatedly.

I recall an incident of criticism that happened when I was a guest speaker at a Toronto church group around 1996. At their minister's invitation, I told the church members the story of my 1979 plane crash Near-Death Experience. I recall one of the church members making a disturbing comment to me after my presentation. "In the past, and up until recently, you would have been charged with heresy for claiming that you had the experience that you just described. Maybe in some churches, you would still be considered a heretic today. In the past, you would probably have been burned at the stake," she said. The minister and several church members agreed with this analysis.

What a chilling comment this was! I shuddered at the thought. I was basically being called a heretic. I responded to this disturbing comment by stating that fortunately, now, in Canada in the 1990s, I would not be burned at the stake as a heretic for talking about my mystical Near-Death Experience. I went on to say that unfortunately, many persons today who have NDEs or other mystical experiences are still being mistreated by society, and today are being mislabeled as mentally ill or delusional.

The audience vocally agreed. With such talk of heresy and burning at the stake being raised when I spoke only about my 1979 NDE, I certainly did not feel safe to publicly talk about my other STE experiences; or some of my new psychic abilities.

I recall another occasion in the late 1990s when I was confronted with misunderstanding and intolerance for mystics like myself. I was presenting a day-long training seminar at a Toronto psychiatric hospital to doctors, clergy, and other healthcare professionals who wished to learn about counseling patients who had NDEs and other Spiritually Transformative Experiences.

During that daylong seminar, I briefly admitted to the group that in addition to my 1979 NDE, I had had another more recent NDE, and some other mystical experiences. I thought those professionals who enrolled in my training seminar would be persons who were interested in and supportive of persons who had experienced STEs.

I was surprised later that day, when one of the workshop participants challenged me and my clinical work counseling STE experiencers, by saying, "Why are you wasting your time with this type of work [with STE patients]? You would make much better use of your professional skills and abilities to try to reach out and help some of the outcasts in our society, like the poor."

I was shocked by this comment. Collecting my thoughts, I quickly said, "Mystics have been outcasts of society for thousands of years, and are still misunderstood and outcasts today. Mystics have been persecuted, called heretics, and burned at the stake. Today mystics are labeled as mentally ill or delusional. I feel called to reach out and help this group of persons who have been outcast by our society." Fortunately, the remainder of the workshop participants agreed with my perspective.

I was met with other types of criticism and misunderstanding in the late 1990s as well. Some critics continued to challenge my authority and credentials for having written my book, *A Farther Shore*. Some individuals challenged my authority to write about mystical experiences because I was not a fully illuminated being. Other critics went further to say that I had no business counseling patients who had experienced STEs as a medical doctor, because I was not an illumined guru or a trained spiritual teacher. A few of my critics went so far as to actively and openly dissuade others from reading my book.

Despite the sometimes harsh criticism, I knew the truth, that I had done much scholarly research as a medical doctor into NDEs and other STEs, and additionally I was convinced of their reality because of my own multiple NDEs and other STEs. I also knew that I had learned a great deal and had amassed much clinical experience in counseling hundreds of STE patients over the past years.

Although I was clearly not an illumined guru or a trained spiritual teacher, I knew that as a medical doctor and a multiple STE experiencer, I had much to share. Additionally, I knew in my soul that Spirit had called me to share what I had learned, to help spread awareness about the reality of mystical experiences including Near-Death Experiences.

Contrary to the criticism and misunderstanding I received from some, the value of my efforts to spread awareness of STEs was confirmed by many others. I had received many hugs and exclamations of gratitude from grateful STE patients whom I had counseled over the years, and thank you notes from persons who had heard me talk about my NDE and STEs at conferences and public events.

I also received several hundred letters from readers of my book, expressing gratitude for my having written the book. Therefore, despite the repeated criticism and misunderstanding from some persons, I continued in my work researching and spreading awareness about NDEs and other Spiritually Transformative Experiences.

Premonitions of my 1995 NDE

When I reflect upon the events immediately preceding the 1995 incident, it appears to me that I had premonitions about the NDE before it occurred. As I described earlier, I experienced several unusual occurrences while I was sitting in the airplane during the hour immediately before my

NDE. I now think these unusual occurrences were premonitions of the impending incident and Near-Death Experience.

As I described in the last chapter, an hour or so before my 1995 NDE, I repeatedly thought about my 1979 plane crash and NDE. As a frequent flyer, these types of recurrent thoughts about the 1979 plane crash were very unusual for me. When I looked out the plane window and saw that ice was starting to form on the wing of the plane, as the plane was bumped by turbulence from a winter storm, it triggered the thoughts about the previous episode. Then later, I misread the date on my newspaper, to read March 27, the date of my 1979 NDE.

At the time, I noticed that these thoughts and events strongly reminding me of my 1979 plane crash and NDE were very unusual, and I had no idea why they were happening to me. However, in retrospect, I think they were all premonitions of the NDE which was about to occur.

Why and how these premonitions occurred, I do not know. I think that by some unknown mechanism, my mind perceived multiple hints from the future, premonitions that I was about to have a powerful Near-Death Experience once again while facing possible imminent death, just as I did while facing the possibility of imminent death in the plane crash of 1979.

My Soul Lesson – Meditation can Speed our Soul Evolution

As I reflect upon the main soul lesson I learned through my 1995 experience, I see that I learned that meditation is a powerful tool to speed up our soul's journey to our ultimate goal – an expanded state of consciousness in unitive communion. During the two months of ongoing communion following my 1995 NDE, I could clearly perceive how life's multitude of experiences were all ultimately designed as learning experiences for our souls.

While in that unitive state of consciousness I could perceive that the true purpose of life was soul evolution, for our souls to learn lessons and grow through our life experiences. Thus, over the course of many lifetimes, all souls would ultimately graduate from the school of life and find their way back home to a state of ongoing God-communion.

While in the unitive state of consciousness, my soul both understood and experienced, how meditation and intentional righteous living could elevate and expand one's consciousness and speed the soul's journey home. Although most major religions teach the importance of righteous living, following the universal spiritual laws such as the Ten Commandments, meditation has not been as widely recognized for its essential role in soul evolution. In my state of unitive communion, I both understood and experienced within myself, that meditation is a secret key to expanding our consciousness and speeding soul evolution.

While in the unitive state, I experienced firsthand that meditation would deepen and expand my state of ongoing communion. During those two glorious months, when my consciousness would begin to contract due to the downward draw of outer-worldly events, I would stop everything. I'd set about stilling myself and meditating for a period of time. My attention was focused on my forehead at the third eye center, and in this way, I could raise my center of consciousness, re-center my consciousness in the Divine realm, and expand my consciousness back into the expansive unitive state of ongoing communion. Meditation was the essential key both to maintaining and deepening my state of communion.

While in the unitive state, I also knew and could perceive that meditation was a powerful tool for everyone to use, to transform and train their consciousness to gradually be able to sustain expanded states of consciousness. When my two months of ongoing communion ended, I knew intuitively that I now had to work hard through regular deep meditations and conscious efforts at self-purification and righteous living, to one day be able to glimpse and sustain that blessed unitive state again.

However, unbeknownst to me, following my 1995 NDE and the subsequent ongoing communion, the Divine hand had not yet finished its work of sculpting my life with powerful STEs.

Chapter 13

MYSTICAL EXPERIENCES IN ISRAEL IN 2000

As my life moved forward, the Divine sculptor continued to mold the course of my life with more unexpected mystical experiences. While traveling in Israel in 2000, I had two powerful episodes that once again changed the course of my life.

As I reflect, I wonder if my consciousness may have been more open or more receptive to having yet other mystical experiences, as a long-term after-effect of my 1995 experiences. I think perhaps it was.

In 2000, five years after my 1995 NDE and ongoing communion, I had two powerful mystical experiences in Israel which impacted me tremendously. They gave me clarity about a recurrent vision I had been experiencing.

Recurrent Visions of my Gurus

After the 1995 NDE and subsequent communion, I outwardly continued my professional life while I inwardly deeply embraced my yogic path of daily meditation, purification of character, and surrender to the Divine will. I knew in my heart that my spiritual path was that of yoga.

Yvonne Kason, M.D.

As I mentioned earlier, since the late 1980s I had been seeing a recurrent vision in my deep meditations of an Indian yogi sitting cross-legged in meditation posture. Somehow, I knew intuitively that this saint was my guru, and had been my guru in a past lifetime.

A few years after the inner visions of my guru began to occur, I finally learned his identity. I trembled inwardly in awe and wonder when I found his photo in Paramahansa Yogananda's book, *An Autobiography of a Yogi*.

I discovered that I had been seeing recurrent visions of Mahavatar Babaji. My inner certainty and conviction that this saint was my true guru from a past life, was the rock within my consciousness which enabled me to firmly and decisively break away from the two spiritual teachers who had around 1995 urged me to accept them as my guru.

However, in my recurrent meditation visions of Mahavatar Babaji, another great Spiritual Master would always appear in the vision as well. In my meditation visions, I would see the form of Jesus Christ standing beside the meditating Mahavatar Babaji. I had no idea what the significance was of my seeing these two spiritual figures together.

I had been raised in a Christian household, and I had deep love and reverence for the Bible and the teachings of Jesus Christ, yet at the same time, I sensed myself to be a yogi, on a spiritual path striving for God-communion through meditation. I felt deep awe and reverence for both of the sacred figures who episodically appeared to me in my meditations, but I did not understand why they appeared together.

In 2000, a powerful mystical experience I had when in Israel finally revealed to me the meaning of my blessed recurrent vision of Mahavatar Babaji and Jesus Christ. At that time, having meditated deeply for over 20 years, and having previously had a kundalini awakening, four NDEs, and multiple mystical experiences, I was in a highly intuitive and deeply receptive state of consciousness. I had several deep spiritual experiences at sacred sites in Israel.

Mystical Experience at the Sermon on the Mount Site

As I discuss in *Touched by the Light*, it appears to me that STE experiencers are more receptive to "darshan," feeling the spiritual blessings, and possibly having a mystical experience when walking, praying, and meditating at holy sites. It seems that the high spiritual vibration of fully God-realized Spiritual Masters leaves a permanent energy or consciousness imprint at the physical sites where the Masters taught and communed with God. Such a darshan experience happened to me unexpectedly in Israel on two shore excursions from a cruise ship.

A powerful darshan/blessing experience, a dramatic mystical experience, came upon me while I was standing at the site overlooking the Sea of Galilea, where Jesus had once stood, as he delivered his famous, "Sermon on the Mount". Here is what happened.

In the summer of 2000, I attended a medical conference that was being held on board a cruise ship that was sailing to several ports on the Eastern Mediterranean. Two of the ports of call were in Israel. I was on a short shore-excursion outing there, visiting some of the Christian and Jewish holy sites.

I had a curiosity about the sacred sites, but was somewhat skeptical, because I had been told there was uncertainty about the locations' historical accuracy. On this day, a tour leader took a group of us close to the Sea of Galilea, to a site where some claimed Jesus Christ delivered his famous first and very profound sermon.

The tour leader walked us around the site. He then began to read out loud Biblical excerpts from the Sermon on the Mount. "Blessed are the poor in spirit; for theirs is the kingdom of heaven. Blessed are they that mourn; for they shall be comforted. ... Blessed are the merciful; for they shall obtain mercy. ... Blessed are the peacemakers; for they shall be called the children of God." [Matthew 5: 2-7]

To my great surprise, as he read these sacred words, I began to tremble inside. I found myself starting to weep silently. I was deeply moved. When the tour leader finished talking, I slipped away from the group to reflect in the serene garden.

As I stood there gazing at the Sea of Galilea, I suddenly felt a powerful *presence* descend on, and permeate me. I knew intuitively, beyond a doubt, that this was the holy vibration of Jesus the Christ. I felt my soul cracked open and felt exposed. I started to sob openly. I felt like a fountain of love was cleansing my exposed soul. Although I heard no words, I intuited the higher guidance, *Be more loving,* and, *Be more forgiving,* relating to relationship difficulties I was having at that time.

I felt like the holy and powerful spiritual vibration at this historical site was not only cleansing me, but also healing something in me, as if dark flecks or energetic knots were being cleansed from my heart. As the tears continued to pour down my cheeks, I felt my heart opening, and felt inner releases happening. I felt I was thereby becoming more loving, and more forgiving. It physically felt as if a weight, that had been heavily constricting my heart, had been lifted away from me. My heart felt open and much freer, as a powerful feeling of Divine love flowed through me.

Feeling lighter, and spiritually cleansed, I slowly dried my tears and began to look around the garden site. Somehow, I intuitively knew that there was a cave nearby, a cave where Jesus and some of his disciples had rested. How I knew this, I do not know. Nobody had told me this and no sign indicated this. I looked around but could see no evidence of a cave.

The quiet gardens were on a hillside facing the Sea of Galilea, and the only feature was a small chapel built there on the slope. My tour group was getting ready to leave, so I slowly walked up the hill along the foundation of the chapel towards them.

As I was slowly walking, a small door marked, "Private. No Entry," opened from the basement foundation in front of me, and a monk walked out. The door remained wide open as I walked by. I peeked inside the door to see what was underneath the chapel. I gazed in amazement, when I saw that there was a small cave in the hillside underneath the chapel. A small altar had been placed at the mouth of the cave. A few rows of benches had been placed in the basement room facing the altar, seats where monks could privately meditate and pray, it seemed. Clearly, my sudden intuition about a cave used by Jesus at this site was absolutely correct.

I left the site with the tour group several minutes later. The powerful healing energy and feeling of Divine love slowly dissipated after I left, but the heart-opening impact on me remained. I knew with inward certainty that this was indeed the correct site. This was definitely where Jesus Christ had walked and talked, and His sacred vibration at the site, remains to this day.

This mystical experience moved me deeply. It is still difficult for me to put into words the depth of the purification that I felt within me resulting from this blessed experience. I felt I had undergone a type of soul healing. I felt chastened, softened in my heart, and at the same time deeply loved by my Higher Power. The soul cleansing aftereffect of this experience is truly indescribable.

The day following this powerful darshan experience, I traveled on another shore excursion from the cruise ship to other Christian sacred sites in Israel, including the Garden of Gethsemane, and the crucifixion and tomb sites in Jerusalem. I had moving spiritual experiences at all of these sacred sites, but the most powerfully transformative mystical experience I had in Israel, happened to me when I visited the site of Jesus' tomb and his resurrection appearance to Mary Magdalene.

2000 Mystical Experience beside Jesus' Tomb

The experience I had while close to Jesus' tomb in 2000, was profoundly deep, and is still very sacred and personal to me. The entire mystical experience is far beyond my capacity to express in words. I am only able to share a small portion of the experience, to convey some of the overall profound meaning this mystical experience had for me.

When I came to the crucifixion site in Jerusalem, and the nearby tomb into which Jesus' dead body had been placed by his disciples, I spied a cordoned-off slab of rock. A sign beside the rock stated that Jesus' body had been laid upon this particular flat slab of rock when his lifeless form was first taken down from the cross after the crucifixion.

The sign indicated that it was here that Jesus' body lay while it was being carefully wrapped in linens by the female disciples who had born witness to Jesus' crucifixion, prior to his body being placed in the nearby tomb. Being highly clairsentient, sensitive to intuitive information picked up through my sense of touch, I knelt down to touch this sacred slab of rock with my right hand.

Immediately upon my touching the sacred rock, I was catapulted into a deep mystical state of consciousness. I was transported into a powerful mystical vision of events occurring 2000 years earlier, on the first Easter Sunday. I suddenly felt as if I were transported back in time. It was an extremely vivid and detailed experience, as if I were actually there.

I could see my surroundings clearly, hear the sounds around me, feel the texture of the earth beneath my feet, and smell the scents in the air. I found myself suddenly present and bearing witness to the profoundly blessed appearance of the resurrected Lord Jesus Christ, as he appeared to the weeping Mary Magdalene on the first Easter Sunday.

I could clearly see the luminous physical form of the resurrected Lord Jesus, standing a few steps up a hill before me. I perceived Mary Magdalene crouched on the ground, weeping, draped over the very slab of rock that I was now touching.

I heard the Lord Jesus say to Mary Magdalene, "Woman, why weepest thou?" The intense spiritual force emanating through those holy words penetrated my soul.

My soul instantly responded. I recognized that voice and that voice's vibration! My heart leaped with joy and soul recognition, as I felt the powerful Divine vibration emanating through the voice of resurrected Lord Jesus. *Rabbi,* [teacher/master] joyously leaped out of my heart. I then went into a state of deep ecstatic communion for an unknown period of time.

This profound experience sucked the air out of my chest. I seemed to stop breathing for the duration of the experience. The depth and the profundity of this sacred mystical experience are far beyond my capacity to express. I remained in a state of beatific ecstatic communion for many minutes. This mystical encounter is etched in my consciousness, and it changed the course of the rest of my life.

Tears of awe, love, and devotion, come to my eyes even to this day, as I think of this profound blessed visionary experience. I was so deeply moved by it, and it felt so intensely private and personal to me, that I did not speak publicly, or write about it for almost twenty years. I hope that my sharing these powerful mystical experiences, that are very sacred to me, may somehow help or inspire others.

Chapter 14

LIFE CHANGES AFTER MY MYSTICAL EXPERIENCES IN ISRAEL

My mystical experiences in Israel in 2000 once again changed the course of my life, this time my spiritual life. They helped me realize who I really was, and who I had been for many lifetimes. These STEs helped me integrate into a whole oneness that fit my soul, that I was a yogi, who was a mystic, and who has been Christian in many incarnations.

I am a Mystic - Multiple NDEs and Multiple Mystical Experiences

These STEs in Israel confirmed to me that I am a mystic—a person that the Divine hand has blessed with many mystical experiences. I think it is important to document this truth in this book, to attest that a normal, high functioning and mentally sound individual like myself can have many powerful STEs over the course of their lifetime, including multiple mystical experiences.

Modern mystics do indeed exist, and I am one of them. I am not sharing these mystical experiences to brag or be grandiose. No, quite the contrary. I hope to normalize mystical experiences for others, to let others know that this is indeed possible for today's ordinary people to have mystical experiences, not just saints of the past.

Yvonne Kason, M.D.

As an STE researcher, I am fascinated by the fact that my life was punctuated by both multiple NDEs and additionally multiple mystical experiences. I think my multiple Near-Death Experiences may have made me more susceptible to having other mystical experiences. My childhood NDEs seemed to have set the stage for several more NDEs and mystical experiences to occur later in my adult life.

It is also possible that something about my consciousness made me susceptible or receptive to both NDEs and mystical experiences, as well as to a kundalini awakening. Perhaps this susceptibility came from genetics, somehow, because I had deeply spiritual grandparents.

Or perhaps my susceptibility to kundalini and mystical experiences came from my past lives. While in the heavenly white light realm in my 2003 NDE, (which I will describe next, in Chapter 15), I was shown that I had powerful mystical experiences in some of my past lives too, as well as a kundalini awakening and NDEs.

Alternatively, perhaps it was my kundalini awakening at age 23 and my life-long practice of meditation, that were the predisposing factors making me susceptible to multiple NDEs and multiple mystical experiences later in life. Perhaps a combination of all these factors contributed to my proclivity for diverse repeated STEs.

Or perhaps the reason for my multiple STEs is ultimately beyond our capacity to comprehend, because the wisdom and the rationale of the Divine sculptor's actions are a mystery far beyond our mortal capacity to comprehend. Only the Divine sculptor knows for certain.

I am humbly sharing the stories of my five extraordinary NDEs and some of my powerful mystical experiences here as a testimonial. The factors contributing to susceptibility to multiple NDEs, and the susceptibility of NDE experiencers to other mystical experiences, will be fascinating areas for future consciousness research.

I am daring to now share the stories of my NDEs and mystical experiences that I previously kept private, because I feel less restrained about sharing them, now that I am retired from the practice of medicine. Being retired, I no longer have concerns about maintaining my medical license if challenged about my mystical experiences.

As a young senior, I also no longer care if skeptics or critics do not believe the truth about the blessed sacred experiences with which the

Divine sculptor has carved out my life. The truth is that I am a modern-day mystic, and I know that other people alive today are as well.

I am a Christian Yogi

My powerful mystical vision in Israel of the resurrected Lord Jesus Christ changed my life profoundly. The experience gave me absolute clarity about my soul's spiritual path. I then knew to the core of my being that I am a Christian, and have been a Christian in many past lives. I also knew to the core of my being that I am a Yogi, and have also been a yogi in past lives.

Somehow, as a result of this powerful mystical experience of the risen Lord Jesus Christ, my soul was able for the first time to integrate these two concepts into the one broader and more complete concept which truly resonates with my soul, *I am a Christian Yogi.*

From that day forward, I have clearly and unashamedly labeled myself as a Christian Yogi. I now almost constantly wear a chain around my neck with a pendant of a Christian cross combined with a yogic lotus. My new inner clarity resolved my many-year-long dilemma around the mystery of why Jesus Christ and Mahavatar Babaji had both repeatedly appeared to me together in visions during my meditations.

The resurrection mystical experience in 2000 somehow opened my heart and soul to the realization that these two great Spiritual Masters were both my gurus! My heart had been expanded somehow, to be able to easily embrace this expansive truth. I was now certain within my soul that I had two gurus, Jesus Christ, and Mahavatar Babaji.

I had known for many years that both Jesus Christ and Mahavatar Babaji are considered gurus within the yogic teachings of Self-Realization Fellowship (SRF). SRF was founded in 1920 by Paramahansa Yogananda, the most recently living guru in the yogic lineage started by Mahavatar Babaji. Propelled by my 2000 mystical experiences in Israel, I intuitively knew that SRF was the hand of Babaji and Christ held out to the West. I then knew with certainty in my heart and soul that SRF was my spiritual path and that I belonged there.

When I returned home to Canada from Israel, I immediately became a member of Self-Realization Fellowship. I had finally found a church where

I fit, with my multiple STEs and as both a Christian and a Yogi. I have been a devoted member of Self-Realization Fellowship church to this day. I am a Christian Yogi.

Thus, my 1995 NDE, plus the two months of unitive communion, and my mystical experiences in Israel in 2000, propelled me into a deeper and deeper commitment to my personal spiritual path seeking self-realization, Divine communion. Ultimately, my mystical experiences in Israel finally gave me clarity about my soul's devotion both to Christianity and to yoga.

The course of my life changed once again, when, based on the revelations of these mystical experiences, I consciously made a deep commitment to the church of my personal spiritual path, Self-Realization Fellowship. I am a Christian Yogi with two gurus: Jesus Christ and Mahavatar Babaji.

Transformed and blessed by the Divine gift of these powerful mystical experiences in Israel, and rejoicing at having found deep clarity about my personal spiritual path, I had no idea that just a few years later, the hand of the Divine sculptor was about to change the course of my life dramatically yet again.

Chapter 15

2003 TRAUMATIC BRAIN INJURY NDE – FULLY DEAD THEN BACK AGAIN

My life changed dramatically and abruptly the evening I had my fifth Near-Death Experience, November 8, 2003. This NDE occurred when I slipped on black ice, fell backward, hit my head hard on the rock cobblestone pavement, and died. I suffered a serious head injury, a "traumatic brain injury" or TBI. This NDE and TBI suddenly and unexpectedly changed the course of the rest of my life.

My life in 2002-2003 was full and satisfying. My professional life had blossomed after the publication of my books, *A Farther Shore*, in 1994, and then *Farther Shores* in 2000. The timing of my book releases coincided with a big upsurge in general public interest during the late 1990s and early 2000s in NDEs. The story of my NDE and my research into NDEs and other Spiritually Transformative Experiences were swept up by this upsurge of public interest, and I became an invited guest speaker at many, many events

I traveled widely from 1994 to 2003, across the USA and Canada, and also to France and Germany, to talk with professional groups, media, church groups, and public groups about Near-Death Experiences, Kundalini Awakening, Mystical Experiences, and other STEs, and their after-effects on consciousness. I networked with professional colleagues also pioneering this field of research, through my involvement on the Board of the Kundalini Research Network, as Co-Chair of the Spirituality in Health-Care Network, as a professional member of the International Association for Near-Death Studies, and as a Mentor of the MD-Psychotherapy Association of Canada. By the time of my NDE in 2003, my medical career as a physician specialized in counseling patients who had diverse STEs was established solidly in Canada.

From 1994 to 2003, numerous television talk shows and TV news shows invited me as a guest to talk about my 1979 plane crash NDE and my research into STEs. In fact, my 1979 Near-Death Experience was re-enacted on two television documentaries, including "Sightings." By 2003, I was a well-known media resource, widely known as the Canadian medical expert on Near-Death Experiences and Spiritually Transformative Experiences.

By the time of my 5th NDE in 2003, the Canadian medical profession had also begun to recognize the phenomenon of Near-Death Experiences and other STEs. I was therefore invited to speak at several major Western medical conferences on NDEs and STEs, as well as on strategies for health care providers to supportively counsel persons who had experienced STEs.

Buoyed by widening mainstream medical interest in STEs, and many diverse healthcare professionals speaking out about the importance of cultural sensitivity including spirituality and spiritual experiences, in December of 2000, I founded the *Spirituality in Health-Care Network* (SHCN), in Toronto, Canada, together with Canadian psychiatrist Dr. John Thornton and 60 other colleagues.

SHCN grew into a vibrant multi-professional and multi-faith network of healthcare professionals, dedicated to integrating spirituality with psychotherapy and health care. I served as Co-Chairman of SHCN from its founding in 2000 until my accident in November 2003. In October 2002, I also chaired the first ever University of Toronto, Faculty of Medicine-sponsored international, multi-professional, and multi-faith conference on Spirituality and Health-Care. It was a smashing success!

To put it simply, I was at the height of my career in November of 2003. I envisioned that I would continue to practice medicine for at least another 20 years. I planned to continue with my work bridging spirituality with health care, and counseling patients with diverse STEs. I loved both these aspects of my career.

My personal life and spiritual life were also happy in 2003. I had a group of professional colleagues and good friends who loved, supported, and respected me and the pioneering work I was striving to do regarding NDEs and STEs. I was deeply committed to my daily Christian-Yoga practice of prayer and long meditation, and I was committed and very involved in my church and spiritual path, Self-Realization Fellowship. In addition, in November 2003, I had many inspirations and ideas for the next two books that I planned to write. I had already started making notes for them.

Thus, on November 8, 2003, the day of the TBI and fifth NDE, I was at the peak of my career, looking forward to many more years of a busy and highly enjoyable professional life. However, unbeknownst to me, God had other plans for my life.

Unusual Signs and Premonitions in the Fall of 2003

In the fall of 2003, in the days and weeks before my accident in November, several small events happened that hinted to me that my life might be changing unexpectedly. I made a mental note of these unusual events, but at the time, I did not sense from these hints how completely my life was about to change.

Two of my regular long-term STE psychotherapy patients were excellent astrologers. They would often tell me during their psychotherapy sessions about astrological planetary alignments and transits that they thought were creating subtle boosts or challenges in their lives. They both had requested to study my natal astrological chart for their own interest. Occasionally, they would tell me about astrological transits which they thought might subtly affect my life.

Although I had a deep respect for Western astrology and Vedic astrology, I also had reservations about the impact of astrology on our day-to-day lives. So, I took their astrological insights and perspectives with a grain of salt.

It was interesting to me in the fall of 2003, that both of these astrologers had informed me that on November 8, 2003, a significant astrological event would occur, a full moon eclipse which coincided with a rare planetary alignment of six planets, an event some called the "harmonic concordance." The six planets involved would be aligned in positions relative to earth similar to the positions of the points of a six-pointed star relative to its center point.

This was supposedly a very auspicious and rare planetary alignment that, from an astrological perspective, could have a beneficial effect on individuals and the planet. Both went further, and informed me that this harmonic concordance on November 8, 2003, would directly impact my natal astrological chart. They both predicted that, because of this, something significant was likely to happen to me on that day, something that would launch me onto my next step spiritually, and/or transform my life in an even more spiritual direction.

I found this astrological perspective about the November 8, 2003, harmonic concordance puzzling. It made no sense to me at all. I recall discussing this point with one of my friends and stating that I could not imagine how my life could possibly become more spiritually oriented than it was already.

At that time, I was meditating two, three, or sometimes four hours per day. In my prayers and meditations, I was dedicating my entire life to serving God and serving others, praying deeply to be God's instrument in all that I do. My medical practice was 90% spiritually oriented psychotherapy, counseling patients with STEs. In my personal time, I was highly involved with volunteering in my church, SRF.

I also volunteered as Co-Chair of the Spirituality in Health Care Network and served on the Board of the Kundalini Research Network. My circle of friends were all deeply spiritual individuals, like me. My life was intensely spiritually focused, both in my professional time, and in my personal time.

As I reflected on the possibility of my life somehow becoming even more spiritually oriented than it already was, the only spiritual deepening that I could imagine as even remotely possible, albeit extremely unlikely, would be if I were to suddenly decide to give up my career and family life to become a nun whose life was entirely dedicated to prayer and meditation on God. However, I had no plan to do this. I had absolutely no intention of turning away from my career, volunteer work, and family responsibilities as a mother, to become a nun. I could not imagine in what way my life could possibly become more spiritually oriented than it was already. I, therefore, put aside the astrologers' comments, although I remembered the comments in my heart.

Something else unusual occurred around the middle of October 2003, a few weeks before my head injury and fifth NDE. I was preparing to give a presentation on STEs to the Spirituality in Health Care Network (SHCN) in Toronto. I recall that a very unusual thought repeatedly popped into my mind as I prepared my notes and audio-visuals for this presentation. *This is my swan song,* I repeatedly thought.

Not surprisingly, I was puzzled as to why I kept thinking this. The thought implied to me that for some reason this October 2003 presentation would be the last time I would be making a presentation to SHCN. I could not imagine a reason why I would not continue to make regular professional presentations at some of SHCN's monthly meetings, the network that I founded and loved, and of which I was the Co-Chairperson.

On the evening of Friday, November 7, 2003, the night before my accident and NDE, another unusual strong thought repeatedly came into my mind. I had an important meeting scheduled for Sunday, November 9, 2003, with my church's managing team, on which I served. I was definitely planning to attend this meeting.

However, on Friday, November 7, 2003, a very strong thought came to my consciousness and would not leave, *I will not be able to attend the SRF meeting on Sunday, November 9,* I thought. I had no idea why I so strongly sensed that I would not be able to attend the meeting scheduled two days later.

But the intuition was so strong and so persistent that I sent an email to my church's managing team, informing them that I would not be able to attend the meeting next Sunday. I was puzzled at the time as to why the inner prompting that I would be unable to attend this meeting was so strong.

November 8, 2003

Saturday, November 8, 2003, I went on a day trip with a friend to Niagara Falls, Ontario. I tremendously enjoyed visiting the falls, and would make the two-hour drive several times a year. My plan for that day was to view the falls and, in the afternoon, walk the tunnels under them, and later watch the full-moon eclipse over the falls in the early evening.

The eclipse was scheduled to peak at about 8:00 p.m. We planned to eat dinner at the restaurant which overlooks the falls, so that while we ate dinner we could watch the eclipse high over the falls. through the restaurant's large picture windows.

The drive to Niagara Falls from Toronto was uneventful. It was a cool autumn day with a clear sky, excellent for viewing the eclipse, I thought. After our arrival, I parked my car in the large parking lot across the street from the crest of the falls. We walked along the sidewalk from the parking lot to the cobblestone viewing area along the edge of the falls.

The view of Niagara Falls was stupendously beautiful, as always. I loved the sound of the roar created by the water cascading over the falls. I enjoyed the feel of the mist from the falls as it sprayed onto my face. I felt blissful and happy, as I gazed at the natural beauty of these stunning falls.

The grandeur and scenic beauty uplifted me spiritually. In awe and wonder, I thought of God's majesty. The song "How Great Thou Art" came to my mind as I gazed at the massive, magnificent falls. Because of the mist rising from the cascading water, rainbows are frequently visible over Niagara Falls on sunny days. So, as usual, I looked carefully for a rainbow in the sky. I smiled contentedly, when I spotted a rainbow above the mist.

After a period of bliss and awe enjoying the view from the top of the falls, my friend and I went down the special elevators to view the falls from the underground tunnels and the lower level observation platform. I loved visiting there, and had done this many times. I especially enjoyed the powerful vibration and deep roar that could be felt and heard underground in the tunnels and at the falls' base, caused by the thousands of gallons of water powerfully pouring over the falls.

I also immensely enjoyed standing and meditating there, while I was permeated by the thunderous roar. As I stood there meditating, it often felt to me like the thunderous roar would transform into the cosmic sound of OM. This powerful vibration and sound would transport me very quickly into a deep meditative state.

I meditated at the tunnel viewing portals, and again for a longer period, while standing on the lower observation platform. It was an unusually profound and deep meditation. To think about that evening's meditation experience moves me to tears to this day, and still stirs deep reverence and gratitude in me. Simply put, while meditating that day, enveloped by the powerful vibration and thundering roar of the OM sound, I found my way back *Home*.

Mystical Communion at Niagara Falls

In my meditation, my consciousness expanded. I slipped into a deep and profound unitive state of consciousness…. the blessed state for which I had been yearning and intensely striving since my coyote-driven experience in 1995. While in this deep mystical state of communion, I opened my eyes, and I could perceive heavenly light around me and above me, in addition to, and superimposed upon, the physical world which I could also clearly see around me.

The sense of my expanded consciousness' direct connection to the infinitely loving Divine source had returned. It was like the Divine communion that I had experienced in those glorious two months in 1995. I was in ecstasy. Tears of joy and gratitude streamed down my cheeks. I was permeated with Divine love, Divine joy, Divine peace, and Divine communion.

As I gazed upwards in this ecstatic, unitive state of mystical communion, with my eyes open, I could clearly see a being of light appear, coming to greet me. His body seemed to be made of luminescent light, and he radiated white light that illuminated his surroundings. He radiated intense love toward me. *Welcome Home,* he said to me telepathically, amidst a wave of intense love that transported me to higher ecstasy.

I immediately recognized this angelic being of light. He was a great saint of my spiritual tradition, a saint whom I revered deeply and loved, the yogic guru who had been appearing to me in my meditations for many years, Mahavatar Babaji. My heart leaped in joy at his appearance. *Master!* my soul cried out, rejoicing. Profound unconditional love flowed from Babaji and permeated every particle of my being.

I reveled in the beauty and joy of the sacred communion. After a period of time, the luminescent and saintly Mahavatar Babaji, disappeared from my view. I remained in ecstasy. The full moon had now risen in the evening sky over the falls, and the eclipse was beginning.

I remained in a beatific state of ongoing mystical communion as my friend and I watched the start of the breathtaking lunar eclipse from the lower viewing platform. Because it was after sunset, it began to get colder and colder. We decided to watch indoors in the restaurant, where it was warm.

As we walked through the tunnels and traveled up in the elevator to the Niagara Falls viewing restaurant, I remained enwrapped in the state of ongoing mystical communion. I was fully aware of the physical world around me, and at the same time, I was fully aware of my expanded, mystical state of consciousness.

I felt/knew I was in a state of God Communion. This may to some sound grandiose to state, but in the state of communion, I did not feel grandiose at all. As I mentioned earlier, communion, by its very nature, is an immensely humbling experience. While in that blessed, mystical state, I was profoundly aware of my smallness and relative unimportance as compared to the vast grandeur of the omnipresent, omnipotent, omniscient Divine source, our creator, that which I call God. Once again, I felt like I was a small wave of the extremely vast ocean of cosmic consciousness, of which we are all waves. At the same time, I felt deeply and unconditionally loved, and knew that all beings were equally deeply and unconditionally loved by our Divine Creator.

"I am *Home* again!" I quietly confided to my friend.

We sat at a window table in the restaurant and ate our dinners while we watched the beautiful full lunar eclipse over the falls. I recall humbly saying to my friend over dinner, "I do not know how long this blessed state of communion is going to last. But now I know, I am certain to the core of my being, that because I have been able to find my way back *Home* once tonight, even if this communion ends tomorrow, I am certain that someday, somehow, I will be able to find my way back *Home* again."

My Fatal Accident

After our dinners were finished, my friend and I decided to take one final look at Niagara Falls from the top viewing platform, before we headed back to my car to drive home. When we stepped outside the building, we discovered that the outside temperature had dropped significantly. It was below freezing. This had caused the mist from the falls to freeze over parts of the cobblestone pavement. There was a thin sheet of ice covering patches of the walkway outside the door of the restaurant. This being the only route to return to my car, we moved forward very cautiously, trying to avoid the ice patches on the walkway, holding railings whenever possible to prevent us slipping.

When we reached the edge of the falls, there was no ice on the walkway anymore. Instead, the cobblestone walkway directly adjacent to the falls was soaking wet with water from the heavy falls spray. We both held the railing and gazed at the magnificent falls for one last time. They were now being illuminated by multi-colored lights, as is done most evenings. The full moon eclipse had not completed yet, and the moon was still partially obscured. It was a beautiful view. My state of ongoing mystical communion stayed strong as I gazed at the spectacular sight.

After several minutes, we decided that it was time to leave. We turned and started walking away from the falls, along the wet cobblestone walkway towards the parking lot. It was very dark along that walkway that night, because of the partially obscured moon and because for some reason the walkway lights were not turned on. We slowly and carefully walked towards the parking lot.

Suddenly, I felt my foot slip out from beneath me. I slipped on an invisible patch of black ice that had formed in an unseen dark pothole in the dark walkway. Instantly, I fell backwards. It happened incredibly quickly. I had no time to try to break my fall with my arms. Before I fully realized what had happened, I fell straight backward onto the rock of the cobblestone walkway. I hit the back of my head very hard with a loud *smack,* and with the full force of the backward slip and fall.

The pain on impact was excruciating. A sharp searing pain pierced my head and brain. It felt like somebody had chopped into my skull with a heavy axe. At the same time, I heard a horrible mushy sound inside my

Yvonne Kason, M.D.

head, similar to what I imagine to be the sound of a watermelon smashing on rock pavement. I now know that at that moment of my head's impact on that solid rock, I sustained a traumatic brain injury.

My battered brain bled, suffering a brain hemorrhage at the point of impact of the fall. My brain bruised with multiple contusions and/or lacerations, both coup and contra-coup injuries, as it bounced back and forth within the confines of my skull, both during and after the fall. My physical body died immediately from the impact of the head injury.

Leaving my Body

At the moment of the impact, my spirit instantly left my body. I felt myself rapidly move upwards through the dark evening sky and up through a dark expanse of space. I felt as if my spirit had been whisked upwards very quickly by some unknown force much greater than myself. I was abruptly pulled away from the earthly scene below.

I briefly glimpsed my body lying lifeless on the ground below me. Then within an instant, I completely lost awareness of my physical body. I felt no more pain. I felt no fear. The sensation of severe head pain from the head injury had only lasted a split second and then disappeared immediately when my soul left my body.

The darkness of the earthly evening sky slowly disappeared as I moved higher. There was complete silence around me. I could no longer hear the earthly sounds surrounding the scene of my accident. I found myself moving up towards an entrance to the realm of white light. My soul made the transition from the earthly plane to the light very rapidly, in just a few seconds.

Welcomed to the Light by Beings of Light

I then found my spirit entering the realm of white Divine Light, the realm which I had seen in my 1979 NDE. Once again, I felt the powerful unconditional love of our Higher Power, what I call God. I felt the welcoming presence of the intensely loving, omnipotent, omnipresent, super-intelligent force which underlies all creation.

The white light of this realm was bright but not glaring. As it had been in 1979, the white light was soft and diffused, similar to the sparkling white luminescence one can view from an airplane as it ascends through the bright glistening top of clouds just before it breaks into the sunny sky above.

At what appeared to me as an entranceway to this white light realm, I immediately saw two angelic, luminous beings of light, who seemed to be waiting for me, to greet me and welcome me into the heavenly realm. Their bodies seemed to be glistening, made of luminescent white light rather than made of physical matter. I instantly recognized them. They were two great saints, Spiritual Masters from my spiritual tradition, saints whom I loved, revered, and considered my gurus – Paramahansa Yogananda and Mahavatar Babaji.

My heart leaped with joy! I felt in awe to be in their holy presence. They seemed to have been waiting for me at my moment of death, and they now lovingly ushered me to the other side, welcoming me into the heavenly realm of Light.

My beloved Spiritual Masters and the Light radiated profound love and great joy towards me, an unconditionally loving welcome. It felt to me as if a loving birthday party or graduation party were being held in my honor in the Light, and I was being very warmly welcomed as the guest of honor at the celebration.

As my spirit entered the heavenly white light realm and began to absorb the powerful feelings of love and joy, the beings of light, my gurus, telepathically informed me that I had died. The communication was all telepathic or intuitive, perhaps by thought transference. Speech was not necessary. Intuitively or telepathically they explained to me that I had died, that my physical body had died.

I was told that my work in the incarnation as Dr. Yvonne Kason was now completed. Intuitively I was congratulated. *Job well done*, I was told. It felt somewhat like a joyous graduation celebration. I had completed the hard work of my lifetime as Dr. Yvonne Kason, and now my loved ones in the Light were celebrating with me on my completion or graduation from that lifetime.

Life-Review Concerns – "Don't worry about it"

For an instant, my intellectual mind took pause, and I remember thinking, *Oh-oh! Here comes my life-review.* By this point in my career, I had learned that many NDE Experiencers who were clinically dead and later returned to life, report a detailed life-review happening after their moment of bodily death. My ego-mind did not look forward to my life-review, because I knew that just like other people, there had been times in my life that I had made mistakes or poor choices, and other times when perhaps I could have been kinder or more considerate than I had been. I had a brief feeling of dread, anticipating some unpleasant moments in my life-review.

It seemed that the two saints by my side were able to read my thoughts, and they were instantly aware of my concerns. I recall the spirit of Yogananda turning his head to glance at me at that moment, and with his glance a deep spiritual understanding was instantaneously transmitted to me, blowing away my concerns as quickly and easily as if he were brushing a fleck of dust off my shoulder. The understanding I suddenly received was, *Don't worry about it.*

I understood instantly through mental transmission accompanying the glance, that the Divine Creator, Mother/Father God, the intelligent power behind the universe, is fully aware that everyone makes mistakes in their soul's journey, incarnation after incarnation. The Divine Parent loves each soul with profound, unimaginably powerful, unconditional love. It's like a wise loving parent understands that, when a young child is learning to walk, it will stumble and make mistakes, perhaps at times falling, skinning its knees, or bumping its head, or even breaking something it fell on by accident. The loving parent understands with compassion that this is all part of the normal learning process for the child. Mistakes and accidents do happen. Likewise, the Divine Mother/Father God, views our mistakes as part of our soul's learning process.

With the thought, *Don't worry about it,* and this deep spiritual understanding being mentally transmitted to me, I let go of all concerns about past mistakes. With new freedom, I opened my heart to absorb more fully the profound love and joy that was surrounding me, and flowing through me in the Light realm. My past mistakes seemed trivial, unimportant, even irrelevant, in the bliss and profound unconditional love of the welcoming Light.

I sensed other beings of light, or spirits, also present in the white light realm. But my soul was elevated in ecstasy and did not focus on details of other beings in the realm of Light. I felt indescribable joy, bliss, and Divine communion. The ongoing mystical communion that I had been experiencing at my moment of death continued, and then markedly and wonderfully deepened while I was in the Light.

Revelations and Past Lives Remembered

I then shifted into a blissful state of pure thought, pure consciousness, a plane glimpsing the infinite stillness and wisdom of the Absolute, with no visual images. In this state, much was revealed to me during what seemed to be timeless time. Information was not communicated to me linearly, one fact at a time, but rather all at once, in an aha experience, or revelation. My expanded consciousness in the heavenly realm was now able to integrate vast amounts of information all at once.

Suddenly, and simultaneously, I remembered all my past lives. It felt like my soul had always known them, but had temporarily forgotten them during my incarnation as Yvonne Kason. It felt as if while I was incarnated in my physical body, and with limited mortal awareness, I could only see a small part of the large complex tapestry of my soul's journey over many lifetimes. It was as if the memory of my soul's experiences across many lifetimes had been obscured from my mortal view by a dark cloth or veil.

Now in the Light realm, it seemed as if the obscuring veil had been pulled away from my mind and memory, so that the whole tapestry of my soul's journey was revealed. I could now see the big picture of all my past lives all at once.

I had previously glimpsed several of my past lives before this NDE, which had seemed like pieces of a giant jigsaw puzzle, with many pieces missing. Now, these past life memories were confirmed, elaborated upon, and put together cohesively with my many other past lives, as if all the pieces of the jigsaw puzzle were finally brought together to form the whole completed picture. I could see/understand the interconnectedness of my

Yvonne Kason, M.D.

many experiences over many lifetimes. With this revelation, many aspects of my life as Dr. Yvonne Kason suddenly made sense to me.

With the memory of my past lives returned, my current incarnation no longer seemed odd or unusual, as I previously thought of it, punctuated with so many NDEs and STEs. I saw and remembered that I had also had NDEs in some of my past lives, and many STEs in many past lives, including Kundalini Awakenings, and mystical experiences in many, many of my past lives. From the perspective of many lifetimes, my present incarnation was not at all unusual. It seemed that my soul was continuing with the pattern of consciousness experiences that I have had for many incarnations.

I remembered incarnations in many cultures and many traditions. I remembered some where I had been a man, as well as many where I had been a woman. I saw myself incarnated in many different cultures, in different countries, with many different skin colors, white, brown, yellow, red, and black. I saw myself raised in many religious and spiritual traditions, in Christian lifetimes, Jewish lifetimes, Native American lifetimes, Hindu lifetimes, Buddhist lifetimes, Muslim lifetimes, and more.

I experienced my soul as multifaith and multicultural, having incarnated in every corner of this planet over the millennia. I saw recent lifetimes, and also lifetimes thousands of years ago. It all made complete sense to me, and remembering my many diverse incarnations made me feel whole, complete, as I now remembered who I truly was.

Timeless Time – Past, Present, and Future Coexist

I communed in ecstasy and bliss in the Light for an unknown period of time. The passage of time in the Heavenly afterlife realm did not seem to correspond with the passage of time on the earthly plane. It felt like "timeless time." Time was not moving forward in a linear fashion as we experience it here on earth. It could loop, and one could travel forward or backward in time. For example, it felt to me that I was on the other side, in the heavenly white light realm, much longer than the length of time my physical body on earth lay dead or unconscious, before my spirit returned to it.

It seemed that in the heavenly realm, what we perceive as past, present, and future, were all happening at the same time, somehow. A person's different incarnations could be occurring simultaneously or overlapping from the worldly linear perspective of time, but this seeming time incongruence seemed quite normal, nothing unusual at all, from the perspective of consciousness in the heavenly realm.

Past, present, and future, all seemed to coexist, or be beyond time. It seemed that by shifting my focus of attention, I could shift from focusing on what we on earth perceive as the past, to focusing on the future, or to focusing on the present.

There is a slight similarity of this altered perception of time with an earthy experience of going to a movie complex with multiple movie theaters, where several different movies are playing simultaneously in the different theaters. We can understand from our worldly linear perspective of time, that one same actor may be acting in several of these films being aired at the same time. We understand that the actor filmed these movies at different times, but they are now being aired at the same time. Somewhat similarly, in the heavenly realm it was understood that what appears to be past, present, and future on earth, can all be perceived and experienced at the same time on the other side.

This and many other aspects of the nature of reality in the heavenly realm of Divine Light, are beyond words and are extremely difficult to describe.

Choosing Whether or Not to Return

At some point, after a period of timeless time, my beloved gurus in their light bodies appeared to me again. Gently and lovingly, Paramahansa Yogananda spoke to me intuitively or telepathically. He said, *You may now choose: whether to incarnate in the body of a baby to further serve Divine Mother; and/or to return to the maimed body of Dr. Yvonne Kason to further serve Divine Mother there.*

This phrasing was perfect for my soul, because for many years my inner prayer had been to be God's instrument. I yearned to serve God/ Divine Mother in all that I do. *Thy will be done,* was my mantra. The prayer of St Francis, *Make me a channel of your peace, Make me a channel of your love,* had been my motto. Also, in the preceding couple of years, my preferred way of relating to God in my prayers was as the Divine Mother.

Interestingly, I was not familiar with the word "maimed" at the time of this NDE, and I had to look it up in the dictionary later to confirm its exact meaning. It means crippled, injured, or impaired with a disability. But somehow, as the word was telepathically communicated to me in the Light, I intuitively sensed its meaning. Something would be injured in my physical body.

I did not think about this choice being given to me by using my intellectual mind, or by analyzing the pros and cons of each choice. Instead, before my ego-mind had time to think, my soul, which was in ecstasy, instantly responded. It felt as though my response physically came out of my heart rather than out of my head or mind. The thought spontaneously leaped out of my heart area, *Master, please guide me. What is the higher choice?*

After a pause, my angelic guru lovingly replied to me intuitively/telepathically, *You can choose.* Implied in these words was the sense that both these choices were good. I do not recall being shown any details about what an incarnation in either of these scenarios would entail.

Once again I did not pause to think about the choice using my intellect or ego mind. Rather, my heart and soul were wide open, in blissful ecstasy, and feeling complete trust in the wisdom of the Higher Power and the Divine Plan. In this state of complete openness and trust, and before my ego-mind had time to think, my bliss-filled heart bowed in reverence before my gurus and inwardly repeated, *Masters please guide me. What is the higher choice? I want to do God's will.*

After another pause, Yogananda's loving inner voice floated through my soul with exquisite sweetness, telepathically saying, *It will be more difficult, but to return.* The implied meaning in these words was to return to my maimed and injured body.

Before I had time to think, and without any hesitation, with complete trust, surrender, and acceptance, my heart and soul instantly responded, *I accept.*

Abrupt Return to my Previously Dead Body

Faster than the speed of thought, I suddenly found myself returned to the previously dead body. As I began my two-word thought response with *I*, I was still fully in the Light in the presence of my two saintly gurus in their light bodies. However, before I could mentally complete my thought, I suddenly found myself in my ice-cold physical body, gasping a deep first breath of life into it. My mind completed its two-word thought with *accept*, with my spirit now suddenly within my reviving body. God and my gurus had known my soul's answer, *I accept*, faster than my soul was able to answer. I was sent back to my physical body in the middle of my uttering the thought.

Returning to my body felt like waking up inside an ice cube. As I gasped my first few breaths of life, I immediately became aware that my body felt extremely cold, with an excruciatingly severe headache. My entire body felt as if I had been in a refrigerator or deep freezer for half an hour. My medically trained mind guesses that my body temperature had dropped significantly after I had died outdoors, on that very cold evening.

At first, when my soul entered my physical body, I could see both realities clearly, the physical world around me, as well as the Divine realm of the white Light and my beloved Spiritual Masters. It felt to me that my angelic gurus had lovingly ushered me back into my injured, previously dead body. They were right there with me. I could clearly see both realms at the same time for several minutes. It appeared to me that the two realms were superimposed one upon the other.

Although I was aware that I was now reawakening in my injured body on the earthly plane, at first the focus of my attention remained almost entirely in the white Light realm, with my beloved gurus Paramahansa Yogananda and Mahavatar Babaji. Slowly, over several minutes, the spiritual realm of the Light and my beloved gurus gradually faded from my view. My expansive state of communion slowly disappeared, and I returned to a normal state of earthly awareness, except for a tiny little spot of the white light realm which I could still perceive. I also had a clear memory of my death experience on the other side.

I was back, re-embodied, re-incarnated in my former body. However, from that moment onwards, my life changed completely. I began a completely new life-stage. I had returned to my body as a disabled medical doctor, a person who had survived a serious traumatic brain injury.

To be more accurate, I was a person who had died from a traumatic brain injury, had a full death transition experience, and then by Divine design, which I accepted, I was returned to my maimed and previously dead body to live on with a physical disability. I had now had five Near-Death Experiences.

Chapter 16

REFLECTIONS ON MY 2003 NDE AND ITS AFTER-EFFECTS

Immediately after my slip and fall accident on November 8, 2003, I did not pause to think about the powerful Near-Death Experience that I had just had. The beauty and grandeur of the hours of ongoing communion and my Near-Death Experience later that evening were pushed out of my conscious mind as I struggled intensely to deal with the challenges of my seriously injured body.

After I awoke in my previously dead body, I lay on the ground dazed for several minutes. I was initially confused after the head-injury, and did not realize that I should have gone to a hospital immediately, for medical attention. With my friend's assistance, I slowly and carefully rose off the ground. I sat down on a nearby seat for a few moments, hunched forward holding my throbbing head in my hands. I had an excruciating headache. Then, with the help of my friend's steadying arm, I walked slowly and carefully to my car in the parking lot.

On reaching my car, I immediately went and sat in the driver's seat as I habitually did. I did not realize how seriously injured I was, and what I now know, that I was cognitively impaired at that moment because of a traumatic brain injury. I put my key into the ignition and placed my hands on the steering wheel to begin to drive. I sat there for a few moments limply slumped over the steering wheel, feeling profoundly drained and weak, my head pounding in pain.

I did not have the self-awareness to know what was wrong with me, but I did recognize that I was not feeling well. "I don't think I can drive the car. Could you please drive me home?" I asked my friend.

In my confused state, I hoped that I would feel better in the morning after a good night's sleep. I insisted on being driven home, rather than to the closest hospital as my friend suggested. She deferred to my request and drove me home to Toronto. By the time we arrived at my home two hours later, as I held a bag of ice we had picked up to my throbbing head, I vaguely realized that I had some sort of head injury. Instinctively, based on my years of medical training and medical practice, I knew that somebody needed to carry out a head-injury routine, that is, to spend the next 24 hours with me and wake me every hour or so to be sure that I could wake up. If I couldn't be roused, they had to call 911 to take me to the emergency department immediately. I asked my friend to stay over in my guest room and do this head-injury routine. Fortunately, I always woke up at the hourly wake-up calls.

Looking back, it is odd to me that in my cognitively impaired state the night of the TBI, I knew enough to ask my friend to carry out the head injury routine, but I did not realize that I should go to an emergency department that very night to have my head injury evaluated with brain scans. Instead, I rested at home, and did not consult a medical doctor until several days later. As my intuition had inferred to me, I was not able to attend the meeting at my church scheduled for the next morning.

Unfortunately, it was a couple of weeks before I was correctly diagnosed as having a traumatic brain injury (TBI) with a brain hemorrhage. I was partly to blame because I did not seek medical attention right away. Feeling exhausted with a very strong desire to sleep, I wanted to just stay at home and rest.

Fortunately, I had two days scheduled off before I needed to return to work in my medical practice. I went to work later that week, despite my throbbing headache and severe fatigue. I felt a loyalty and a strong sense of responsibility to my patients, and I did not want to cancel my office hours if I was still physically capable of coming to work.

On the day I returned to work, as doctors often do, I had a hallway consultation with one of the other doctors in my group practice. Between both of us seeing our scheduled patients, I told him briefly in the hallway about hitting my head in the slip and fall accident, and my resulting throbbing headache, mental sluggishness, and fatigue. In my cognitively impaired state, I was not sure whether I had lost consciousness or not.

In those early days after the TBI, I had not yet integrated my NDE and did not realize I had been dead or unconscious for some time. Without any proper examination, and with inaccurate information from me, my colleague told me that probably I had a concussion, and then he rushed off to see his next patient. I still did not realize that I should have gone to a hospital and had a proper assessment for my head injury. Instead, I continued trying to live my regular life, presuming incorrectly that I had a mild concussion.

I struggled to try to carry on with my normal daily activities, but I simply could not. I felt mentally foggy, had a severe constant headache punctuated by frequent additional migraine headaches, and had marked fatigue, dizziness, short-term memory problems, and sluggish thinking. I started cutting down the time I spent in the office, and took naps during my lunch breaks. I asked my secretary to start canceling some non-urgent appointments.

About one week after the injury, I finally booked a proper appointment to see a family doctor. I insisted that I felt there was something wrong with my brain, "My brain is not working right," I told him.

He suggested I could go to the local emergency department for testing and brain scans, or he could send me for an outpatient CT scan of my brain. Still not realizing the severity of my injury, I chose the out-patient CT scan which would be done a week later. I was feeling so poorly and was so fatigued that I did not want to have to endure the many hours of waiting normally needed in an emergency department.

The next week, I had a CT scan of my head, which clearly showed my brain hemorrhage and suggested possible further brain injury. My family doctor urgently referred me to a neurologist, who immediately told me to stop working. The neurologist told me I was probably cognitively impaired.

The neurologist ordered an MRI scan that revealed that I had indeed had a TBI with a brain hemorrhage and contusions (bruising) and/or lacerations of both of the frontal lobes of my brain. I was then referred to a top cognitive neurologist who specialized in traumatic brain injury. She told me to take at least six months off work, to give my brain time to heal.

When I was finally correctly diagnosed, I felt a great sense of relief. Although I loved my professional work, and hoped to be able to return to medical practice soon, I knew I needed time to heal. My struggle to live my normal life was not working.

Slowly, the severity of my brain injury began to hit me more and more clearly. I started neuro-rehabilitation and underwent large amounts of testing, which helped identify my areas of loss. As it turned out, my brain did not heal in six months, or two years, or five years. I had become a disabled person.

My life after the traumatic brain injury was profoundly challenging. Due to my new disabilities, I could no longer do almost everything that I used to be able to do. I was suddenly unable to continue my career and professional work as a doctor and medical professor/teacher. I had to stop my numerous volunteer activities, writing of books and articles, public speaking, serving at my church, and volunteering in my son's school activities. Even day-to-day activities such as grocery shopping, driving downtown, and housekeeping, became very challenging to me. I often told others that although I could still think, walk, and talk after the TBI, it felt as if it completely destroyed and wiped out everything else of my former life and abilities, as if an atomic bomb had hit and wiped out everything else in my life.

To make matters worse, even though I was unable to work, struggling with severe fatigue and multiple physical and cognitive symptoms, for many months after my injury I had to struggle intensely to try to get some financial support. I had to battle with my insurance providers to finally acquire the disability benefits to which I was entitled. I eventually had to hire a lawyer to help me in my struggle to receive disability benefits and compensation for my personal injury and loss of my career.

In total, my life immediately following the 2003 slip-and-fall accident was extremely stressful. It took years of neuro-rehabilitation for me to learn how to compensate for some of the cognitive challenges I now had to live with. I also had huge psychological stresses after the TBI, adjusting to my dramatically changed life as a newly disabled person, and struggling for years to try to gain some financial security.

My need to take legal action added yet another level of major psychological stress to my life. These major, practical, challenges in my life consumed almost all my mental energy, and I had very little time or energy left to reflect upon my period of ongoing communion or the NDE.

In the first few years after the head injury accident, I felt like I was in a war for my very survival, constantly fighting battle after battle, to move forward on my healing journey. There are many stories that I would like to share about those challenges during my healing journey, but this tale is far too long and complex to include in this book.

Immediate Impact of my 2003 NDE

I have had a clear memory of most of my beautiful 2003 Near-Death Experience from the moment it occurred until now. Thinking about it during those first difficult post-TBI years would elevate my mood. Just thinking about my mystical communion at the base of the falls, remembering being welcomed into the heavenly light by my loving gurus in their light bodies, or thinking about my ecstatic communion in the white light, would partially bring back those elevating experiences to my consciousness.

Those reflections would make me feel joy, inner peace, and inner certainty that I was loved and cared for by God. To this day, when I think about this NDE, I still enjoy the same elevating shifts in my mood and consciousness.

Immediately following that NDE, it felt to me that the doorway in my mind did not close fully, so as to separate my normal conscious awareness from the perception of the heavenly realm of Divine white light. After my spirit was abruptly returned to my previously dead body, I initially could see both realities clearly, the gross physical reality of the world around me, and the subtle realm of loving Divine light with my gurus.

Slowly, over the course of several minutes, the subtle spiritual realm of white light gradually faded from my view, but it did not disappear totally. I always felt that somehow the door of my perception of the heavenly realm remained open just a crack. I felt that although I could no longer clearly peer through to the other side, a shaft of light still poured through the open crack in the doorway of my consciousness, and blessed me in an indescribable way. Inwardly, I still perceive it to this day.

This tiny crack has given me comfort, strength, and upliftment, especially in my darkest hours. During the first few weeks and months after the TBI and NDE, I was very aware of this crack in the door of my consciousness. The shaft of light felt to me like a life-ring that I could cling to, which had been thrown to me by the grace of the Divine. I clung to it with all my might, as I was buffeted by the stormy seas of my worldly life immediately following the dire accident. In those early days, this crack of light, my Divine life-ring, was a great source of strength to me.

Spontaneous Soul Retrieval of NDE Memory Fragments

Although I now fully remember the 2003 NDE, interestingly, for the first several months after my accident, I had no memory of the final part of it. I clearly remembered the beginning and middle parts. It is quite fascinating how the memory of the final part came back to me, the choice of whether or not to return to my maimed body. This memory fragment came to my awareness through a spontaneous soul-retrieval experience that was triggered by a visit to a Native American sacred site, "The Petroglyphs", north of Peterborough, Ontario.

This active sacred site is known to the Nishnaabe (Ojibway) people as *Kinoomaagewaabkon*, or *The Teaching Rocks*. It is an outcropping of crystalline marble in the Canadian Shield, a place where shamans have been coming for hundreds of years to go on vision quests. The shamans would carve images into the rock, petroglyphs, inspired by their vision quest experiences. There are many carvings on the rock face, depicting turtles, snakes, birds, humans, canoes, and more.

I had visited The Petroglyphs many times before my head injury. Intuitively, or clairsentiently, I sensed that this was a power-place on the planet, a place where the veil between worlds was thin. The vibration was conducive to STEs. Over the years, I have had many powerful STE experiences while meditating there.

A fascinating phenomenon would occur each time I visited The Petroglyphs. I would always find one particular image would stand out for me, and intuitively I would sense a meaning or message that the particular image had for me, relating to my life issues at that time. For example, I visited there again last month. The image that immediately caught my attention was of a person carrying a large load or burden on their back. Behind that person was a Spirit that, to me, seemed to be invisibly helping the person carry their load.

I understood the message from Spirit that day at the *Teaching Rocks*, was to remember that Spirit is invisibly helping me through the many challenges life was currently giving me. Metaphorically, Spirit was helping me carry my burden. Each time I would visit The Petroglyphs over the years, a different image or series of images would speak to me, giving me a different intuitive healing message. This is indeed a powerful healing place on our planet.

Several months after the TBI, when I visited The Petroglyphs for the first time since my head injury, I had a very odd experience. When I looked at the rock carvings, every image that caught my eye looked to me like somebody having their head chopped into with an axe. *How horrible,* I thought. Surprised and distressed, I would intentionally look away, but the next image that would catch my eye would again appear to me to look like somebody having their head chopped into with an axe. This happened repeatedly.

I wondered to myself, *Why is this happening to me? Do I know anybody who had their head hit by an axe?* As I paused to reflect on my question, I suddenly remembered my head injury accident. *Oh, it's me,* I realized. I had received a blow to my head, albeit not with an axe, of course.

Then, another carving strongly caught my attention. It was a carving of a boat or canoe with a shaman sitting in it. I saw an explanatory sign posted on the viewing platform railing. It explained that this image symbolized the shaman journeying into spirit worlds to do a soul retrieval, to recover soul fragments that had split off from someone, and bring them back, so that the person could re-integrate and heal. As I read this I pondered, *I wonder if I have any soul fragments that need to be recovered?*

I then left the site and returned to my nearby cottage. As I prayed and contemplated this experience, suddenly vivid memories popped into my consciousness. With blazing clarity, I suddenly remembered the excruciating pain I felt on impact during my head injury. It felt like my head had been chopped into with an axe! Until that moment, I had not remembered the pain of impact. Now, suddenly, that memory came back to me in full force. I clutched my head and gasped, as I clearly recalled the excruciating pain.

Then, suddenly, I found myself re-experiencing the entire Near-Death Experience. Yes, I now remembered the pain of impact, but I also re-experienced how immediately after the impact, my spirit was instantly whisked up out of my body. The pain disappeared in that moment. I then remembered and re-experienced the entire NDE in full detail, entering the Light realm, being greeted by the 2 saints, the joy, love, and revelations while in the light, and recalling all my past lives. Then something wonderful happened. I clearly remembered and re-experienced the final segment of the NDE, something I had not yet remembered until this soul-retrieval experience.

I now clearly remembered how the two beings of Light, the saints Paramahansa Yogananda and Mahavatar Babaji, reappeared to me at the end of my sojourn in Heaven, and how they gave me a choice. I was given the choice of either returning to my maimed, injured body and/or reincarnating as a baby, to further serve the Divine Mother in both situations. I now remembered being given this choice, and I recalled how I accepted and surrendered willingly to Divine will, the higher choice, to return to the injured body, although this path would be difficult.

Remembering both the pain of the impact, and the choice I made to return at the end of my NDE, had a tremendous healing effect upon me. I felt more whole. I felt like a gap within me had now been filled. I was actually glad to recall the pain of the impact, because now my memory felt right, correct and complete. The missing piece of memory had been put in place.

Similarly, remembering that I had been given a choice and that I had chosen to return, that I voluntarily and willingly accepted to return to my injured body, was profoundly healing to me. It made sense now. I understood now. I had accepted Divine will, leading me to take the more difficult path.

As I look back, I now realize that I had a spontaneous soul retrieval experience that day, where Spirit brought me back two memory fragments/soul fragments. Integrating them into the rest of the TBI and NDE memory had a powerful healing effect on me, exactly as the soul retrieval explanation sign described. My current NDE memory now includes the final choice of whether or not to return. The memory fragments are fully integrated.

I sometimes wonder if there are other details of my 2003 Near-Death Experience that I do not currently recall. My intuition says, *Yes*. Other revelations may have been veiled from my current memory, to be revealed, if necessary, in the future, on a need-to-know basis.

Spiritual Impact of my 2003 NDE

As I now reflect on the after-effects of this experience, I realize that the NDE definitely transformed me spiritually. My spiritual devotion, and awe of the Divine mystery, increased significantly after it. I was moved deeply by the wonder and beauty of my death transition, and my time in the heavenly white light realm. The hymn *How Great Thou Art* would frequently slip into my mind.

My certainty of the immortality of my soul impacted me greatly after this NDE. As I struggled with the numerous challenges faced by my physical body, I was less affected emotionally than one might expect, because I strongly identified with the fact that I was an immortal soul. I was not the physical body.

I knew to the core of my being that the physical body was my soul's covering, like an automobile that I was riding in to move around in the world. By this analogy, I was the driver of the automobile, not the car itself. Although my vehicle, the car, was damaged/injured, I was just fine. I knew as an experienced truth that I was the immortal soul living within my physical body, but I was not the physical body itself. My physical body may have been seriously injured, but my soul was not injured at all. This gave me great comfort and equipoise immediately following the TBI and NDE.

Additionally, in the months immediately following the experience, I felt cradled in Divine love. I felt as if somehow some of the profound unconditional love that I basked in, had come back with me, when I returned to my physical body. It felt to me as if I still had some of that love and white light in my soul, nourishing me, giving me hope, and giving me strength through my numerous arduous healing battles.

NDE Features of my 2003 Head Injury NDE

After the 2003 head injury, I was immediately certain that I had had another Near-Death Experience. However, this one was different from the other four that I had earlier in my life. This time my physical body had died for a period of time. To me, this clearly distinguished it from my earlier experiences. I sometimes make this distinction by calling my 2003 head injury experience my "Death Experience" NDE, while I call my other NDEs my "Near-Death" NDEs.

Comparing the features of my 2003 NDE with the features first defined by Dr. Raymond Moody, it is clear that my experience included eleven of the fifteen classic NDE features. These were:

1. *Ineffability*: The experience had aspects that were far beyond words, and are very difficult for me to describe to others.

2. *Strong feelings of peace*: A strong feeling of peace was with me at all times, right from my moment of death at the beginning of my NDE. Because the accident happened suddenly and unexpectedly, I never experienced any fear. The strong sense of peace remained with me throughout the duration of my NDE. My pain disappeared the instant my spirit left my body.

3. *Floating out-of-body: An out-of-body experience.* My spirit and point of perception left my physical body immediately at my moment of death. I instantly found my spirit being whisked upwards through the evening sky by a force greater than myself, away from my physical body and the earthly plane. I quickly lost all awareness of what was occurring around my physical body that had just died.

4. *Dark tunnel:* I found my spirit moving upwards very rapidly through a dark expanse of space. The darkness around me very rapidly became lighter, and within moments the darkness disappeared and I found myself in the light.

5. *Meeting Spirits: Mystical Visions:* I was greeted into the light by the welcoming figures of two radiant and luminescent beings of light, who radiated intense love towards me. I immediately recognized these beings of light, Paramahansa Yogananda and Mahavatar

Babaji, two beloved saints and gurus of my spiritual tradition. Telepathically they informed me that my body had died. I was welcomed warmly and openly into the afterlife.

6. *White Light Experience:* I found my spirit moving into a heavenly white light realm that is truly indescribable. Its beauty and magnitude are beyond my capacity to express in words. I felt permeated with profound unconditional love of the Higher Power. I was in a profound state of mystical communion, Divine ecstasy. It was a state of bliss, profound joy, and mystical union. Much was revealed to me while I was in the Light, in a type of revelation. This was not linear learning, but much was revealed at once. I suddenly remembered my past lives, in a manner that made me feel like I had always known them, but somehow forgot while incarnated. The events of my life as Dr. Yvonne Kason suddenly made much deeper sense to me in the context of the interconnection of many of my past lives. It seemed as if I were in timeless time. Much more time seemed to pass while I was in the Light than seemed to transpire on the earthly plane.

7. *Life Barrier:* After an unknown length of time in blissful communion in the white light realm, I was suddenly told that it was time to choose whether to return to my maimed body and/ or to reincarnate in the body of a baby. It was clear my timeless time of basking in ecstasy in the afterlife had now ended, and I needed to choose.

8. *Abrupt return to the body:* When I mentally thought *I accept* [to return to my maimed body], faster than the speed of thought I found myself in my ice cold previously dead body. With the thought *I,* I was still in the white light realm. Suddenly I found my spirit in my physical body, gasping a deep breath of life before I completed my thought with *accept.*

9. *Conviction of the reality of the experience:* I have a clear memory of my 2003 NDE and of when I reawakened in my injured, previously dead body. This memory has remained very clear in my mind despite the passage of over seventeen years.

10. *Transformational impact:* This NDE transformed me on many levels:

    a. *Spiritually,* I was humbled, and in awe of the fact that the two great saints/gurus whom I loved and revered were there to greet me and help me cross over into the afterlife at my moment of death. My spiritual devotion, awe, and gratitude for the grace of the Divine mystery deepened in me after this NDE. My certainty of God's love gave me the inner strength to endure the numerous ongoing and extremely difficult challenges that faced me after my return. My strong faith and spiritual conviction that God-communion was indeed humanly possible, gave me the inner strength to struggle for many years to regain my ability to meditate deeply.

    b. *Psychologically,* the 2003 NDE psychologically impacted me tremendously as well. I identified strongly with my immortal soul and was therefore less emotionally impacted by the new physical disabilities I faced. I was absolutely convinced by my NDE experience that God's Divine plan for all souls is inherently good, and perfect.

    I also knew to the core of my being that my spirit's return to the physical body was not any sort of punishment. This gave me great psychological strength as I struggled with the many physical and worldly obstacles and challenges I had to deal with as a newly disabled person. It also gave me the psychological strength to ignore misguided persons who claimed that I was being punished by God via my new disability.

    c. *Psychically,* I was transformed and opened. My intuition became even deeper after this NDE than it had been previously.

11. *New Views of Death:* I had previously lost my fear of death in 1979. The 1995 NDE had given me the additional certainty of the reality of reincarnation. Now, this 2003 NDE was the first time that I had experienced dying completely. This was the first time I experienced something that many other people who died completely for a period of time have reported: that upon their death, loving spirits were there to greet them and usher them to the other side.

I rejoiced in discovering that my gurus were waiting for me, welcoming me, helping me transition into the afterlife. This gives me even greater comfort in the prospect of my final death transition. I feel confident I will be lovingly helped in the final crossing over when my final hour truly does arrive.

As I reflect upon the features of this experience, it is clear to me that this was indeed another Near-Death Experience. Subjectively, my 2003 Near-Death Experience felt much deeper to me than the other four NDEs that I had earlier in my life. It is fascinating to me, as an NDE researcher, that all my NDEs had a similar number of classic features, eleven or twelve. Even though I died completely for some time in 2003, and it felt to me like this experience was much deeper than my other NDEs, it did not have more NDE features than my earlier experiences. I find this very interesting and somewhat puzzling. Perhaps additional NDE criteria will need to be added to Dr. Moody's list, such as complete death of the physical body, and revelations/new information communicated to the soul while in the Light.

Spiritually Transformative Impact

On reflection, I realize that this NDE definitely transformed me spiritually. My reverence and awe of the Divine mystery deepened afterwards. Many of the beautiful aspects of my NDE moved me deeply, and still move me profoundly to this day. It increased my sense of wonder and gratitude towards the Divine. I felt and feel spiritually humbled, and in awe of the beauty of the Divine plan.

I feel deeply moved by the beauty and love inherent in my death transition, how the Divine lifted my soul up and brought me to the Light at my moment of death. I am struck by the comforting fact that I did not have to search or struggle to find my way to the Light after I died. Instead, a force far greater than me instantly took control, whisked my spirit out of my newly dead body, and transported me almost instantly into the realm of white light.

I feel deeply comforted by the fact that during my death transition, by loving Divine design, I did not need to search or struggle to find loved ones on the other side. Instead, I was welcomed into the realm of heavenly light by two beings of light who loved me. They welcomed me, assisted me, and explained to me that my body had died.

I was and am profoundly moved by the fact that, at my moment of death, it was my beloved gurus Paramahansa Yogananda and Mahavatar Babaji, who were there waiting for me. This fact inspires me very deeply, to this day. It was immensely humbling to have been welcomed by these saints. Their loving welcome gives me great comfort when I think about the prospect of my final death transition.

Another spiritual impact was that my conviction became even stronger, that it was indeed humanly possible to reach a state of ongoing mystical communion. Having once again glimpsed that blessed state of ongoing mystical communion for a few hours before the accident, and experiencing a much deeper state of ecstatic mystical communion while I was in the white light realm during my NDE, I knew it was possible to attain. I strongly yearned to once again experience that blessed state of unitive consciousness.

My commitment to deepen in my practice of daily prayer and meditation intensified after. Unfortunately, one of the very challenging sequelae of my frontal lobe brain injury, was that I completely lost my ability to meditate. My ability to concentrate had been severely injured. My intense yearning to once again experience mystical communion, combined with my strong faith and spiritual conviction, gave me the inner strength and determination to struggle for many years to gradually regain my ability to meditate for long periods.

Psychological Impact

Psychologically, this NDE impacted me tremendously. I was convinced by my communion and revelations during the NDE, that God, in Its infinite intelligence and infinite unconditional love, had a beautiful, innately loving Divine plan for all souls. I knew, somehow, that the Divine plan was inherently good and perfect. I also knew to the core of my being that my spirit's return to once again incarnate in my body was part of God's perfect plan for me, and it was not any sort of punishment.

However, I did not know the reason why, in God's wisdom, I was to return to living on earth in a body with a serious disability. Nonetheless,

I implicitly trusted God's plan for me after my NDE, and I knew it was a good plan. I did not need to understand the reason. I trusted in God's wisdom. That was good enough for me.

My new deep conviction of the perfection of God's plan gave me great psychological strength, as I struggled with the many physical and worldly obstacles and challenges I suddenly had to deal with. My trust in the inherent goodness in the Divine plan, my clear memory of the profound unconditional love with which I was welcomed, and my memory of the loving choice given me as to whether or not to return, gave me great psychological strength. It enabled me to ignore the sometimes hurtful statements made by misguided persons, who claimed that I was being punished for some bad karma.

Another transformational after-effect of this most recent experience, came from my new deeper understanding of many of my past lives. Before this NDE, I had sometimes wondered about the rather unusual course of my life. In addition to my very extensive, *normal,* higher education and my well-respected career as a traditionally trained Western medical doctor, my life had also been punctuated with many *paranormal* experiences.

In all, these were five Near-Death Experiences, a spontaneous kundalini awakening, multiple mystical experiences, and numerous psychic phenomenon. Before my 2003 experience, I did not understand why I had these stark contrasts in my life. However, during my revelation during this NDE, my past lives were simultaneously revealed to me. I was then instantly able to see the interconnectedness of many of my past lives with the course of my present lifetime.

Suddenly, the mix of normal and paranormal in my life all made sense to me. I saw that in many past lives I had been a mystic, with multiple STEs, including NDEs. I also immediately understood why certain significant life events had happened to me in the way that they had. They were but a continuation of experiences that had happened to me in previous lives. Earlier glimpses of past lives I had seen before this NDE were confirmed. This multi-lifetime perspective of the events of my current life, relating to my past lives, gave me a much deeper psychological insight into the events of my current life.

Yvonne Kason, M.D.

Psychic Impact

Psychically, I was also transformed and opened after the 2003 NDE. I found that I was even more intuitive than I had been before it. This heightened intuition was a great asset to me, as I struggled through the many battles of the first many years after the TBI. When I followed my intuition, the results were always to my advantage. In my state of severe fatigue and multiple worldly challenges, I relied heavily on my enhanced intuition after the traumatic brain injury.

A New Life-Stage Begins

On reflection, I think that the 2003 Near-Death Experience launched me into yet another new spiritual life-stage, similar to how my previous 1979 and 1995 ones each launched me into a new spiritual life-stage. Previously, after my 1995 experiences, my spiritual urge shifted into an intense yearning for spiritual deepening and psychological purification. I began to research mysticism and stages on the mystical path. I strived to detach from ego issues, and to surrender to the Divine will in all things. I sincerely prayed *Make me your purified instrument*, and *Thy will be done*.

However, following the 2003 experiences, my spiritual focus shifted again. Surrender to Divine will had by now become an automatic habit for me. Due to the reality of the traumatic brain injury and the resulting disability, I was forced to surrender even more, and let go of virtually all that I was capable of doing in the world before the TBI.

I no longer needed to work spiritually at surrendering, because all had already been taken away from me. Since I identified myself as my immortal soul, although disappointed, I did not feel crushed or broken by having lost all of my former worldly positions and abilities.

Further, during the NDE, my soul had voluntarily and completely surrendered to the Divine instruction that my spirit should return. Therefore, although I struggled intensely in my efforts to heal after the TBI, spiritually, I totally accepted whatever was God's will for my life. I gradually accepted the new shape of my re-incarnated life as a disabled person, and let go of my previous able-bodied life. Surrendering to the Divine will had become second nature to me.

My new spiritual focus after my 2003 NDE was my intense desire for spiritual expansion, a deepening communion. Having lost the ability to engage in my previous outer worldly life, my inner life became the most important focus for my soul— my quest for spiritual deepening. I intensely yearned to re-experience the state of ongoing communion that I had once again glimpsed for a few hours before the head injury. My deep-rooted personal relationship with my Higher Power, God, and my daily spiritual practice of prayer and meditation became the most important things in my life, in my new life-stage.

Determined to Relearn How to Meditate

Of all my new physical and cognitive disabilities after the traumatic brain injury, one of the most distressing to me was the loss of my ability to meditate. I had a very strong yearning for deepening communion. Before the TBI, I had been an avid meditator for over 25 years. As I described earlier in this book, propelled by my 1979 and 1995 NDEs, and especially stimulated by my period of ongoing mystical communion after my 1995 NDE, I became a highly committed meditator.

I deeply yearned for greater spiritual unfoldment and hoped to one day again glimpse that blessed state of ongoing mystical communion. In the three years immediately before my head injury, I was regularly meditating for a minimum of one hour twice a day, morning and evening. I did a longer meditation, three to four hours in length, at least once a week. Several times a year, at meditation retreats and special events, I meditated for even longer periods, five, or six hours in a day.

I enjoyed my regular twice-daily meditation periods immensely, and I cherished my longer meditations. I found I became able to go quite deep in my long meditations, in which I had been blessed with many beautiful spiritual experiences. My practice of prayer and meditation was the backbone of my life.

I was shocked to discover after the 2003 traumatic brain injury, that I had completely lost my ability to meditate. I was informed by my specialist doctors, that the location of the lacerations and/or contusions in the frontal lobes of my brain, were in the regions that govern attention and concentration. Due to these injuries, I had lost my ability to concentrate, an ability essential for meditation, (and for working as a doctor).

The effect of these frontal lobe injuries was to suddenly give me an extremely poor and short attention span. I felt as if I had suddenly developed a severe case of Attention Deficit Disorder. My mind wandered very quickly, and I was unable to concentrate on anything longer than a few moments. I would quickly forget what I was doing while mid-activity, and wander off to another activity. In this state of extremely poor attention and concentration, I found I was completely unable to meditate, not even for a few minutes. At the time, I was very distressed by this new development.

In my soul, and with all my willpower, I was absolutely determined to rebuild my ability to meditate. I intensely yearned to re-experience the intense peace and bliss that I felt in my meditations. I also deeply yearned to once again strive for that blessed state of ongoing mystical communion. I knew from my years of study and practice of yoga meditation, that regular and long meditations were necessary to prepare and expand one's consciousness to be capable of sustaining an ongoing state of mystical communion.

My persistent efforts to re-learn how to meditate was an intense struggle after my brain injury. This struggle lasted for many, many years. I do not know if my brain cells slowly found new routes around the damaged cells in the concentration areas of my frontal lobes, or if my brain's neuroplasticity gradually stimulated new healthy brain cells to grow through the damaged frontal lobe areas. Whatever the biological mechanism was, by my persistent and determined effort to increase the length of my meditations, over the course of twelve years, I slowly but gradually regained my ability to meditate.

At first, after my head injury, I could not even concentrate for five minutes before I would get distracted, forget what I was doing, and wander away from my meditation spot. I tried to force myself to sit in my meditation chair wrapped in my meditation shawl morning and evening, as had been my custom before the TBI.

In an effort to prevent me from absent-mindedly wandering away from my meditation spot within a minute or two, I resorted to writing myself notes, to remind myself that it was time to try to meditate. My mind was incredibly restless in the early months, and it rebelled at the thought of my sitting still in silence for more than a few seconds. I found short prayers to God, singing hymns to express my love to God and my gurus, and repeating short affirmations such as "I love you God," worked best for me in those early days after the TBI.

After a few weeks, I began to force myself to sit and try to meditate twice daily, starting with five minutes at a time. This was a rigorous struggle. Then, very gradually over the weeks and months that followed, I pushed myself to concentrate and meditate for progressively longer periods: ten minutes, then fifteen minutes, then twenty, then twenty-five, and so on. It took about three years of persistent daily effort to gradually increase the length of time my mind was able to meditate to one hour. I meditated for one hour twice daily from that point onwards.

Resuming Long Meditations

Some five or six years after my head injury, I felt the strong inner prompt to try to meditate for two hours. I was in the extremely supportive environment of the Self-Realization Fellowship (SRF) silent meditation retreat, in Encinitas, California. I had been staying at this oceanside meditation retreat for a glorious two-week stay of deep daily meditations, interspersed with long invigorating walks along the Pacific Ocean beach, much rest, and delicious vegetarian meals.

Additionally, the high spiritual vibration, the *darshan* of the great saint and guru Paramahansa Yogananda permeated the retreat. The chapel was built upon the very spot where the saint had meditated and communed with God, many times during his lifetime. I felt spiritually uplifted by the strong spiritual vibration at this holy site.

On the second last day of my retreat, following my inner prompt to try to meditate for two hours for the first time since the TBI, I went to a two-hour long group meditation scheduled at the nearby SRF Encinitas Temple. Meditating for two hours that day was extremely difficult for me. My mind became intensely restless and rebellious during the second hour. I had to use all the strength of my willpower to keep myself seated in the temple.

Yvonne Kason, M.D.

My rebellious mind repeatedly urged me to bolt out of the room, and leave my meditation. Repeatedly, I strived to tame my restless mind, and bring it back to thoughts of God and meditation. I prayed intently for help from God and my gurus to assist me to make it through the two-hour meditation. I forced my restless mind to focus on my meditation techniques. Somehow, using all my willpower and determination, I made it through the ordeal.

After this first attempt, I began to force myself to do a two-hour group meditation a few times a year, whenever I had the opportunity. Very gradually, over the course of a couple of years, my mind adjusted to two-hour-long meditations.

Another couple of years later, while I was again on a two-week-long silent meditation retreat in the SRF Encinitas retreat, the inner prompt came to me to try doing a three-hour-long meditation. So, towards the end of my stay, I went to a three-hour group meditation held at the nearby SRF Encinitas Temple. I was determined that no matter how rebellious my mind might become, I would force myself to sit through the three hours of meditation. Well, to my delight, through the grace of God and my gurus, that meditation sailed by with relatively little difficulty.

After that first three-hour meditation, I felt jubilant. "Satan be Gone!" my heart sang out in joy. I wept tears of joy because I felt my soul had won a significant victory in a battle against Satan. I felt that after I had lost my ability to meditate from the TBI, the force of darkness, what I call Satan, had fiendishly attempted to dissuade me or discourage me in my attempt to seek deepening God-communion. I felt the dark force of delusion wanted me to despair, to think it impossible to regain God-communion, to give up my difficult quest to regain my ability to meditate.

Once I had successfully completed my first three-hour-long meditation, I somehow knew in my soul, that through my hard effort, and through the grace of God and the invisible blessings of my gurus, I would now be able to do long meditations again. This inner victory of my first post-TBI three-hour meditation was a significant milestone for me, a turning point in my journey to rebuild my ability to meditate. I now had the confidence that with time I would definitely be able to do yet longer meditations. And in fact, this has been the case.

From that day forward, I regularly did a two or three-hour meditation each week, in addition to my regular one-hour meditation twice daily. Gradually over the next five years I progressively attended a four-hour meditation, then the following year a five-hour meditation, then the next year a six-hour meditation. I now do two-hour or three-hour meditations regularly and attend a six-hour meditation up to three times a year. These long meditations have helped me tremendously to deepen my spiritual practice.

Misunderstood by Others

Unfortunately, I was frequently met with misunderstandings from others following the 2003 events. During the immensely challenging first few years, I found myself cruelly judged by several people. For example, one small group of people I knew was openly spreading the false story that I had faked the traumatic brain injury because I was lazy and did not wish to work to earn my living any longer.

Further, I was accused of faking the severity of my symptoms in order to get my disability benefits. Fortunately, I knew this to be a lie, and my doctors had shown me the MRI scan of the brain injury. Nonetheless, this cruel and baseless insult stung.

Another person whom I knew stung me with another hurtful comment, based on his misunderstanding. This quite religious friend told me that he was convinced that I had done something very bad in the eyes of God when I published my books on NDEs and STEs. He vehemently told me that I was now being punished by God as a result of my sin of the things I had written in my books.

Fortunately, due to my lived experience of the unconditional love in the heavenly light, and the congratulatory welcome I received into the light realm during my NDE, I absolutely knew that I had not committed some horrible sin in the writing of my books. Further, the profoundly loving way that everything was explained to me, and my being given the choice about whether or not to return, gave me absolute certainty that my disability was not some sort of wrathful punishment. I chose to ignore this person's hurtful comments.

Another misunderstanding I had to deal with was a few people's cruel attitudes that I had nothing of value to say or contribute, because I was now *brain-damaged* [their words]. These insensitive and misinformed individuals cruelly dismissed my opinions on issues, and my insights on any matter, with rolled eyes, and hurtful comments about my being brain-damaged.

I knew I had multiple physical challenges after the traumatic brain injury, including cognitive challenges with my attention and concentration, and short-term memory difficulties. However, I had not lost any of my intelligence, sound judgment, years of life experience, strong intuition, or deep spiritual awareness. This outright dismissal of the value of all my opinions and experience due to my new disability was very disturbing. Fortunately, I had found deep inner strength in my 2003 NDE, and I was able to distance myself from those persons who treated me in such an obviously inappropriate and disrespectful manner.

Yet another source of insult and misunderstanding thrown at me was online criticism by a reader of my book, *Farther Shores*. The author gave me and my book a scathing review, claiming that I had no business talking about NDEs because my one and only NDE had happened over 20 years earlier, in 1979. They dismissed everything I wrote in my book as fabrication and exaggeration of a "want-to-be" Near-Death Experiencer. As I reflected on this insult, I was disappointed, but knew the criticism to be unfounded. Wincing a little I thought, *Well, everyone has the right to have an opinion.*

The other type of misunderstanding I encountered several times, was from some people who firmly believed that I had nothing of value to say about NDEs or other STEs, because I was not fully enlightened, a trained spiritual teacher, or a guru. I learned to shrug off these criticisms as well. I know that I am not fully enlightened, and am not a guru. I do not pretend to be.

However, for some reason in God's great and beautiful plan, I have been blessed with five NDEs, a kundalini awakening, and several mystical experiences over the course of my lifetime. Further, I have extensively researched the literature on NDEs and STEs, and additionally have had the clinical experience over my 25-plus years as a doctor, of counseling many hundreds of people who had STEs. I know in my heart that I have much to say based on my personal and professional experience. And I too, have the right to have an opinion.

Premonitions of my 2003 NDE

When I reflect on my 2003 experiences, it is clear to me that I had two premonitions that something major was going to happen to me that day. I do not consider the astrological predictions that November 8 would change my life as a premonition. I would consider this to be an unusual sign forecasting a change. However, I did have two other strong experiences in the fall of 2003, which I think were premonitions of the fatal accident occurring.

As I prepared my notes for a presentation to the Spirituality in Health-Care Network (SHCN) in October 2003, I repeatedly had the thought pop into my mind, *This is my swan song.* I immediately realized that this recurring thought suggested that, for some reason, I would not be making more regular presentations to SHCN. At the time, I could not think of a reason why this could possibly occur, and I had no idea why this thought kept popping into my mind.

Then, the day before the head injury accident, I had a very strong inner intuitive sense that I would not be able to attend an important church meeting scheduled for the day after the TBI. The inner thought *I will not be able to attend the SRF meeting on Sunday,* kept nagging me that day. The intuition was so strong, that I informed my church committee that I would be unable to attend the November 9, meeting. I had no idea why.

It is fascinating to me that I had these premonitions about my 2003 accident. It seems to me that somehow in consciousness, past, present, and future, can sometimes cross, and communicate.

A Deathbed Vision Before my Death?

When I reflect on my powerful meditation experience a few hours before I died, when I slipped into a state of ongoing mystical communion, I now wonder if this might have been a *Deathbed Vision* experience. A Deathbed Vision is a phenomenon that has been identified by many health care providers. It is sometimes called "nearing-death awareness," or an "end-of-life experience." Deathbed Visions occur to many people when they are going to die soon. They usually occur several hours or even a few days before the actual moment of death.

They are a type of mystical experience, and often have several typical NDE features including: a sense of peace and calm, a loss of fear of death, a mystical vision of a being of light, (often the luminous spirit of a deceased loved one), a dark tunnel with a loving white light at the far end, and/or a mystical vision of an angel, prophet, or important spiritual figure from the dying person's religion.

Deathbed Visions have also been described as an experience where it seems that the veil between the physical realm and the astral heavenly realm of light becomes very thin. The person who is about to die is able to perceive aspects of the heavenly realm of light, and communicate with the spirits of deceased loved ones.

Unbeknownst to me, I was about to die on November 8, 2003, a few hours after I went into my glorious mystical state of ongoing communion. During it, the veil between matter and spirit had been removed from my perception, to reveal some aspects of the heavenly realm of light. I felt profound peace and calm, and a great joy. I indeed saw a luminous being of light, an important spiritual figure from my faith tradition, one of my gurus, Mahavatar Babaji. In fact this beloved guru who greeted me hours before my death was one of the two gurus who later ushered and welcomed me into the light at my actual moment of death later that evening.

It is quite possible that my mystical vision and three hours of mystical communion before my NDE, was actually my Deathbed Vision. Perhaps for some reason in the great Divine plan, the Divine was preparing me for my final transition which was going to occur later that evening, in the same way that the Divine has prepared many other persons for their final transition, with a Deathbed Vision.

It is also possible that, by Divine design, it was simply time for me to once again glimpse that beatific state of ongoing mystical communion, one more time before my death and NDE. I can only speculate about these points, as I cannot know this for certain. However, little did I know as I slowly adjusted to life as a disabled person, that the Divine Sculptor had more beautiful surprises in store for me in the years ahead.

Chapter 17

A HEALING STE: 2016 HEALING FROM TRAUMATIC BRAIN INJURY

My healing process was very slow and difficult. Initially after the TBI, I took a temporary sick leave from my medical practice, hoping that my disability would be temporary and I would one day be able to return to my work as a doctor. However, very little improvement occurred in my disabling symptoms over the first six years after the TBI.

After three years of no significant improvement, despite my intensive efforts in neuro-rehabilitation, my neurologist advised me that it was time for me to officially retire from medical practice. She wisely advised me to shift my focus away from thinking I was on a temporary sick leave, to focus on adjusting to a long-term and perhaps permanent disability.

My neurologist was both a realist and an optimist, for which I am very grateful. She informed me that in her professional opinion, since I was still significantly disabled three years post-TBI, it appeared extremely unlikely that I would ever be able to return to my former career as a doctor, author, and medical teacher. However, she told me to never give up hope, and that some healing may continue to happen.

Yvonne Kason, M.D.

Adjusting to Chronic Disability

I pursued neuro-rehabilitation intensively for a total of seven years. I clung to the faint hope that one day I might be able to return to my beloved career as a medical doctor counseling STE patients. I tried many mainstream medical and alternative holistic healing modalities, as I continued to strive for physically recovery. After my official transition to retirement and long-term disability at three years post-TBI, my neuro-rehabilitation focus became to learn strategies to adjust to and compensate for my long-term or permanent disabilities. I found learning compensating strategies to be extremely helpful in expanding the range of day-to-day activities I was capable of doing. This improved the quality of my life significantly.

I continually and intentionally strived to "optimize my adaptation" to my long-term condition, that is, to make the best of what I was still able to do, despite my disabilities. I consciously chose to look at the positives in my disabled life, focusing on the skills and blessings that I still had in my life, rather than negatively focusing on what I had lost.

So, I tried to focus on my abilities, rather than on my disabilities. I deliberately focused on the positive, soul-nurturing things I was still able to do, like meditating each day (to the best of my capacity), going to my church's annual convocation each year, and going on episodic two-week-long meditation retreats in sunny California. Reading was difficult for me in the early years, so instead, I would listen to CDs or watch DVDs of inspirational talks.

I intensely embraced my personal daily practice of yoga and meditation. I was deeply propelled by my yearning to once again experience glimpses of the Divine, whether it be during my deep meditations, in further mystical experiences, or ultimately in that blessed state of ongoing mystical communion which I had previously experienced. I consciously and intentionally made spiritual deepening the focus of my disabled retirement years.

I even coined the phrase "spiritual retirement" to describe a retirement such as mine, one in which the retired person makes spiritual deepening the highest goal of their retirement years. I slowly accepted that my previous career as a medical doctor and author was part of my past life before the TBI, beyond my post-TBI capabilities.

2016 Sudden Brain Healing – A Miracle

After 12 years of being so significantly disabled that writing more books or public speaking seemed physically impossible, something miraculous happened. Suddenly, something healed within my brain. Somehow, perhaps through a miracle of neuroplasticity, and/or through the grace of God, in February 2016, over twelve years after the head injury, I had a spontaneous brain healing while meditating, and my inspired creativity, my ability and inspiration to write, suddenly came back.

In the preceding few years, several times when I was deep in meditation at the SRF meditation retreat in Encinitas, California, I had the strong inner intuition, *You will write again.* I always surrendered this thought to God with my prayer, *God's will be done.* It seemed far beyond my disabled physical capabilities to write books again, but I kept this inner intuitive guidance in my heart.

On February 24, 2016, while I was deep in a three-hour-long meditation in the SRF Encinitas retreat, the inner intuition came extremely strongly to me again, *You will write again!* But this time, I suddenly inwardly saw a fountain of liquid light erupt in the center of my brain.

This extraordinary liquid light flowed from the base of my skull up into the center of my brain and brightly illuminated and lit up a region in the center of my brain that had previously been in darkness. I felt like the lights were literally turned on in the center of my brain. Inwardly, it felt like the central part of my brain suddenly "woke up," after being "asleep" for twelve years after my TBI. It had been reactivated by the inner flood of liquid light energy pouring into it.

At the same time, in the stillness of my deep meditation, thoughts and ideas for what I should write in my next few books started rapidly flooding through my consciousness, as if a floodgate had been opened. My thoughts and inspirations that had been held back for twelve years now had suddenly burst forth. At the end of the meditation, the inner flood of light ended, and I rushed to my retreat room to write several pages of notes of the inspiration and ideas that continued to flow through me.

From that day onwards in my subsequent deep meditations, it was as if the floodgate in my mind remained open, and the waters of writing inspirations were repeatedly rushing through my consciousness in huge gushes.

Every day, and in every meditation, the inspiration and ideas for writing books continued to flow. I spent hours writing my inspired ideas into my journal after each meditation. By the time I left the retreat, I had already been writing notes for my next books every day for almost a week.

At first, I felt almost overwhelmed by the voluminous amount of ideas and inspiration flowing through my consciousness. The medically trained part of me wondered if perhaps I had gone manic. However, my inner inspirations were based on my previous research and clinical experience and were clearly formulating themselves into at least four separate books that I planned to write, including this one.

The inner impulse to write these four or more books was powerful and persistent. I felt a strong inner prompt, *It is time to write, NOW!* I made prolific notes and slowly started to divide my notes according to which of my future books I would discuss each topic.

Pass on What You Have Learned

At first, I did not have confidence in my physical ability to write all these books, to express all my ideas in the manner my inspired creativity was prompting me. I was concerned, because, despite the marked healing of my creativity and inspiration to write, I still continued to suffer from the post-TBI physical challenges of Chronic Fatigue Syndrome, Fibromyalgia, and other health issues. I recall one day after writing many, many pages of inspired ideas that clearly would need to be written into several different books, I turned inwardly to God in prayer, and asked, *Lord, you do know that I have a physical disability, don't you?* I felt unsure that my physical stamina and energy would be sufficient to write these books.

The inner response to my query came through loudly in my intuition, *Pass on what you have learned!* Indeed, my long-term memory and spiritual insights about STEs had not been lost due to the TBI. Additionally, my spiritual understanding had deepened during the twelve years of intense spiritual striving. But the doubt nagged me: did I have the stamina to write these books?

The day after I surrendered my doubts to Spirit in prayer, it seemed to me that the Higher Power gave me a response to address my stamina concern, through a true story that I heard. This story showed me what I recognized to be the right attitude that I should have about the large new task Spirit had placed in front of me.

I refer to a true story I heard about SRF's past president, Sri Daya Mata. It concerned an incident that occurred to her when she was a young disciple of Paramahansa Yogananda. He had given her the assignment to complete a task that young Daya Mata thought was far beyond her capability. It was to organize the very first Self-Realization Fellowship world convocation.

It is reported that young Daya Mata first balked at the huge assignment, telling Yogananda that she was simply not able to complete this task. Allegedly, soon afterwards, Daya Mata regretted that she had refused Yogananda's request, and humbly returned to his study to inform him that although she felt the task was beyond her capabilities, she would do her best to complete it. It is reported that Yogananda then smiled at her and told her [approximately] "All you ever have to do is your best in serving God. Leave the rest up to God."

This story and Yogananda's teaching comment, "Do your best … [and] leave the rest up to God," inspired me. I cast aside my doubts due to my own continuing health challenges, and I focused on doing the best I could in my effort to complete the task ahead of me, to pass on what I have learned. I became determined that I would do my best to write these books that Spirit within me was inspiring me to write.

Writing Books Again

After I returned home to Toronto, the writing inspiration continued strongly throughout 2016, through 2017, and has continued on and off to this day. I felt like my knowledge, experience, and intuitive wisdom had finally been set free after being imprisoned and locked in my brain and consciousness during the twelve years of post-TBI disability.

My insight and intelligence were intact after the TBI, but the physical injuries to my brain and the severe post-TBI fatigue had made me incapable of expressing my insights in written form. Suddenly, on February 24, 2016, my brain was healed. My inspired creativity had reawakened that glorious day, and inspiration was flowing through me like a fast-moving river.

Not only that, but my mental stamina also dramatically improved, and it has continued to improve gradually over the next years. I began to write prolifically. I wrote the complete first draft of two books, *Touched by the Light* and this book, *Soul Lessons from the Light*, in 2016, in the first year following the miraculous brain healing.

I felt tremendous joy as I wrote, a joy to be able to serve and help others again, through the printed medium of my books. I had missed being able to serve and help others after the disability began in 2003. I previously greatly enjoyed being of service to others through my medical practice counseling of STE patients, my many media, public, and professional presentations, through my volunteer work, and through my books.

After the healing, I felt great joy that I was able to serve others and serve God in some small way again, through my writing of books. I was delighted that I was once again able to share my thoughts and creativity with others. But, I wondered whether my other disabilities had also healed in 2016. To my delight, I soon learned that, yes, they had.

Public Speaking Again

With time, it became clear that my ability to speak publicly had also been healed simultaneously with the writing recovery. I knew that after I wrote the first draft of my new books, I would have to promote them in some way. In August 2017, an invitation came to me to speak, at the International Association for Near-Death Studies annual conference in Denver, Colorado.

It was there, that I made my first post-TBI major presentation, about my multiple NDEs. I was quite nervous before my talk, unsure if my ability to public speak had been given back to me or not. I was delighted when, at the end of my talk, I received a standing ovation. It was then clear to me that my ability to give talks and presentations was also healed. Since then, I have resumed public speaking regularly and giving many media interviews.

I feel great relief that my insights and intelligence are no longer locked inside my head. I feel humbled and in awe of this miracle in my life, that, after twelve years of being physically incapable, somehow God, through his miracle of neuroplasticity, has healed my brain's writing and public speaking abilities. Beyond this, my inspired creativity has reawakened too, and inspiration flows through my consciousness almost daily. For this, I am deeply grateful.

I am sharing the story of this profound healing miracle with humility and gratitude, in the hope that perhaps some aspect of my story might be helpful to others. Medical science used to say that neurological healing after a traumatic brain injury stopped after about two years. My miracle healing proves that this is not correct. Neuroplasticity of the brain is real. Healing can and does sometimes occur, even as many as twelve years after a traumatic brain injury. And further, with God, all things are possible. Miracles and healings do occur!

Possible Factors Contributing to my Miracle Healing after 12 Years

I often wonder what factors may have contributed to my sudden brain healing after twelve years of disability. I think my regular daily meditation practice and my commitment to lengthening my meditations helped stimulate my brain's neuroplasticity to continue to heal my brain. Some recent medical research into the effects of meditation on the brain suggests that meditation does indeed stimulate brain neuroplasticity, encouraging the growth of new brain cells to bypass damaged brain cells. Pioneering psychiatrist and brain researcher Dr. Norman Doidge has now documented several other cases of extraordinary neurological healing through the poorly understood phenomenon of neuroplasticity of the human brain.

Additionally, I wonder what role the kundalini mechanism may have played in my brain's spontaneous healing twelve years post-TBI. According to yogic theory, when the kundalini mechanism is awakened, it causes a reversal of the outward direction of flow of "prana"/life energy, to an inward flow up the astral spine and physical spine to the brain, combined with an inward upward flow of "ojas"/sublimated sexual energy. This inward and upward flowing prana and ojas nourishes the brain and enables the spiritual transformation of consciousness and STEs.

I think this kundalini mechanism has continued to be active in me to some degree since 1976. Subsequently, repeatedly over the years, I have had many signs of ongoing kundalini activity, including repeated rushes of energy moving up my spine, luminosity and inner light sensations, inner astral sounds, and inner sensations of the chakras. Having been blessed with three NDEs and multiple mystical experiences in my adult lifetime, I felt them each associated with an increase in kundalini-type physical symptoms.

Initially after the TBI in 2003, my kundalini symptoms seemed to be decreased significantly for some years. It felt to me intuitively that all my prana/life energy was needed outwardly for my body and brain's difficult physical healing processes. However, gradually over the twelve years after the TBI, my kundalini symptom of energy rushes up the spine started occurring again, especially as I started doing longer and longer meditations regularly. In the year immediately preceding my spontaneous brain healing in 2016, the rushes of energy up my spine started occurring much more frequently.

On February 24, 2016, the day that my spontaneous brain healing occurred, I had many distinct experiences of rushes of kundalini energy moving up my spine. From that day forward, I have continued to feel recurrent rushes of energy moving up my spine, often coinciding with my realization of a deep spiritual insight which I feel prompted to share in one of the books I am writing.

The kundalini mechanism is still poorly understood by Western medical science. Most Western doctors and scientists either do not know about kundalini or are not convinced that it is a real biological-psychological-spiritual mechanism that can sometimes activate in a human body. Regardless of this Western lack of awareness, as I detail in my book, *Touched by the Light,* I and many highly respected individuals from around the world, including Gopi Krishna, Paramahansa Yogananda, Dr. Carl Jung, Dr. Lee Sannella, Dr. Bonnie Greenwell, Dr. Ken Ring, and Dr. Bruce Greyson, have researched and written about the existence of this spiritual energy phenomenon.

In my heart and soul, I believe that many factors may have contributed to my spontaneous healing: the grace of God; the blessings of my saintly gurus; the healing attributes of an active kundalini mechanism; and my daily meditation practice with gradually increasing frequency of long meditations.

My personal healing efforts probably also contributed to my body's capacity to heal. They included: careful attention to a nutritious diet; avoidance of food sensitivities; nutritional supplements; detoxification; avoidance of pesticides and other chemical exposures; adequate rest; and regular physical exercise. Only the Divine knows for sure which combination of factors contributed to the sudden healing and subsequent writing inspired creativity. But no matter what the exact healing factors were, I am deeply grateful for this healing.

Prompted to Write Books

I intuitively feel Spirit prompting me to write several books. The first two I felt prompted to write, *Touched by the Light,* and this book, *Soul Lessons from the Light,* are now complete. I know it will take me several years of continued hard work to write the other books that Spirit is prompting me to produce, sharing my insights and life experiences.

Writing continues to be challenging for me because my post-TBI Chronic Fatigue Syndrome was only partially healed in 2016. It has been healing slowly but surely, but I still do have to pace myself and rest regularly, to not risk slipping back into full-blown Chronic Fatigue Syndrome. Unfortunately, recent episodes of covid-19 have temporarily aggravated my fatigue. However, although I may sometimes only have the stamina to write for half a day, I choose to celebrate my cup half-full, rather than focus on the half-empty side. Each half-day of writing is another half-day closer to completing my next book.

I also feel a certain urgency about my book writing. I remember how my beautiful experiences of ongoing mystical communion in 1995 and 2003 were both temporary. Those beatific states of consciousness only lasted for a period of time, two months in 1993, and three hours in 2003, then they went away. This makes me wonder if perhaps my new gift of restored inspired creativity and ability to write might also possibly go away in the future. I am therefore striving to record as many of the ideas and inspiration that are flowing through my consciousness, as quickly as I possibly can.

Having been blessed with five Near-Death Experiences, I am well aware that ultimately God is the source of everything in the Universe. I remind myself that ultimately God is the only doer in my body. Therefore, if, for whatever small reason in the great cosmic drama, the Divine Higher Power wishes me to write more books to share what I have learned, then surely the Divine Higher Power will continue to give me the energy and inspiration to do so. In that I trust. I surrender to God's will. *God's will be done.* I will do my part, and make my best effort to complete my Divinely prompted writing assignment.

My Soul Lesson – There is Always Hope for a Better Tomorrow

As I reflect on the key soul lesson that I learned from my fifth NDE in 2003, on my intense and challenging healing journey afterward, and on my brain healing in 2016, I realize I learned that, with God, there is always hope for a better tomorrow.

I understood to the core of my soul, while I was in the realm of Divine Light, that every facet of life and creation is all a part of the Divine's omnipresent plan. I had the revelation that the Divine plan is perfect in all ways and profoundly loving. This revelation gave me great inner peace and equipoise as I struggled with adjusting to life as a disabled person post-TBI. I trusted that God's plan for my life was perfect, even if I could not understand the wisdom or higher purpose behind my struggles.

I also had the revelation in the Light, the clear understanding, that the Higher Power, what I call God, in its infinite love and omnipotent power, can change anything in the Divine plan. My soul knew that there was always hope for healing of the post-TBI symptoms, despite my bleak medical prognosis. My heart and soul refused to give up hope, that through the grace of God, some healing might still occur.

My miraculous spontaneous brain healing, coupled with the reawakening of my writing inspired creativity, healing of my ability to write books, and regaining of my public speaking ability, are physical demonstrations of the truth of my soul lesson: there is always hope. There is always hope for a better and brighter tomorrow. Miracles do happen. With God, all things are possible. I am a living testimonial to that truth.

Chapter 18

FOUNDING
SPIRITUAL AWAKENINGS INTERNATIONAL

After *Touched by the Light,* the first book I wrote after my brain-healing, was published in 2019, I was invited to do many media interviews, podcasts, and presentations, including on the *Dr. Oz Show* twice, and on the *Coast to Coast* radio show. I was delighted to realize that my abilities for public speaking and to do media interviews had also healed in 2016. Through these experiences, it gradually became clear to me that Spirit was also helping me regain my self-confidence in my healed ability to assume leadership positions again.

Joining a Board of Directors

In 2018, I was invited to join the Board of Directors of IANDS, the International Association for Near-Death Studies. At first, I hesitated. I had served on many volunteer Boards and University committees before my head injury, and I knew how much time and energy they could take. Further, I was very protective of my time to focus on the mission I had been given by Spirit after my brain healing *Pass on what you have learned.* However, despite my concerns, my inner intuitive guidance was to accept the invitation. I, therefore, joined the Board of Directors of IANDS in September 2018.

In the summer of 2019, I was asked by several Board members to accept the nomination to be elected President of the IANDS Board of Directors.

I was cautious, because I wanted to focus on doing what Spirit was guiding me to do. *Thy Will be done,* I prayed. *Guide me clearly, what you would have me do.* I put the decision in God's hands and waited to receive clear guidance.

Spirit later intuitively prompted me, *Accept the nomination to become IANDS President.* I then followed that guidance and accepted the nomination.

By this time, another new Board member, a businessman, Robert Bare, had been nominated to become IANDS Vice-President.

Following Higher Guidance

My intuitive Higher Guidance was strong and clear once again, guiding me to contact Robert Bare to discuss the possibility of running as a slate for IANDS President and Vice-President. I, therefore, phoned Robert to get to know him, and to learn whether our values and perspectives were compatible.

We immediately connected. We discovered we had very much in common. We were both multiple STE experiencers and multiple NDE experiencers. We were both highly intuitive as a result.

During our first long conversation in the summer of 2019, Robert told me he received an intuitive download, strong Higher Guidance, telling him that he and I were destined to do something else together outside of IANDS. His guidance was that we were being called by Spirit to found a new organization together, an international organization with a much broader focus than IANDS.

I reflected on his guidance, and responded that I would have to meditate and pray about his idea. When I went into meditation following our conversation, to my amazement and surprise, I, too, received a strong download of Higher Guidance. I was guided, *Yes, you and Robert should start a new organization, and call it "Spiritual Awakenings International".*

I was also given a vision of the Spiritual Awakenings International (SAI) mission: to focus on the whole spectrum of Spiritually Transformative

Experiences, including NDEs, which I had always focused upon in my professional career. SAI would focus on raising awareness globally about the many diverse types of STEs, provide a safe harbor for STE experiencers to share and learn, and promote networking between STE experiencers and support groups around the world.

I told Robert that my inner guidance confirmed his, and that it had also given me the name for the new organization, *Spiritual Awakenings International.*

At first, I was quite surprised that Spirit was guiding us to start this new organization together, because I hardly knew Robert. However, it also made logical sense. My medical career had always focused on the whole spectrum of Spiritually Transformative Experiences, not just exclusively the Near-Death Experience. I also had a great deal of professional leadership experience before my head injury, serving on Boards of Directors, and Chairing Boards and senior medical committees. Additionally, I had much administrative experience, organizing speaker events, and organizing and running conferences. I had the professional and administrative skills to lead a new non-profit organization focused on STEs.

Robert had other skills that would be needed. In addition to being a retired police officer, he had earned a Master's degree in Public Administration, and a PhD. By 2019, he was an in-demand business consultant, who had years of experience working with non-profit corporations in the USA and internationally. He knew all the corporate and business steps that would be necessary to successfully set up a new non-profit corporation in the USA. Together, we had the combined skills necessary to plan and then launch Spiritual Awakenings International on a solid business footing and anchored in solid STE research and experience.

Robert and I quickly realized how our two skill sets and respective professional experience complimented each other, and that we could work as a team, both as President and Vie-President of IANDS, and, in the future, in founding Spiritual Awakenings International.

In early December 2019, I was elected President of IANDS, and Robert was elected Vice-President. We worked efficiently as a complementary team. We did our best to support and guide IANDS during our terms in executive office. However, we both knew Spirit was calling us, at some point in the future, to found another organization.

Higher Guidance sets SAI's Timetable

By March 2020, Robert and I both knew we would be stepping away from the IANDS Board soon, in order to start Spiritual Awakenings International together. On March 27, 2020, on the anniversary of my 1979 medevac plane crash NDE, an auspicious day for me, the date that I annually call my *re-birthday*, I received strong inner guidance: *Today you resign as IANDS President*. I informed Robert. We both resigned from the IANDS Board that day, with friendly letters of resignation.

Robert immediately began taking the first business steps to register Spiritual Awakenings International as a new non-profit business in the State of Oregon where he lived. Together, we developed a business plan for the birth and eventual launch of SAI. We found two colleagues willing to serve on our founding Board of Directors. Carefully following legal advice, we established our SAI Bylaws. The new Board of Directors elected me President, and Robert Vice-President.

Together, we went through the required steps to prepare to launch the organization. One of our first business tasks was to develop a website. We found a website developer that my intuition said *Yes* to, and I started working long hours writing the content, developing the design, and selecting images for the website.

Every stage and decision was guided by Spirit. I always prayed and meditated, asking for Higher Guidance, before I made decisions. I developed all the content for the website, much of it based on my 40 years of STE research and personal experience, and material from my newly released book *Touched by the Light*.

Spiritual Awakenings International® Launches June 15, 2020

Suddenly, in early June 2020, I received another strong STE, a download of Higher Guidance: *Launch Spiritual Awakenings International on June 15, 2020*. That gave me only 2 weeks to finish writing the website content. I worked long hours, frantically, to complete writing the content by the deadline Spirit had given me. But with God's help, I did it, assisted with hard work by our website developer.

We defined SAI's mission as: "To spread awareness globally of Spiritually Transformative Experiences. Spiritual Awakenings International® (SAI) is a non-profit worldwide network of individuals and groups who are interested in collaborating to raise awareness, network, and share personal experiences relating to diverse types of Spiritually Transformative Experiences, "STEs," to raise global spiritual awareness."

Spiritual Awakenings International® Grows Rapidly

Spiritual Awakenings International® has blossomed and grown exponentially since we launched in June 2020. In the first year, we gained close to 2,000 subscribers from 58 countries around the world. This showed me that there clearly was a need for such an organization. SAI turned two years old in June 2022. SAI had grown to close to 3,000 subscribers from 75 countries around the world, from every continent except Antarctica.

The organization now hosts monthly online English language featured speaker events, monthly *SAI Experiencers Sharing Circles*, and an annual online conference. In the first year, Spiritual Awakenings International also launched its own YouTube Channel, so that people all over the world can view the videos of all our speaker events.

In 2021, SAI expanded, and added a Spanish language program, with monthly events in the Spanish language, featured speaker events and Spanish *Experiencers Sharing Circles*. The SAI website was also translated into Spanish. We plan to translate the website into more languages in the future, and to host events in other languages too, to reach out to more and more of the world community, raising awareness about STEs and our true spiritual nature.

Passing on What I Have Learned Through Spiritual Awakenings International®

I am delighted that Spiritual Awakenings International® has become a new online forum where people can pass on and share what they have learned about Spiritually Transformative Experiences. Our monthly speaker events, annual conferences, and Experiencers Sharing Circles are a forum that can reach people all over the world. The SAI website shares a summary of my classification and descriptions of types of STEs. The Spiritual Awakenings International YouTube Channel shares videos both of my presentations, and of all other SAI speakers on STEs.

I feel grateful and blessed that the miraculous brain healing of 2016, not only healed my ability to write books, and give presentations, but it also restored my ability to be a leader and administrator, to serve as Co-Founder and President of Spiritual Awakenings International.

www.spiritualawakeningsinternational.org.

Chapter 19

PURIFYING THE HEART: STAGES ON THE SPIRITUAL PATH

Reflecting on the after-effects of my life's multiple Spiritually Transformative Experiences, I realize that major psychological and spiritual shifts happened in my personal and spiritual goals after many of them. As I reflect, I can now see that each of my three adult mystical NDEs propelled me onto new life-stages.

It is clear to me that my 1979 plane crash Near-Death Experience launched me into a new life-stage. That NDE, combined with the kundalini awakening I had in 1976, propelled me to begin a quest to learn about mystical experiences, NDEs, kundalini awakening, and other Spiritually Transformative Experiences. For almost twelve years after this NDE, I privately searched for a deeper understanding of my experiences through my research, reading books from many sources, and learning from teachers of diverse spiritual traditions.

After I had my calling mystical experience in 1990, I was once again launched into a new life-stage. Although I continued with my research into STEs, I now felt strongly called to be of service to others. I felt called to share what I had learned about STEs, to advocate for STE experiencers, and to strive to help others who were experiencing them. I began to share the story of my 1979 NDE publicly, and I openly specialized my medical practice in counseling STE experiencers.

I then networked with other professionals and colleagues from around the world who were also seeking to learn about kundalini awakening, NDEs, and other STEs. As part of my efforts to help other STE experiencers, in 1994 I published my first book on STEs, *A Farther Shore.*

Then, following my 1995 NDE and the two-month long period of communion afterward, I was propelled into yet another new life-stage. I was launched into a stage where I felt a deep desire to strive for spiritual deepening, through surrender to the Divine will, and purification of my character.

With the ecstatic memory of ongoing communion emblazoned into my consciousness, I intensely yearned to once again experience that unitive state. I became a much more zealous spiritual aspirant, deeply committed to my yogic path with regular daily meditation, and intentional purification of character – self-development. Surrendering to Divine will and letting go, detaching from ego desires, became central to my psychological and spiritual work. My inner prayers became ones of surrender to Divine will, *Make me your purified instrument*, and, *Thy will be done.*

Although I continued to learn more about STEs and to serve others through my professional work and volunteer work as I did before this NDE, in my private time my focus shifted much more deeply inwardly, into my personal spiritual practice and self-purification of character, and learning to let go of ego attachments.

My 2003 head injury NDE propelled me onto yet another life-stage. I was forced by the traumatic brain injury symptoms to rapidly detach, and let go of my past worldly activities and desires. My spiritual focus after this became my intense inner desire for deepening communion during my meditations. My inner life in meditation became the backbone of my post-TBI life. My deep personal relationship with my Higher Power, God, and my daily practice of prayer and meditation practice were the most important things in my life during this life-stage.

Purifying the Heart: Stages on the Spiritual Path

As I reflect on the successive spiritual life-stages that I went through over the course of my life, propelled forward by my NDEs and peak STEs, I see that the stages correspond with the spiritual life-stages described by

Swami Sri Yukteswar, the guru of Paramahansa Yogananda, in his book *The Holy Science*. He described a model for the progressive stages that a spiritual aspirant of any faith tradition will go through on their journey to self-realization/god-communion.

Sri Yukteswar called these stages and the spiritual transformation process underlying them, *Purification of the Heart*. I have found this model of the universal stages on the spiritual path to be both beautiful, and extremely helpful. It has helped me understand the shifts in spiritual and psychological focus that occurred in me after my successive NDEs and STEs, and in the past, it also helped me to counsel STE patients.

My interpretation of the progressive spiritual life-stages according to Swami Sri Yukteswar are as follows.

1. The Dark Heart Stage

The stage that all persons are on before they have a spiritual awakening, is called the "dark heart" stage. Sri Yukteswar describes a person in the dark heart life-stage as thinking that the gross physical portion of creation is the only reality and that nothing else exists beyond this. This stage is marked by materialism, self-centeredness (at its extreme, cruelty), lack of self-reflection, and blind following of dogmas. Persons in the dark heart stage have no real awareness of and no personal experiences of spiritual states of consciousness.

2. The Propelled Heart Stage

After a spiritual awakening, a spiritual seeker enters the second spiritual life-stage, that Sri Yukteswar called the "propelled heart" stage. A spiritual awakening may occur due to an NDE, another type of STE, or sometimes a powerful life experience. This stage is marked by spiritual seeking and spiritual searching.

During it, a seeker may study and learn from many different sources, including diverse spiritual teachers and different faith traditions. They will question what they have been told to believe and will seek deeper understanding. They will begin their personal healing and recovery work, begin to move out of denial, and take personal responsibility for their actions and choices in their life.

They begin to develop deepening respect for others, and a sense of mutual love, now discovering how much they can learn from others. They will tend to associate with other spiritual seekers. This is a very long stage, and some individuals may remain in the propelled heart stage for most of their life, or for several lifetimes.

As I reflect on my life, I can now see clearly that I was launched onto the propelled heart life-stage after my 1979 plane crash NDE. I became a spiritual seeker. That NDE propelled me to begin a quest to learn about them and other STEs. For years after my 1979 NDE, I searched for a deeper understanding of my experience through reading books from many sources and by learning from teachers of diverse spiritual traditions.

3. The Steady Heart Stage

According to Sri Yukteswar, the "steady heart" is the next spiritual life-stage in purifying the heart. This stage is marked by expanding humanitarian love, a deep desire to be of service to others, and commitment to your selected spiritual path. Aspirants now have expanded in their sense of love and respect for others throughout the propelled heart stage. They show a deepened humility and they have increasingly realized their errors and shortcomings, and repented.

These aspirants have developed mutual respect and multi-faith tolerance for others. Their heart has expanded to the point of feeling all of humanity as their greater family. As a result, a desire to be of service to others becomes very strong.

In addition, a spiritual aspirant at this-stage has reached a personal conclusion from their wide spiritual searching in the previous stage. They have now determined within themselves which spiritual path resonates with their heart and soul.

Having found their heartfelt spiritual path, the spiritual aspirant now stops searching for new teachers and teachings, and instead shifts his/her focus to deeply embracing the teachings and practices of their heartfelt spiritual tradition and lineage. The aspirant chooses to drink deeply from their chosen spiritual well, rather than sampling lightly from many different wells, as they did previously.

As I reflect, I now see that my calling mystical experience in 1990 propelled me onto the steady heart spiritual stage of my life. After my profound calling mystical experience, I felt intensely drawn to serving others, by sharing what I had learned throughout my spiritual searching and research of the previous twelve years. I felt powerfully drawn to help other STE experiencers, to advocate for experiencers, even at the risk of harm coming to me through criticism, censure, and misunderstandings from the medical professional and medical governing bodies.

I felt strong respect for the followers of diverse faiths, and from diverse cultures, whom I perceived as my spiritual brothers and sisters under our one cosmic parent, God. This call to service, my desire to serve others, was incredibly strong. From 1990 onwards, my professional life became primarily focused on helping patients with STEs from a multifaith perspective, volunteering to serve on boards for groups supporting STE experiencers, and educating the public and medical profession about the reality of STEs.

By 1990, when I shifted onto the steady heart spiritual stage, I had also become certain of my personal spiritual path. I knew I was a yogi. Although I had learned from the teachings of many spiritual traditions over the previous twelve years, by 1990 I was certain of and deeply committed to my spiritual path of yoga and meditation. From the time of my 1990 calling mystical experience onwards, I was clearly at the steady heart spiritual life-stage.

4. The Devoted Heart Stage

According to Swami Sri Yukteswar, if purification of the heart continues to deepen in a spiritual aspirant, through continued spiritual and psychological efforts, the aspirant will eventually move into the "devoted heart" life-stage. This stage is marked by an increasing interior focus on the Divine, deep surrender to the Divine will, deep embracing of self-purification, self-improvement, personal healing and recovery work, and, deepening love for the Divine.

Yvonne Kason, M.D.

The aspirant willingly detaches from personal ego desires and worldly ambitions, and surrenders to Divine will in all things, desiring to become a more and more purified instrument of Divine will on the planet. Now, through experience the aspirant has learned the superior joy and peace found in following the wisdom of Divine guidance and Divine will, and the bitter consequences of succumbing to the whims of ego desires and unhealthy habits.

In this stage, the aspirant has already had several mystical experiences, STEs, and/or periods of ongoing unitive communion. Having repeatedly tasted of the exquisitely beautiful nature of the inner spiritual realm, unitive mystical consciousness, the heart of the aspirant can now gradually abandon the notion of finding true soul happiness in the outer world. Instead, there is an increasing yearning to find its true soul satisfaction in the inner spiritual realm, in the direct experience of Divine communion.

As I reflect on the after-effects of my 1995 NDE and communion experience, I see that they definitely propelled me onto the devoted heart life-stage. I realized, after my unitive communion, that my true soul happiness could only be found inwardly, when I was in a state of ongoing Divine communion.

Having experienced communion for two months, I yearned deeply afterward to experience that blessed state again. My personal reverence and love for God, and trust in the wisdom of the Divine plan, deepened tremendously. In my deep meditations, I willingly and consciously strived to detach from my worldly thoughts and ego desires.

I knew in my soul, through the 1995 experience, that God's infinite wisdom and God's plan were perfect. I therefore eagerly and willingly surrendered myself to God's will, and God's inner purification process. I deeply embraced my personal healing and recovery work, in my desire to be molded into God's purified instrument.

I intensely desired to surrender to God's will for me in all things in life. In my service to others, I yearned to be God's instrument. *Thy Will be done*, became my affirmation. I now see that these psychological and spiritual shifts that occurred within me after my 1995 NDE are typical of the shift onto the devoted heart life-stage.

5. The Clean Heart Stage

According to Swami Sri Yukteswar, the final spiritual life-stage is the "clean heart" stage. The focus of spiritual attention at this stage, in addition to continuing the tasks of the earlier stages of spiritual commitment, service to others, surrender of ego attachments, and surrender to Divine will, becomes very much the inner life, efforts to deepen in communion with the Divine source.

As a spiritual aspirant continues to progress in their interior life of meditation and purification of character, "journeying Godward," the aspirant's heart and psyche become increasingly purified and clearer. They develop deeper and greater inner realization. At the clean heart stage, through long and deep meditations, the heart and psyche of a spiritual aspirant becomes more and more purified into a clean clear state, devoid of external attachments. They thus become capable of perceiving, comprehending, and sustaining, expansive Divine communion states of consciousness. At the clean heart life-stage, the spiritual aspirant has had repeated mystical experiences and/or periods of ongoing mystical communion.

The Swami also states that at the clean heart life-stage, the spiritual aspirant completely surrenders ego desires, and the ego self, to the Holy Spirit, to the Divine. They have a deeper realization of the immanence of the Divine, of God's omnipresence permeating them, and all of Creation. The mystic experiences/realizes that nothing exists separate from the Divine Source, there is no separation from the Divine Source.

The advancing spiritual aspirant has the lived experience of non-duality. They increasingly feel dissolved in communion or oneness with the universal source, God. Ultimately, the advanced clean heart stage aspirant shifts into a state of ongoing mystical communion. They begin to reflect and also manifest Divine light, Divine love, and Divine wisdom.

As I reflect on my spiritual focus after my 2003 head injury Near-Death Experience, I think I began to shift into the early stages of the clean heart life-stage. My primary spiritual focus was on my inner life. My intense desire now was for spiritual deepening. I deeply yearned to re-experience mystical communion, which I had once again glimpsed prior to the accident.

I, therefore, struggled intensely for many years after the TBI to regain my ability to meditate deeply. Once my ability to meditate was restored, my focus became to continually go deeper and deeper in my meditation practice, seeking more expansive communion through regular and long meditations.

Although my primary spiritual focus now was my interior life and my daily efforts for deepening communion, I still had to continuously pay attention to the purification of my character, and my detachment from emotionality, thoughts, and desires during my meditations, just as I needed to during the previous stage. However, by 2003, my inner attention to self-purification and emotional detachment from ego desires had already become a strong habit within me, so the focus of my attention became much more on my efforts for spiritual deepening.

As I understand the spiritual life-stages of purifying the heart, when a spiritual aspirant moves forward over time from one life-stage to the next, they must still continue to use the spiritual attributes and psychological skills that they developed in earlier stages. It seems to me to be an additive process, just like skills that we learn in school.

Skills learned in grade one in school, like basic addition and subtraction, must still be used in grades six, seven, and eight. However, by the time a student reaches the higher grades, the basic addition and subtraction skills learned in grade one have become almost automatic. Although these more basic skills must still be used in higher grades, the focus of learning is on more advanced skills in the higher grades.

I think a similar cumulative learning process occurs across the several spiritual life-stages in the purifying the heart model. Thus, the spiritual and psychological skills learned earlier, must continue to be used by one who is focusing on deepening communion.

Anyone Can Slip at Any Stage

I think it important that I share a word of warning here. Anyone, at any stage of the Purifying the Heart spiritual life-stages, may slip in certain circumstances, make an error, and fall back to a lower stage. This is comparable to how even an esteemed university professor may occasionally make a mistake in simple arithmetic.

I can attest to experiencing such psycho-spiritual slips, and I have observed them occur to other very dedicated spiritual seekers. I think we must always remain humble, and realize that we are all imperfect, no matter what stage of life we are in, and that we can all sometimes make mistakes.

What I have learned over my career as a medical doctor and psychotherapist, plus during my many years as a devoted spiritual seeker, is that we must continuously self-reflect with honesty and humility, and admit when we have made an error or slip. It is all too easy to slip into excess emotional reactivity or be caught in ego desires when we are surrounded daily by very tumultuous worldly events.

When we realize a slip or error has occurred, I have found the best recourse is to pray for help and guidance, then to meditate deeply until peace of mind is restored. Intense meditation will re-center the self in Spirit and bring back emotional equipoise and clarity of thought. In the clarity of mental equipoise, the manner to deal with or make amends for one's error will usually become clearer.

Sometimes this might involve seeking professional counseling or spiritual guidance. Other times, a sincere apology, efforts to improve one's attitude and behavior, spending more time in meditation, going on a meditation retreat, and/or efforts to make amends to others, might be required.

I have found Swami Sri Yuktewar's model of the Purifying the Heart spiritual life-stages extremely helpful. This model has helped me understand the major shifts and changes in spiritual focus that happened to me during my life's spiritual journey. I also found this model most helpful for counseling and advising my STE patients in my medical practice, to help them understand the changing spiritual yearnings they experienced over the years, in the aftermath of their STEs.

As I reflect, it appears that each of the NDEs that I experienced as an adult propelled me forward onto my next spiritual life-stage. This demonstrates to me the powerful spiritually transformative impact that all these experiences have had upon my life.

Chapter 20

SPIRITUALLY TRANSFORMATIVE EXPERIENCES: "IN MY FATHER'S HOUSE ARE MANY MANSIONS"

JESUS CHRIST. JOHN 14:2

My five Near-Death Experiences and multiple other Spiritually Transformative Experiences have been extraordinary and blessed gifts in my life. The stories of my NDEs and other STEs that I shared in this book may seem unusual to some people, but to me these experiences are precious. Each of my mystical experiences and adult NDEs was beautiful and had many positive after-effects. They uplifted me, and changed me in positive ways. My childhood out-of-body NDEs also expanded my awareness of our true spiritual nature, at a very young age.

However, they also created new life challenges for me. As I have shared, as an adult I had to struggle with balancing the responsibilities of my studies and later my career as a medical doctor and responsibilities as a mother, with having intense STEs that were generally poorly understood, and at times outright misunderstood. I had to deal with others telling me that my NDEs and other STEs were hallucinations, flights of my imagination, grandiose fantasies, or dismissed as nothing of value.

However, I knew in my heart and soul that my NDEs and mystical experiences were sacred, peak events, which changed the course of my life.

I saw how STEs transformed other experiencers too. I, therefore, persisted on my life path of raising awareness about STEs, as called by Spirit.

I was amazed and grateful at how well my books about STEs were received by readers around the world. Many hundreds of people wrote me letters, expressing how grateful they were, stating that my clear definitions of types of STEs, and my description of the yogic model of conscious and kundalini awakening, had helped them and their loved ones come to a deeper understanding of their powerful STEs and the after-effects they experienced. The huge number of letters of gratitude I received touched my heart deeply.

My wish in this book is to inform and inspire readers by sharing my personal spiritual awakening story, the true stories of my five Near-Death Experiences, kundalini awakening, and multiple mystical experiences. My deepest hope is that reading my personal STE stories will make readers feel greater love, reverence, and emotional closeness towards our profoundly loving Divine creator.

I also hope that some of the Higher Power's profound unconditional love that permeated my soul during my NDEs and mystical experiences, somehow rubs off on readers, and uplifts them.

Further, I hope other people having STEs will feel supported and normalized, to know they are not alone. I, and many other people alive today, are having multiple Spiritually Transformative Experiences.

Every Near-Death Experience is Unique

Each Near-Death Experience I had was unique. By looking at the NDE features first defined by Dr. Raymond Moody, each of my NDEs had multiple classic features. Although each was similar to the others in some ways, each also differed from the others in many ways.

Many Near-Death Experience researchers have noted that each person's NDE is unique. My own five Near-Death Experiences suggest that in persons who have multiple NDEs throughout their lifetime, each is still unique, one from the other. The multiple NDE experiencer will be an interesting area for future research.

As I look back on how varied my five NDEs were one from another, I wonder why this was so. Perhaps they varied according to my state of personal and spiritual growth at the time. For example, in my 1995 near-miss plane incident NDE, I had a life-review that included re-experiencing three peak STEs that I had earlier in my life. I could not possibly have had a life-review including these three STEs until I had lived long enough to have those experiences.

Additionally, in my 1995 NDE, when I was facing what I thought was certain imminent death, I chose to die consciously, by letting go of my earthly life and going deep into meditation, in search of the white light realm. I did not learn about the concept of conscious dying until many years after my 1979 plane crash NDE. Thus, my spiritual understanding and meditation experience in 1995 were factors that seemed to have contributed, to some degree, to the nature of the 1995 NDE.

I also think my 2003 head injury NDE may also have been influenced by my spiritual understanding at that time. During my 2003 NDE, I was greeted by two beings of light whom I immediately recognized, Paramahansa Yogananda and Mahavatar Babaji, two great saints and gurus of my spiritual path, Self-Realization Fellowship (SRF). I joined the SRF church in 2000.

I am unsure whether or not I would have been greeted by these two saintly gurus if I had died completely during an NDE earlier in my life, before I had found my way to my spiritual path, SRF. Perhaps I would have still seen these saints, or perhaps I would not have. There is no way for me to know this for certain.

Even if my deepening spiritual understanding over the years did influence in a small way the specifics of what I experienced in some of my more recent NDEs, I do not think that it was the main cause for my multiple Near-Death Experiences. I know many people who are long-time devoted meditators with deep spiritual understanding, who have never experienced an NDE, even when they had close brushes with death. Why some people have NDEs when they are close to death or facing death, and others do not, also remains a mystery.

Further, it is now well documented that individuals from all faith traditions, or of no faith tradition, and having all levels of spiritual awareness from low to high, including atheists and agnostics, have experienced a highly spiritual NDE. In my earlier books, *Farther Shores* and *Touched by the Light*, I shared examples of individuals who were atheists, like Howard Storm, or who had highly unspiritual backgrounds, like Dannion Brinkley. Both had dramatic spiritual conversions after their NDEs, and felt propelled afterward to become strong vocal proclaimers of the reality of the universally loving Higher Power. Having no deep spiritual understanding before a Near-Death Experience does not at all seem to be a limiting factor governing who will have a highly spiritually transforming NDE. It seems anyone can have a powerful NDE.

God Manifests to us in Countless Diverse Ways

I have another theory to account for the great diversity and uniqueness of these spiritual experiences. It relates to the immense vastness, multiple dimensions, and complexity of the Divine Higher Power behind the universe.

As I, and many others, have glimpsed in NDEs, the Divine Higher Power, God, our blessed Source, seems infinite in size, omniscient, omnipresent, and omnipotent. The infinite Source exudes profound unconditional love, which is truly beyond our comprehension.

Additionally, the Higher Power does not seem to be constrained by the linear perception of time, such that a blending of past, present, and future, is possible within the Divine realm of loving light. The unfathomable omnipresent vastness, infinite intelligence, and omnipotent complexity of the Divine Source are by their very nature incomprehensible to our limited human capacity to perceive.

I think our diverse and varied glimpses of the Divine Higher Source reported in many people's NDEs, reflect our limited human capacity to glimpse only one small aspect of the infinite diversity and multiple dimensions of the omnipresent Higher Power, like one small facet of a massive multifaceted diamond. A popular Indian fable depicts this quite well.

> *A group of blind schoolchildren was assigned the task to wash the body of a large elephant. Each child was led to one spot beside or below the elephant and instructed to wash the*

portion that was within their reach with the wet rag they were provided.

After the blind children were finished washing the elephant, their teacher called the students together and asked them to describe what an elephant looks like.

The first student answered, "An elephant looks like a tall tree in the forest because it has a thick, round trunk that reaches up to the sky." This child had been washing one of the legs of the elephant.

"No!" exclaimed another student. "The elephant looks like a huge plant and has very large flat leaves." This child had been washing a huge ear of the elephant.

"No!' exclaimed the next student. "The elephant looks like a rope vine, hanging from an unseen branch high on a tree." This student had been washing the rope-like tail of the elephant.

"You are all wrong" exclaimed another student. "The elephant looks like a rock-hard spear, jutting forward ready for battle." This student had been washing a tusk of the elephant.

"No, no, you are wrong" exclaimed yet another student. "The elephant looks like a soft coiling snake" This student had been washing the trunk of the elephant.

"Nonsense," said the last student, "The elephant looks like the ceiling of a cave. It is a hard solid roof over our heads." This student had been washing the underbelly of the elephant.

Laughing, the children's teacher responded to the children's confused and varied responses. "You are all correct," the teacher stated, "but you are also all wrong. Parts of the elephant are indeed like a tree trunk, like a large leaf, like a rope vine, like a spear, like a snake, and like a ceiling. But the whole elephant has all these attributes and many more attributes that you were not able to touch or feel. The truth is that the elephant is a combination of what you each felt, plus much more that you were simply not capable of perceiving."

This Indian fable capsulizes my thoughts as to why I think NDEs differ so much one from another. The infinite nature of the Divine Higher Power is so vast and multifaceted, that with our limited human perceptive capability we only glimpse small varied aspects during each of our NDEs or mystical experiences. The totality of our loving Creator's nature is far beyond our human capacity to perceive.

Further, because the one infinitely loving Higher Power is the cosmic parent to all persons of all races and religious traditions, the Divine may manifest itself to individuals in the manner that suits each individual perfectly for their current culture and state of consciousness. The Divine can be like a shape-shifter.

Some persons may glimpse the Higher Power in the form of a Divine Mother. Others may glimpse the Divine very differently, as such things as the Spirit underlying all of Nature, as a silent Force of Love throughout the cosmos, as our Heavenly Father, as a Spiritual Master such as Jesus, as an angel, or as the nameless undefinable universal Creator.

I think that the nature of the Divine Higher Power, God, is so vast, complex, multi-dimensional, and multifaceted, that like the limited perceptions of various aspects of the elephant, all the STE perceptions of the Divine may indeed be true glimpses, and at the same time, all these perceptions are incomplete.

Premonitions of NDEs – Past, Present, and Future Coexist

Looking back on my five Near-Death Experiences, I find it fascinating that I had premonitions before three of them, those I had during my adult life. I wonder how it is possible that some part of my being knew in advance that I was going to have these serious accidents and NDEs?

Prior to my plane crash experience, I had a premonition in the form of a strong and very unusual impulse to eat some cookies just before I went into the medevac airplane. It appears that when I got the strong inner impulse to eat some cookies, on some unconscious level, my soul knew in advance, that later that day I would be having an extremely intense physical ordeal, struggling for my survival.

Similarly, in the two hours immediately before the near-miss plane incident, I had several premonitions. I repeatedly had thoughts pop into my mind about my previous medevac plane crash and NDE. This was very uncharacteristic for me at the time.

Additionally, a few minutes before the incident, my eyes repeatedly misread the date on my newspaper to read March 27, the date of my 1979 plane crash. It took several minutes of blinking and staring at the date on my newspaper until mysteriously the print seemed to shift before my eyes until it finally read the correct date, which was February 27. It appears that some part of my mind knew that I was about to have another NDE that day, and my mind was giving me premonitions, hints to forewarn me.

Prior to the 2003 fall at Niagara Falls, I also had two premonitions that something major was going to happen to me. A few weeks before, I had the strong intuition that my scheduled presentation to the Spirituality in Health-Care Network, would be my last presentation. *This is my swan song,* repeatedly popped into my mind, for reasons at the time unknown to me. Now, I realize this was a strong premonition of the accident.

Again, on the day before the accident, I had another strong premonition. The thought, *I will not be able to attend the meeting on November 9,* repeated over and over in my mind. It nagged at me to the point that I emailed the other committee members to inform them that I would not be attending that meeting. My premonitions had both been correct.

I find it fascinating that I had premonitions for three of my five NDEs. When I consider how it could be possible for a part of my mind to know in advance that something major was going to happen to me, I think about my experience of *timeless time* in the Heavenly Light realm during my fifth NDE. While my body was dead, and my spirit was in the Divine Light during the NDE, I had a strong clear perception that time was fluid and flexible in that realm.

Time was not linear there, as it is experienced here on earth. Past, present, and future, seemed to comingle, or coexist. Thus, in the Divine Light, it was possible to see into what on earth we perceive as the past, and it was also possible to see into what on earth we perceive as the future.

The speed of time passing also seemed different in the Heavenly Light realm. During my 2003 experience, the length of time I was in that realm, seemed to be much longer than the length of time that passed on earth, before I once again awoke in my previously dead body. It felt to me as if time looped, or bent, to fit my long astral Heaven experience into a shorter worldly time frame.

As I reflect on the fluidity and flexibility of time in the Heavenly Light realm, I think it is possible that in some extraordinary circumstances, our souls, or some part of our minds, might receive glimpses or hints of the future. I think this is absolutely possible, based on my experience of timeless time. This could account for the premonitions that I had of all three of my adult Near-Death Experiences.

NDEs & Mystical Experiences are Etched into my Memory

Another aspect of my NDEs and peak mystical experiences that I find quite extraordinary is how clearly the memory of each of them is etched into my mind. Despite the passage of time, I still have an extremely clear memory of them all. The clarity of these memories stands out and is vastly superior to my memory of other events that happened throughout my life. It is as if the memories have been permanently etched into my memory somehow.

Another striking feature of the memories of my three adult NDEs and peak mystical experiences, is that when I focus on remembering a specific experience, not only do I remember the events and feelings that occurred before and during it, but I also begin to re-experience the beatific state of consciousness I had during that STEs. Thinking about them makes me begin to re-experience the blissful, elevated, expansive, love-filled state of consciousness that I felt during them. Even writing about them in this book has lifted my consciousness to re-experience some of the beatific states.

I find this phenomenon of re-experiencing the spiritual elevation when thinking about these events to be another extraordinary way that the memory of them differs from my memories of other events. Thus, it appears that both the memory of, and the upliftment in consciousness that occurred during them, are by some unknown mechanism permanently etched into my conscious memory.

Yvonne Kason, M.D.

Soul Lessons from my NDEs and STEs

As I reflect on the key lessons that I learned from all my STEs, I realize that I learned four fundamental soul lessons that have shaped the course of my life. These lessons have become a part of my being, an integral part of who I am, and what I know to be true.

These soul lessons are not a belief or a faith based on some external doctrine or teaching. These are my reality. I know these things to be true because I have experienced them myself.

As I now reflect on my life's experiences, my four soul lessons have become clearer and more complete. I can now summarize them as follows.

Lesson 1 – We are Immortal Souls – in Bodies to Learn and Grow

My experiences, leaving and returning to my body, revealed that my soul is separate from my physical body. This has also been reported by hundreds of other NDE experiencers.

My experiences also showed me that my soul would indeed live on after the death of my physical body, just as the founders of the world's great faiths have attested. In my head injury NDE in 2003, my physical body was actually dead for a period of time. I experienced firsthand being welcomed into the afterlife by saintly beings of light, and feeling embraced by the welcoming unconditional loving light of the Higher Power.

What also became clear to me is that, according to some Divine plan, upon embodiment as human babies, we forget the truth of who we really are, immortal souls, who are actually never separate from God. Instead, we seem to become body identified. When we incarnate, for some reason, we forget the time we spent living as souls in the heavenly realms between lives. We also forget our many past incarnations. This forgetting of our true soul nature when we incarnate lays at the core of the Divine mystery of Creation.

Feeling extraordinarily blessed, I can clearly recall my spirit being alive while out of the body and in the Light realm. I can clearly recall many of my past lives that were revealed to me there. I can also clearly recall the moment that my soul re-entered my body after each NDE induced sojourn on the other side. By the miracle of these experiences, I _do_ remember that I am truly an immortal soul, temporarily living within my present physical body.

During my two-month period of ongoing Divine communion after my 1995 NDE, I could clearly perceive and understand within my being, that all of life's experiences were ultimately designed as prods – tools to help us learn our necessary soul lessons. It was clear to me while I was in that expansive unitive state, that the happy and the challenging experiences of life were all ultimately designed, by the infinitely intelligent plan underlying the universe, to help our souls learn and grow. I could see the exquisite beauty of the Divine plan, how slowly with time and over many incarnations, as we learn our moral soul lessons, every soul will gradually make their way back *Home*, to self-realization, ongoing God-communion. There is ultimately a happy ending for us all. The cosmic design is for every soul to successfully complete their spiritual evolution of consciousness over many lifetimes. My NDEs taught me the soul lesson that we are all souls, on an incredible journey of learning and growth.

Lesson 2 - We Are All Loved by the Universal Higher Power

The second, and most important soul lesson that I learned is that a Higher Power exists, and we are all loved profoundly, and unconditionally by our Divine Creator, our Mother/Father God. Whether we call this Higher Power the Force, Brahma, the Creator, God, Divine Mother, Great Spirit, Allah, or another name, this One Cosmic Force exists, and can be glimpsed in Near-Death Experiences and other mystical experiences. It is the same one God that is being worshipped and sought by all the world's great religions, albeit in somewhat different ways, with different rituals, and with somewhat different understandings.

My experiences revealed to me that this one Higher Power underlies all the universes. It is immensely vast, permeating the entire cosmos in multiple dimensions, and infinitely intelligent. This intelligence underlies all aspects of creation, and is profoundly loving in nature. This immensely powerful love is inexpressible in its magnitude, and is also totally unconditional. Of that, I am absolutely certain, because I have experienced it repeatedly, in my NDEs and mystical experiences.

I have experienced our Divine Higher Power as being immanent in all Creation, omnipresent, interpenetrating all of Creation. No distance separates us from our beloved parent, God, because every atom of creation is an outpouring of God, a ray of the Divine Source. We are each like rays radiating from the Divine Sun, or drops forming a part of the cosmic ocean of God. We are all diverse expressions of our one Creator, God. God is within each and every one of us, in our hearts and in our souls. There is no separation. We have merely forgotten, lost sight of our connection with the Divine.

Every time we love or feel loved, every time we manifest kindness, compassion, forgiveness, courage, endurance, or generosity, we are expressing a small aspect of the God within our hearts and souls. Our Divine Parent God is ever-present within all of creation, smiling at us through every beautiful sunset, in the beauty of flowers, in the sweet song of birds, in the goodness in human actions, and in the inspiration of human genius.

These are all expressions of the immanent, omnipresent profoundly loving God manifesting throughout creation. In truth, we all are souls who are a part of God. Like waves of the Divine cosmic ocean, we always remain a part of the Divine ocean, even if we have forgotten this truth, or have lost awareness of that one-ness. In Spirit there is no separation. That Divine cosmic ocean is also always loving us, profoundly and unconditionally, regardless of whether we are aware of it or not.

My experience of the Divine Higher Power is that It is like both an infinitely loving Divine Mother force, who loves us completely and unconditionally, and also like a wise discerning Divine Father force, who teaches and disciplines us when we make errors, to help us to learn and grow. It appears to me that God has designed the cosmos giving us each free choice. It's done in such a way that we "children" souls may have many interesting incarnate experiences, in order to learn our soul lessons, grow and learn from our successes and errors. Ultimately, we find our ways back *Home* to a state of ongoing God-communion, where there is no separation, no duality.

No matter how many times we might stumble in the multifaceted journey of our many lifetimes, our unconditionally loving Creator/Cosmic Parent is invisibly prodding us in the correct direction. It's rooting for us to pick ourselves up when we fall, learn our soul lessons, transcend our problems and shortcomings, and slowly find our way back *Home* to self-realization, Divine communion, non-duality. My NDEs taught me the soul lesson that this is the true goal of the loving Divine plan, for every soul to find their way back *Home*, to communion in the loving arms of our shared Divine Cosmic Source.

Lesson 3 – *Meditation and Moral Living can Speed Soul Evolution*

The third soul lesson that I learned is that it is possible to speed up our soul learning, our soul evolution. It is possible to hasten our journey back *Home* to self-realization, God-communion. The key to this acceleration is practicing regular deep meditation, and right living following the universal spiritual laws.

I found meditation a powerful tool to speed up my spiritual evolution of consciousness. I am not alone. For thousands of years, the yogi sages and Buddhist adepts have affirmed that meditation is a key to spiritual deepening. Through daily deep meditation, anyone can expand their consciousness, to make it more capable of perceiving the vastness of Divine communion. Through attention to personal growth and refinement of character, we purify our consciousness, making it more capable of sustaining expanded spiritual states.

Over the years, as we expand and purify our consciousness through daily meditation and self-development, we begin to realize, to actually experience, the immanence of God. We begin to increasingly get glimpses of the Divine within us, around us, and within all things. Ultimately, duality vanishes, and we experience or realize our oneness with all creation, with the Divine Higher Power, in ongoing unitive mystical states of consciousness.

At the start of my near-miss plane incident NDE in 1995, it was through deep meditation that my spirit was able to quickly slip out of my body and into the NDE. During my two months of ongoing communion after this NDE, I discovered that meditation and right living were the keys to keeping my consciousness in its expanded unitive state.

When my consciousness would begin to contract, deeply meditating with my attention focused on my third eye center on the forehead, would re-expand my consciousness into the full unitive state of communion. Further, while in the fullness of the unitive state, meditation would make my consciousness expand even further and go into even deeper states of communion. I experienced firsthand, how meditation directly stimulates deeper spiritual expansion of consciousness.

Similarly, while in the unitive state, it was perceptible to me how humble, moral living, and positive spiritual attitudes of mind were also essential for mystical communion. While in the unitive state, I could directly perceive both in myself and others, how negative thinking, emotionality, and emotional attachments, and lowering the attention of one's consciousness away from Divine thoughts, would contract and lower the consciousness away from Divine communion. I could also clearly perceive how emotional equipoise, spiritual thinking, and letting go of emotional attachments, would raise our consciousness. When a humble, loving attitude was combined with deep meditation, expansion of consciousness could occur.

On November 8, 2003, a few hours before my slip and fall, I once again found that through deep meditation I shifted into an expansive state of ongoing unitive communion. This state of ongoing mystical communion lasted several hours and continued to the moment I died and began my death experience in the NDE.

These NDE-related meditation experiences taught me the soul lesson which confirms what adepts and sages have attested for eons, that meditation and right living are indeed keys to speeding our spiritual journey *Home*.

Lesson 4 – There is Always Hope for a Brighter Tomorrow

The fourth soul lesson I learned is that there is always hope for a better and brighter tomorrow. The omnipotence and omniscience of the Divine Higher Power are infinitely greater than any of the challenges we are facing as individuals, as nations, or as a planet. Meditating deeply, turning to the Divine within, and seeking Higher Guidance about life matters, can always bring some light and hope, even to the most challenging situations. Never give up hope for a better tomorrow. With God, all things are possible

I have experienced several miracles in my life, many of which I shared in this book. My sudden healing in time for Christmas, following my fervent childhood prayer, was a clear miracle to me at the age of twelve. The multiple synchronistic events that led to my being rescued, and my life saved after the 1979 medevac plane crash, were, in my opinion, more miracles in my life. To me, being blessed with two months of ongoing Divine communion in 1995, is another powerful miracle in my life.

The healing I experienced in 2016 was, indeed, miraculous, maybe generated through a neuroplasticity miracle. To me, it is a testimonial to the grace of God.

After the 2003 traumatic brain injury, I never gave up hope that I might experience further healing in the post-TBI symptoms, even though medical science had decreed my injuries as permanent. I think this is another important soul lesson I learned from my Near-Death Experiences and multiple mystical experiences, to never give up hope for a better tomorrow. With God, all things are possible.

Due to my personal experiences of multiple STEs and miracles in my life, I know that there is always hope for a better tomorrow. We must never lose hope. Of course, we must continue to do our part to strive for a better tomorrow, while we attune ourselves to the Divine will the best we can, through moral living, prayer, and meditation, and then surrender the outcome to God. If we turn to the Higher Power in our hearts, the Divine hand might unexpectedly intervene, and invisibly reach out to offer assistance, healing, or guidance in our time of need. I know this to be true because I have experienced it many times.

There Are Many Mansions

In conclusion, as I reflect on the multiple STEs I've written about, the soul lessons I learned from them, and the ways that they impacted my life, I am struck by how profoundly diverse those experiences were one from the other. Although each NDE gave me a partial glimpse of the profoundly loving Higher Power underlying the universe, it is striking to me that each experience was so different from the others in many ways. Each also gave me the clear perception that the Divine Cosmic Source, our Higher Power, is vastly larger and infinitely more complex than our limited human capacity to perceive.

The infinite vastness of the Divine, and the similarities and the differences between my many experiences, have drawn me to conclude, as Jesus Christ once said, "In my father's house are many mansions" (John 14:2).

To me, this means that in God's infinite universe, there are many, many ways that our loving Higher Power may reveal glimpses of his/her infinite nature to us – like glimpses of many diverse rooms in the Creator God's immense mansion of loving universal creation. The Higher Power's multi-dimensional "mansion" is far beyond our capacity to grasp in its totality.

I hope that readers have felt inspired and uplifted by reading the stories of my five Near-Death Experiences, to know that a loving realm of Light and joy awaits us after our death. There is nothing to fear in death. All we have to do is sincerely turn to the Light in our hearts, to the Higher Power as we understand it. I sincerely hope this knowledge will comfort and give hope to persons when facing death themselves, and to persons when dealing with the death of a loved one.

I also hope that by sharing my stories, I have given some support and validation to other NDE and STE experiencers. I hope my reflections on them have given other experiencers a deeper understanding, to help them integrate their own experiences and the many powerful after-effects.

Finally, I hope that reading these stories, and the soul lessons I learned from them, has helped readers deepen in their love and trust for the Divine power behind the universe. I hope every reader will put down this book trusting deeply in what I learned to be true, that we are all dearly loved and precious to our shared Cosmic Parent, the Higher Power, God.

BIBLIOGRAPHY

The following bibliographic references are listed in the order that I mentioned them in each chapter.

Chapter 2

Moody, Raymond A., Jr. *Life after Life: The Investigation of a Phenomenon—Survival of Bodily Death*. New York: Bantam, 1975.

Kason, Yvonne. *Touched by the Light: Exploring Spiritually Transformative Experiences*. Toronto: Dundurn Press, 2019.

Chapter 3

Kason, Yvonne, and Degler, T. *A Farther Shore: Exploring How Near-Death, Kundalini, and Mystical Experiences can Transform Ordinary Lives*. Toronto: Harper Collins Canada, 1994.

Kason, Yvonne. *Farther Shores: Exploring How Near-Death, Kundalini, and Mystical Experiences can Transform Ordinary Lives*. Toronto: Harper Collins Canada, 2000, and Bloomington, Indiana: iUniverse, 2008.

Kason, Yvonne. *Touched by the Light: Exploring Spiritually Transformative Experiences*. Toronto: Dundurn Press, 2019.

George Lucas, Irvin Kershner, Director. *Star Wars Episode V: The Empire Strikes Back*. Film, 20th Century Fox, 1980.

Joel Schumacher, Director. *Flatliners.* Stonebridge Entertainment, 1990.

Burpo, Todd and Lynn Vincent. *Heaven is for Real.* Thomas Nelson, 2010.

Neal, Mary C. *To Heaven and Back: A Doctor's Extraordinary Account of Her Death, Heaven, Angels, and Life Again.* Colorado Springs, CO: WaterBrook Press, 2011.

Moorjani, Anita. *Dying To Be Me: My Journey from Cancer, to Near Death, to True Healing.* Carlsbad, CA: Hay House Inc., 2012.

Chapter 5

Krishna, Gopi. *Kundalini: The Evolutionary Energy in Man.* Boulder, Colorado: Shambhala, 1967, 1970.

James, William. *The Varieties of Religious Experience.* New York: New America Library, 1958.

Underhill, Evelyn. *Mysticism: The Nature and Development of Mystical Consciousness.* Oxford, England: Oneworld Publications, 1993.

Kason, Yvonne. *Touched by the Light: Exploring Spiritually Transformative Experiences.* Toronto: Dundurn Press, 2019.

Chapter 6

Waller, Adrian. "Down in Devils Gap." *The Reader's Digest*, February 1981. pp 25-30

Chapter 7

Denver, John. *I Want to Live.* 1977

Krishna, Gopi. *Kundalini: The Evolutionary Energy in Man*. Boulder, Colorado: Shambhala, 1967, 1970

James, William. *The Varieties of Religious Experience*. New York: New America Library, 1958.

Bucke, Richard Maurice. *Cosmic Consciousness*. New York: E.P. Dutton, 1969.

Moody, Raymond A. *Life after Life: The Investigation of a Phenomenon – Survival of Bodily Death*. New York: Bantam, 1975

Chapter 9

Kason, Yvonne, and Degler, T. *A Farther Shore: Exploring How Near-Death, Kundalini, and Mystical Experiences can Transform Ordinary Lives*. Toronto: Harper Collins Canada, 1994.

Lukoff, David, Frances Lu, and Robert Turner. "Towards a More Culturally Sensitive DSM-IV: Psychoreligious and Psychospiritual Problems," *Journal of Nervous and Mental Disease* 180, 11 (November 1992).

American Psychiatric Association. *Diagnostic and Statistical Manual of Mental Disorders*, 4th ed. Washington, D.C.: American Psychiatric Association, 1994.

Chapter 10

Grof, Stanislav, and Grof, Christina. *Spiritual Emergency: When Personal Transformation Becomes a Crisis*. Los Angeles: Jeremy Tarcher, Inc., 1989.

Krishna, Gopi. *Kundalini: The Evolutionary Energy in Man*. Boulder, Colorado: Shambhala, 1967, 1970.

Yogananda, Paramahansa. *Autobiography of a Yogi*. Los Angeles, California: Self-Realization Fellowship, 2007.

Kason, Yvonne, and Degler, T. *A Farther Shore: Exploring How Near-Death, Kundalini, and Mystical Experiences can Transform Ordinary Lives.* Toronto: Harper Collins Canada, 1994.

Kason, Yvonne. *Farther Shores: Exploring How Near-Death, Kundalini, and Mystical Experiences can Transform Ordinary Lives.* Toronto: Harper Collins Canada, 2000, and Bloomington, Indiana: iUniverse, 2008.

Kason, Yvonne. *Touched by the Light: Exploring Spiritually Transformative Experiences.* Toronto: Dundurn Press, 2019.

Chapter 10

Kason, Yvonne, and Degler, T. *A Farther Shore: Exploring How Near-Death, Kundalini, and Mystical Experiences can Transform Ordinary Lives.* Toronto: Harper Collins Canada, 1994.

Chapter 12

Underhill, Evelyn. *Mysticism: The Nature and development of Mystical Consciousness.* Oxford, England: Oneworld Publications, 1993.

Yogananda, Paramahansa. *Autobiography of a Yogi.* Los Angeles, California: Self-Realization Fellowship, 2007.

Yogananda, Paramahansa. *God Talks With Arjuna: The Bhagavad Gita: Royal Science of God-Realization.* Los Angeles, California: Self-Realization Fellowship, 1995.

Sams, Jamie, and David Carson. *Medicine Cards: The Discovery of Power through the Ways of Animals.* Santa Fe, New Mexico: Bear & Company, 1988.

Kason, Yvonne. *Farther Shores: Exploring How Near-Death, Kundalini, and Mystical Experiences can Transform Ordinary Lives.* Toronto: Harper Collins Canada, 2000, and Bloomington, Indiana: iUniverse, 2008.

Kason, Yvonne. *Touched by the Light: Exploring Spiritually Transformative Experiences*. Toronto: Dundurn Press, 2019

Chapter 17

Kason, Yvonne. *Touched by the Light: Exploring Spiritually Transformative Experiences*. Toronto: Dundurn Press, 2019

Doidge, Norman. *The Brain That Changes Itself: Stories of personal Triumph from the Frontiers of Brain Science*. New York, NY: Penguin books, 2007.

Doidge, Norman. *The Brain's Way of Healing: Remarkable Discoveries and Recoveries from the Frontiers of Neuroplasticity*. New York, NY: Penguin books, 2015, 2016.

Krishna, Gopi. *Kundalini: The Evolutionary Energy in Man*. Boulder, Colorado: Shambhala, 1967, 1970.

Krishna, Gopi. *Higher Consciousness: The Evolutionary Thrust of Kundalini*. New York: Julian Press, 1974.

Yogananda, Paramahansa. *God Talks With Arjuna. The Bhagavad Gita: Royal Science of God-Realization*. Los Angeles, California: Self-Realization Fellowship, 1995.

Yogananda, Paramahansa. *The Yoga of the Bhagavad Gita: An Introduction to India's Universal Science of God-Realization*. Los Angeles, California: self-Realization Fellowship, 2007.

Jung, Carl. *The Psychology of Kundalini Yoga: Notes of the Seminar given in 1932 by C.G, Jung*. Ed. Sonu Sham Dasani. Princeton: Bollingen Series, Princeton University Press, 1996.

Sannella, Lee. *The Kundalini Experience*. Lower Lake, California: Integral Publishing, 1987.

Greenwell, Bonnie. *Energies of Transformation: A Guide to the Kundalini Process*. Cupertino, California. Shakti River Press, 1990, 1995.

Ring, Kenneth. *The Omega Project: Near Death Experiences, UFO Encounters, and Mind at Large*. New York: William Morrow, 1992.

Greyson, Bruce. "Near-Death Experiences and the Physio-Kundalini Syndrome." *Journal of Religion and Health,* Vol. 32, No. 4, Winter 1993, 277-290.

Chapter 19

Yukteswar Swami Sri. *The Holy Science*. Los Angeles: Self-Realization Fellowship, 1990.

Kason, Yvonne. *"Purifying the Heart: 5 Stages on the Spiritual Path."* Presentation made to the Spirituality in Health-Care Network, Toronto. October 2, 2010.

Kason, Yvonne. "Purifying the Heart: A Roadmap to the 5 Stages on the Path of Life." Presentation made to ACISTE, American Center for the Integration of Spiritually Transformative Experiences, Chicago, and October 7, 2018.

Kason, Yvonne. "Purifying the Heart: A Roadmap to the Spiritual Path." presented to Spiritual Awakenings International, August 21, 2021. Video on the Spiritual Awakenings International YouTube Channel.

Chapter 20

Kason, Yvonne, and Degler, T. *A Farther Shore: Exploring How Near-Death, Kundalini, and Mystical Experiences can Transform Ordinary Lives*. Toronto: Harper Collins Canada, 1994.

Kason, Yvonne. *Farther Shores: Exploring How Near-Death, Kundalini, and Mystical Experiences can Transform Ordinary Lives.* Toronto: Harper Collins Canada, 2000, and Bloomington, Indiana: iUniverse, 2008.

Kason, Yvonne. *Touched by the Light: Exploring Spiritually Transformative Experiences.* Toronto: Dundurn Press, 2019.

Storm, Howard, in *A Message of Hope: The Near Death Experience – Accounts and Perspectives.* Video by M. Taylor Bach. Ft. Thomas, Kentucky: The counseling Institute, 1987.

Brinkley, Dannion. *Saved by the Light: The True Story of a Man who Died Twice and the Profound Revelations He Received.* New York, New York: Harper Collins, 1994.

ABOUT THE AUTHOR

Dr. Yvonne Kason MD, MEd, CCFP, FCFP, is a family physician and transpersonal MD psychotherapist (retired), author of 6 books, and public speaker, previously on faculty at the University of Toronto, Faculty of Medicine. She is the President and Co-Founder of Spiritual Awakenings International® www.spiritualawakeningsinternational.org. Dr. Kason has had five Near-Death Experiences and multiple Spiritually Transformative Experiences.

Dr. Kason first coined the phrase "Spiritually Transformative Experiences" (STEs) in her groundbreaking 1994 book, *A Farther Shore.* This term has now been adopted by foremost researchers in the field. She is an internationally renowned expert on Spiritually Transformative Experiences, who is in demand as a media resource and keynote speaker internationally.

Dr. Yvonne Kason had a powerful Near-Death Experience (NDE) in a 1979 medevac plane crash which propelled her to become the first Canadian medical doctor to specialize in research and counseling of persons with NDEs and other Spiritually Transformative Experiences. A pioneer in the field, she co-founded the Kundalini Research Network, the Spirituality in Health-Care Network, and Toronto Awakenings Sharing Group www.torontoawakenings.org. She is also a Past-President of IANDS, the International Association for Near-Death Studies.

Dr. Yvonne Kason is a mother and grandmother, and a devoted long-time practitioner of yoga meditation. She speaks three languages, English, German, and French. She divides her time between living in Toronto, Canada, and snowbirding winters in Encinitas, California, or Florida, USA.

Website: www.dryvonnekason.com

Printed in the United States
by Baker & Taylor Publisher Services